Studies in the Life of Women

Abigail Scott Duniway, Writing Oregon's Equal Suffrage Proclamation

ACKNOWLEDGMENT

My thanks are due to resident capitalists, business men,
wage-earners and men and women taxpayers of
Portland, whose advance orders have
enabled me to publish the first
edition of this book.

THE AUTHOR

Abigail Scott Duniway, Signing Oregon's Equal Suffrage Proclamation, in Presence of Governor Oswald West and Mrs. Viola M. Coe.

PATH BREAKING

AN AUTOBIOGRAPHICAL HISTORY OF THE EQUAL SUFFRAGE MOVEMENT IN PACIFIC COAST STATES.

BY
ABIGAIL SCOTT DUNIWAY

With a New Introduction by Eleanor Flexner

SECOND EDITION

SCHOCKEN BOOKS · NEW YORK

Reprinted from the James, Kerns & Abbott edition of 1914

First SCHOCKEN PAPERBACK edition 1971

Introduction copyright © 1971 by Schocken Books Inc.
Library of Congress Catalog Card No. 79–162285
Published by arrangement with Source Book Press
Manufactured in the United States of America

INTRODUCTION TO THE
PAPERBACK EDITION

This account of Abigail Scott Duniway's leadership of the woman suffrage movement in the Pacific Northwest was first published more than half a century ago. It is being reissued at a time when still another group of Americans is being enfranchised, those between eighteen and twenty-one years of age. Although this step has been under discussion for several years, it seems to have come about almost by itself, naturally and gradually, out of the changing roles in our society, the earlier maturing of youth, its search for new responsibilities, its participation in the bloodiest external war in our history.

The enfranchisement of this latest group has little in common with earlier such advances. Black Americans supposedly received the vote after the war that was also supposed to "free" them; yet they had to wait for an entire century before a beginning was made at implementing the Fourteenth and Fifteenth Amendments to the Constitution in the southern states.

Most Americans are not even aware of when American women were given the vote and the circumstances that led to their enfranchisement. We are so used to women sitting at the Board of Elections tables in our polling places, to women's names (however few) on the ballot, to women serving (even if infrequently) in community, state, and national bodies, that the idea of their *not* having the vote simply does not occur to us. Nor will it occur to most eighteen-, nineteen-, and twenty-year-old women, as they line up outside the polling place to vote in their first election, that, had it not been for long effort and many sacrifices, only the young men would be waiting there to cast their ballots.

vii

The Nineteenth (woman suffrage) Amendment to the United States Constitution was proclaimed law on August 26, 1920, following its ratification by the requisite assent of two-thirds of the states in the Union. Behind that action lay fifty-three years of incessant work, beginning with the first referendum in Kansas in 1867 on the question of giving the vote to women by amending a *state* constitution. During those fifty-three years there was always a campaign, or several campaigns, in progress somewhere in the United States for either state or federal action on the issue.

> Millions of dollars were raised, mainly in small sums, and expended with economic care [wrote Carrie Chapman Catt, who led the struggle for many years]. Hundreds of women gave the accumulated possibilities of a lifetime, thousands gave years of their lives, hundreds of thousands gave constant interest and such aid as they could. It was a continuous, seemingly endless chain of activity. Young suffragists who helped forge the last link of that chain were not born when it began. Old suffragists who forged the first link were dead when it ended.*

One of the women who gave "the accumulated possibilities of a lifetime," and who died before the end had been achieved, was Abigail Scott Duniway of Oregon. Beginning in 1870, when she founded her newspaper, *The New Northwest,* until the victory for woman suffrage in Oregon in 1912, Abigail Duniway lived primarily for that cause and worked in the campaigns of three states: Oregon, Washington, and Idaho. Together with Wyoming, Colorado, Utah, and Montana, these made up a block of states that gave women the vote ahead of any other section of the country.

* Carrie Chapman Catt and Nettie Rogers Shuler, *Woman Suffrage and Politics* (New York, 1932), pp. 107–8.

Abigail Scott came to Oregon in a covered wagon as a girl of seventeen in 1852, only six years after a treaty with Great Britain made the area part of the United States, and only three years after the beginning of the California Gold Rush. (She lived until 1915, and the beginning of World War I!) Her mother died of cholera on the journey. Although Abigail had attended a log-cabin school back in Illinois only "at intervals," she was able to pass an Oregon teacher's certificate examination and taught for a few months, until she married Ben Duniway and went to live on a frontier ranch.

Duniway was energetic and able, but he lacked business judgment. In addition, the law gave him complete control over his property and his wife's earnings from making butter (a profitable sideline for many pioneer farm women). In consequence the family was ruined:

A man came up from the village to our woodpile, where my husband was at work, and asked him to become surety for a considerable sum. . . . The two men parleyed for a while and then went into the house. It dawned upon me suddenly, as I was picking a duck, that it would ruin us financially if these notes were signed. I tried hard to be silent, being a non-entity in law, but my hands trembled, my heart beat hard, and I laid the pinioned duck on its back and repaired to the living room to investigate. My husband had already signed two notes and was in the act of signing the third, when I leaned over his shoulder and said, tremulously, "My dear, are you quite certain about what you are doing?" The other fellow looked daggers at me, but said nothing, and my husband answered, as he signed the last note: "Mama, you needn't worry; you'll always be protected and provided for!" I wanted to say: "I guess I'll always earn all the protection I get," but I remembered that I was nothing but a woman; so I bit my lips to keep silent and rushed back to to my work, where for several minutes I fear that duckflesh suffered, for I didn't pluck the feathers tenderly (pp. 13–14).

The notes were defaulted, and Mrs. Duniway's forebodings were fulfilled. Shortly thereafter Duniway was largely incapacitated for life by an accident, and his wife had to support them and their children—a girl and five boys—by teaching, taking in boarders, and running a millinery business, until the boys could help take care of their parents.

And help they did. It was her sons who largely made it possible for Abigail Duniway to put out the newspaper that served as her voice and that of the nascent suffrage movement to which she had been converted, first by her mother's bitter experiences and then by her own harsh life. Not only did she edit and largely write *The New Northwest;* the self-educated woman also wrote fiction and poetry, which, besides helping to fill her paper, appeared as books. After Susan B. Anthony visited Oregon to stir up the issue of suffrage in 1871, Mrs. Duniway added lecturing to her other activities and travelled thousands of miles to win subscribers to the paper and fresh forces for the suffrage cause:

> It was no small task to travel, often by night, over the terrible roads of the Pacific Northwest, lecturing from three to five evenings every week, writing serial stories for "The New Northwest," illustrative, always, of various phases of my theme, and furnishing editorial correspondence often covering a full page of the paper. Added to all this was my necessary work of canvassing for the paper, meeting all sorts of social activities, "talking shop," at retail, with the women in their homes, ministers in their studies, and judges in their court rooms, often departing by stage, at night, after a lecture, for the next way station to make preliminary arrangements

for another series of meetings and repeating the same process at every settlement large enough to warrant a stopover (p. 52).

For a few brief years, between 1886 and 1893, there was some dissent against the Duniway leadership in Oregon. She gave up the newspaper, by then a losing battle, and worked in Washington and Idaho instead of Oregon. Then she came back into leadership, personally directing five of Oregon's six suffrage campaigns—in 1887, 1900, 1906, 1908, and 1910. Only a major illness dictated her withdrawal from the final drive in 1912. She died three years later, just before her eighty-first birthday.

It was an extraordinary life. Certainly Abigail Scott Duniway was one of the most gifted and able women to come out of the first era of the woman's rights movement (as distinguished from a second era beginning to take shape today). Nevertheless, the qualities that were her greatest assets—her tremendous drive, her ready gift of words as speaker or writer, her organizing ability, and her self-confidence—sometimes became acute defects. Her caustic wit could degenerate into withering sarcasm, and this was never more true than when she was pitting her strength against some of the national leaders of the suffrage movement (particularly Dr. Anna Howard Shaw) or the temperance and prohibition organizations; in both cases she could be indiscriminately abusive.

Her belief in her own powers and judgment eventually turned into unbridled vanity, of which there is unfortunate evidence in her autobiography, *Path Breaking*. It even seems possible that the record number of suffrage campaigns in Oregon can be charged, in part, to Mrs. Duniway's ability to antagonize those who did not agree with her, and also to arbitrary personal decisions that proved to be errors in judgment. No other state in the country voted on woman suffrage six times. (South Dakota came closest, with five). When one considers the expenditures of time and energy, not to mention money, one can legitimately wonder whether Mrs. Duniway's leadership was always in the best interests of the cause.

Path Breaking itself bears some evidence of her complex personality. It is the record of an egotist, rendered more so by age; it is heavily charged in some places with a bitterness that did not turn to forgiveness after the victory of 1912. The latter portions of the book contain chapters assembled from earlier speeches and articles, or from clippings culled from the press by not very discriminating campaign followers. It is also not free from errors. For instance, there was no vote on woman suffrage in Oregon in 1909 (as indicated on p. 188). The wording of the measure as presented to the voters at the 1910 election, on which Mrs. Duniway puts a good deal of emphasis (it was to be based on women *taxpayers* receiving the vote), was actually the same as in former years, due to error—either malicious or otherwise—in the state office responsible for printing the ballot.*

Nevertheless, *Path Breaking* must be read for what it is, not for what it is not. The perceptive reader will find a great deal, including the occasional eloquent sentence which wraps up a historical era in a few words: "My father, being of an adventurous disposition, started, with his invalid wife and the nine surviving children of their family of twelve, to travel with ox teams and covered wagons across the plains to Oregon" (p. 3). She documents the speed with which the frontier moved, in half a century, across half a continent. She found Portland in 1871

a village . . . of about eight thousand pioneers . . . an ambitious little city-to-be . . . one principal street

* I am indebted for this fact and others in the life of Mrs. Duniway to Miss Leslie Roberts' Reed College senior history thesis, 1969: *Suffragist of the New West: Abigail Scott Duniway and the Development of the Oregon Woman Suffrage Movement.*

along which flourished double rows of drygoods
stores, meat markets, a primitive hotel or two, and
once in a while a Chinese laundry. An occasional
saloon peeped out on the Wilamette River (p. 31).

Within her lifetime it had become a city of 130,000 with
the lineaments of the city we know today.

Along with the city grew the social forms and institutions that had existed in the communities from which the
settlers came. Some of them had made it from the eastern
seaboard in one move; others had paused briefly on the
way; still others, like the Duniways, came from a generation that had settled in Illinois or Kentucky or Ohio. Most
found their places relatively quickly in a society stratify-
ing into familiar patterns: political parties, labor unions,
and the Grange, or women's clubs, the WCTU, and
"society."

Within this rapidly shifting, enormously active frontier milieu, Abigail Scott Duniway fought the fight for
woman suffrage with tireless energy, a superb gift of
extemporaneous oratory, and endless wit. In those days
public meetings, like a good sermon, were among the few
diversions available to a hard-working, hard-living popu-
lace, and audiences loved the Duniway style of eloquent
idealism well laced with repartee. She never failed to
regale them with the incidents of her endless and strenuous travels, such as one occasion when the stagecoach in
which she was traveling reached Yakima on a cold winter
evening at dusk:

I saw the men on seats behind myself and the driver
passing a bottle, which I pretended as usual, not to
notice. Finally, one of them, who had evidently become more mellow than the rest, accosted me, saying:
"Madam! you ought to to be home, enjoying yourself, like my wife is doing. I want to bear all the
hardships of life myself, and let her sit by the fire,

toasting her footsies." I didn't answer and nobody
else said anything. It was almost dark when we
reached town, and the obliging driver went out of
his way to leave this fellow-passenger at his own
door yard, where we found his protected wife, busy
with an ax, chopping away at a pile of snow-covered
cord wood. . . . I afterwards heard that the men who
saw the incident nicknamed the husband "Old footsie
toaster" (pp. 89–90).

She could turn almost any occasion into a platform
with a receptive audience around her. On a river-boat
trip down the Columbia River, she accepted the captain's
charge of a quartet of disheveled, hungry children whom
the authorities were redeeming from a home where they
were receiving neither food nor care. She did her best to
get them fed and occupied and then became absorbed in
her omnipresent newspaper work. The other female passengers watched critically while the children ran wild and
Mrs. Duniway continued at work, and finally reproached
her with neglecting "your children." "Can't you see that
you are wasting your time, advocating woman's rights,
when your children need proper care?"

I drew from my satchel a portfolio of photographs
and said, "Here are my six children." Then, rising
to my feet and speaking to all the women who had
been discussing me, I told them to their evident
surprise, that my children were all engaged, after
school hours, in setting type for the Equal Rights
newspaper, The New Northwest; and we were hoping to see the day when all mothers would be as
successful with their children as I had been with
mine. I distributed copies of my newspaper among
them, and, after trying in vain to quell the noisy
waifs in the cabin, returned to my writing (pp.
91–92).

The book also makes clear how physical factors dictated the development of politics and reform. Settlement and everyday living had to follow the rivers and passes, cluster in the valleys, and accommodate to the distances and the climate. Topography dictated concentration in the major cities, loosely knit organizations, and printed communication (hence Mrs. Duniway's newspaper), rather than gathering groups together for frequent or regular meetings which, in large stretches of the area, was simply not practical.

But most of all, *Path Breaking* dramatizes the impact of emigration and settlement on the women—their burdens, their courage, the inequities under which they suffered even in a relatively unstructured pioneer society —and the stature of Abigail Scott Duniway herself. There are other such women whose lives are still buried. The re-publication of this book is a welcome addition to our knowledge of those who helped shape the society in which women today are taking an increasing part in determining their destiny and that of our world.

ELEANOR FLEXNER

Northampton, Massachusetts
May 1971

INTRODUCTION

It was not my expectation, or design, when beginning my work, in 1871, for securing equal rights between the mothers and fathers of the race, to encounter a conflict between the two contending elements of force and freedom, known as prohibition of the liquor traffic and prohibition of woman's right to vote. But this history will bear me out in stating that whenever the conflict has been forced upon me, I have met it without flinching, and with due regard for the inalienable rights of everybody, keeping always before me the immortal words of our martyred Lincoln: "By no means excluding women."

If we formulate laws to shut away from the child the tree of knowledge of good and evil, he grows to maturity as a moral weakling. When thus bereft of the power of resistance, he falls an easy prey to evils which he will surely encounter somewhere in his journey through the world.

The man who is only honest because everything he might be tempted to steal is hidden beyond his reach, or destroyed, or driven from use, or abuse, by the fiat of man-made laws, is never safe from his own moral delinquency, unless restrained of his liberty by prison walls. But, as it would be both impossible and unjust to deprive all men of their natural inheritance of self-government because of the infirmities of the weak or dishonest few, it ought to be universally manifest that all men should not be denied the power of self-control over human appetites because some men abuse them.

The only rational cure for the woes of the drunkard's wife is the power to protect herself from the condition of servitude without wages in the home, of which she is now a defenseless victim. "Give her of the fruit of her hands," said Solomon, "and let her own works praise her in the gates."

Since God has put alcohol among the elements of our planet, and for aught we know, throughout the universe, it is indestructible, and as necessary as air or water or fire or food. But, as each of these elements was made by omnipotent power, for human use under proper, man-made regulations by his own consent, the same rule must apply to one element as to another. We build houses to protect humanity from storm and flood and fire, but we cannot prohibit their existence, or use, under proper restrictions for their control. We have pest houses for men who catch the smallpox, but we do not compel all men to be quarantined. When man is taught from childhood that all power for good or evil depends upon himself, he will grow to manhood in voluntary obedience to the God-given right of self-control; or, if he disobeys this law, he must do so at his peril.

I have little doubt that the present conflict will continue to exist (ostensibly) in spots, outside of the penitentiary, the insane asylum and the jail for years to come. But I can foresee a time when free enfranchised women will be wise enough, and morally strong enough to quit the business of marrying inebriates, or mothering drunkards or criminals. When the business of mothering the race shall become recognized in its true relation to the race itself, the mother will be held responsible, as she ever ought to have opportunity to be, for the character of the child she releases to the world. But to transmit character-building power to her children, she must first, herself, be free and independent of all restrictive influences and laws opposed to the God-given right of individual liberty.

ABIGAIL SCOTT DUNIWAY.

Portland, Oregon, April 9, 1914.

CONTENTS

Contents

DEDICATED

By the Author

IN LOVE AND SYMPATHY

To

Every friend of human liberty and individual
responsibility who may read this book

CHAPTER I.

Author's Childhood—Married Life on a Farm.

I HAVE been importuned for many years to write a history of the Equal Suffrage Movement in Oregon, Washington and Idaho. These requests invariably call for statements, in autobiographical form, beginning with the personal history of myself, and the causes that led me before the public as the original advocate and leader of the Equal Suffrage Movement in the Pacific Northwest. Hitherto, when thus importuned, I have procrastinated, always offering as an excuse that my work would not be completed till the enfranchisement of women, which cause I had chosen at the age of 36 as my life work, was fully accomplished throughout my chosen bailiwick, which comprised the Pacific Northwest, originally the whole of Oregon, known in later years as "Old Oregon," now formed into the three Equal Suffrage states of Oregon, Washington, Idaho, and including parts of Montana and Wyoming.

I was not an easy convert to Equal Suffrage. I had been led from childhood to believe that women who demanded "rights" were man-haters, of whom I certainly was not one. But a long train of varied pioneer experiences led me at last into the light, which, when it burst upon me, found me willing to take up the burden of efforts, through which, as I look backward over the receded years, I can recall so much that is worthy of record, that the trouble is to decide what to omit in this recital, rather than what to transcribe.

GROUP OF EQUAL SUFFRAGISTS

MARTHA J. FOSTER
December 1870, Albany, Ore. One of the
Three Founders of the Oregon State
Equal Suffrage Association in 1870

MRS. MAY ARKWRIGHT HUTTON
Of Spokane. Eastern Washington Suffrage
Leader and Philanthropist

MRS. DUNIWAY
As a Teacher at Twenty-Seven, and Keeper
of a Boarding House

ABIGAIL SCOTT DUNIWAY
President Oregon Equal Suffrage
Association

MRS. ALICE WEISTER
President of Psychology Movement and
Leading Suffragist

ABIGAIL SCOTT DUNIWAY
December 1870, Albany, Ore. One of the
Three Founders of the Oregon State
Equal Suffrage Association in 1870

ADDIE GRACE BARLOW
Trained Writer and Leading Suffrage
Co-Worker of the State of
Washington

My parents, who were Kentuckians by birth, had first met as young people in the wilds of Illinois Territory. They were married October 22, 1830, in Pleasant Grove, Tazewell County, Illinois, where they lived till March, 1852, when my father, being of an adventurous disposition, started, with his invalid wife and the nine surviving children of their family of twelve, to travel with ox teams and covered wagons across the plains to Oregon.

I was born October 22, 1834, just four years after my parents' wedding day, I being the third of their rapidly increasing family of a dozen, the eldest of whom had died in infancy, before the second child, a daughter, had seen the light. Their disappointment, when this second child was born a daughter, was severe; and when, about seventeen months after, I was born, I remember that my mother informed me on my tenth birthday that her sorrow over my sex was almost too grievous to be borne.

My earliest recollection of any important event was standing by the bier of my paternal grandmother, Frances Tucker Scott, who died of pulmonary trouble when I was less than 4 years old. I remember seeing half-dollars resting upon her partly closed eyelids and noting the extreme pallor of her clay-cold face. But my parents did not take me to the cemetery, nor tell me anything about the burial, and I did not know till long afterwards why I couldn't see my grandmother any more.

How I learned to spell, read and recite bits of rhyme I do not know, though my busy mother must have taught me, just as in after years I taught my own children the alphabet as soon as they were able to speak plainly, or could read and count the numerals in the old Webster's Elementary Spelling book I had smuggled across the plains by stealth in an ox wagon when I was 17 years old. It was a little battered book that would have been destroyed in the fire that consumed our cabin and belongings in 1855, if it had not been loaned to a neighbor to whom I had taught the alphabet and to spell some easy words, which, after learning, she desired to teach her little children, as rapidly as she was able. Just what became of that little book, with its thumb-worn pages and ragged corners, I do not know, but I would give a handsome price for it if I could get it now.

The home of my birth, a little one-story and a half frame building, with a log-built kitchen and loomhouse attached, stood a few hundred feet from the main highway, or lane, between Pekin and Peoria, through which long lines of covered wagons were driven daily, in Spring and Summer, laden with the crude belongings of emigrants, bound for Missouri, at that time the anticipated goal of the restless path breakers who left their homes in Kentucky, Indiana and Illinois to plant for themselves new habitations in a newer West. I remember troops of bare-foot children coming to our home at sundown, carrying hickory and walnut sticks to bear away the fire coals my mother kept covered with ashes for her own use at cooking time, and that she always had brands, or coals, at hand to divide with the wayfarers in the lane.

I must have been 9 or 10 years old when my father brought home the first cooking stove I had ever seen. It was a huge, awkward affair, and my mother said it was more trouble to keep it in order for baking than it was to do her cooking by the fireplace, as her neighbors did.

I could not have been more than about 4 years old when a great sorrow befell my beloved paternal grandparents, in the unfortunate death of a brilliant and favorite son, the younger and only brother of my father, who had been sent to a high-class university, in an older state, where, as too often happens among the sons of prosperous pioneers, he fell into evil ways, and when

under the influence of intoxicants, committed some petty
crime for which he was overtaken when escaping from
arrest, and whipped to death by the border ruffianism
of the times.   I have often thought in later years that
this tragedy must have hastened my grandmother's death.
Of one thing I am certain: it threw my grandfather and
my father into financial difficulties that dragged them
into poverty and drove my father into bankruptcy.   To
satisfy his creditors, my father gave up his farm, where
six children had been born, and moved to a village called
Wesley, on the banks of the Illinois River, where he
leased a sawmill, spending a Winter with his family in
a well-appointed, though tiny, steamboat cabin of several
apartments, where the seventh living baby came to them.
Our parlor-kitchen contained a heater, which was also
a cooking stove, more modern than its predecessor; but
the most I remember about it was that my young brother,
afterward known to fame as the great Oregon editor,
Harvey W. Scott, sat one day upon the hearth to get
warm and narrowly escaped death, from which my older
sister and I rescued him with much effort.

It was while we were living in Wesley that I made
my maiden speech, never dreaming that I was doing an
unwomanly thing.   William Henry Harrison was the
presidential candidate, and, my father being an uncompromising Whig, I naturally partook of his ardor.   I
remember calling the village children together under the
shade of a sycamore tree, where I climbed to a horizontal
limb and harangued them about "Tippecanoe and Tyler
too."   To this day I have vivid recollections of that "log
cabin and hard cider campaign," which long ago passed
into history.

One raw, blustery morning—it was the 9th of March
—we older children were called home from a neighbor's,
where we had spent the night, and were conducted to our
mother's bedside where we were shown a baby sister.

Another baby of only fifteen months lay in a trundle bed near by, begging for "mama," who, occupied with the newcomer, was weeping in her helplessness and begging, without avail, that the older baby should be brought to her.

I am not pretending to follow the events of my childhood, or of this history, as they recur to me in chronological order, but I remember my return to the farm, the home of my birth, after our mother was able, or felt obliged to call herself able, to resume her many cares.

I also recall a dapper-looking business man from Pekin, our county seat, who had closed out my father's ownership of the farm, causing us to give it up and seek shelter in a log cabin, on some land inherited from my grandfather. This visitor haughtily demanded the return, to the farm my father had lost, of many movable articles, and we children, not understanding the intricacies of the law, wondered, after he had departed from his bootless errand, if the man were cloven-footed, like a person of historical notoriety whom we called "Old Splitfoot." I do not remember how long it was, or whether before or after this, to us, unnecessary event, that one day when my mother was busy at the loom in an adjoining cabin, our little sister Catherine, afterwards known to fame in many useful ways, as wife, mother, widow, home-maker, teacher and editor, toppled forward from her chair and fell into the fire. I remember my sister and I trying to catch her as she fell, and, failing, joined a chorus of children's screaming voices and brought our agonized mother to the scene. To this day, I cannot recall that incident without a shudder. My baby sister, too young to remember it, did not suffer after all, as we older ones did, who always felt that we ought to have known enough to have kept her away from the fire.

Work in the maple sugar camp was one of the annual employments of my childhood's days that I recall. My father, who was at one time recovering from a long illness, was just able to tap the trees and adjust the spiles and troughs for catching the sap, when he suffered a relapse, and I and my sister, seventeen months older, collected the sap, gathered branches from fallen trees, built the fires and boiled the syrup, which we carried to the house in pails for mother to "sugar-off."

There was a little log school house about a mile distant, which we attended at intervals, though my sister and I suffered many severe physical afflictions at times, which kept us away from school, resulting, as we afterwards knew, from exposure in the sugar camp.

Then, too, I recall many hot Summer days, of seemingly interminable length, when we were kept busy at picking wool by hand, or paring and coring apples, stringing the quarters on twine for drying in the sun; such monotonous occupations often confining us from daylight until dark. When the "rolls" came home from the woolen mill, spinning by hand was next in order; then "spooling," "reeling" and "hanking" had also to be done, and our dear mother experienced great relief when the yarn was sent to the factory to be dyed and woven into cloth and blankets for household use, relieving her from much of her former labor as a manufacturer in the home.

We had no mothers' clubs in those days. It was the universal belief that children could not hurt themselves at work; but when my brother and I were sent to plant a ten-acre cornfield, we must have thought differently, for we grew so tired that we skipped an entire "land" in the middle of the field to shorten the job; but we realized our mistake when the fraud was discovered, almost too late to correct it.

The circular sawmill craze began at last to reach

our county, and my father, aided by Deacon Huntington, an estimable Christian gentleman, imported the first
such sawmill ever seen west of Ohio. Its motor power
was horses, and the driver was the deacon's son.

Our fortunes began at once to mend. A smaller
house was built for occupancy by my grandfather, his
second wife and our dear great-grandmother, and we
were moved to the big elm tree homestead, where we
lived in comparative comfort and plenty until my father
caught a new installment of Western fever, and decided
to cross the plains to Oregon.

How we regretted leaving the dear, familiar haunts,
and how our mother grieved as she, for the last time,
visited the hallowed spot in the pasture, where the remains
of her first-born son were buried, are incidents engraved
upon my memory as indelibly as the light of the sun
would be if I should never see it again.

I remember standing at the bedside, when another
little sister came to our crowded home, and my mother
said, through her tears: "Poor baby! She'll be a woman
some day! Poor baby! A woman's lot is so hard!"

* * *

That long and perilous journey across the Great
Plains, over the Oregon Trail, has been so often described
in other histories, that repetition in these pages is unnecessary. Suffice it to say that our gentle, faithful, self-
sacrificing mother became a victim to the hardships of
the journey, fell ill of the cholera and died, on the 20th
day of June of that memorable year. My late lamented
brother, Harvey W. Scott, who was then a boy in his
early teens, mourned her death with the intensity of feeling characteristic of his strenuous nature. He told me
once, as I lay helpless on a bed of illness caused by my
own hardships as a pioneer path breaker, that sometimes
he would awaken in the night, and recalling our mother's

arduous lot, would rise and pace the floor, the victim of unavailing retrospection and regret. "Yes, brother," I said in reply, "and her memory, added to my own experiences and those of our surviving sisters, led me long ago to dedicate these maturer years of my life to the enfranchisement of women."

* * *

My father, after a brief visit in French Prairie, Oregon, at the home of his brother-in-law, Rev. Neil Johnson, who had preceded us to Oregon in 1851, moved with his remaining family to the village of Lafayette, the county seat of Yamhill County, where we spent the Winter among his pioneer cousins, James, Lemuel and Lawson Scott.

The following Spring found me installed as a district school teacher on the banks of the little river, Rickreall, near its junction with the wider Willamette, in the village of Eola, then known as Cincinnati, and looked upon for a time as a rival of the City of Salem. It was here that I met my fate in the person of Mr. Ben C. Duniway, a young rancher of Clackamas County, who took me, a bride, to his bachelor ranch, where we lived for four years. Two children, Clara and Willis, were born to us here. It was a hospitable neighborhood composed chiefly of bachelors, who found comfort in mobilizing at meal times at the homes of the few married men of the township, and seemed especially fond of congregating at the hospitable cabin home of my good husband, who was never quite so much in his glory as when entertaining them at his fireside, while I, if not washing, scrubbing, churning, or nursing the baby, was preparing their meals in our lean-to kitchen. To bear two children in two and a half years from my marriage day, to make thousands of pounds of butter every year for market, not including what was used in our free hotel at home; to sew and cook, and wash and iron; to bake and clean and stew and fry; to be, in short, a general pioneer drudge, with never a penny of my own, was not pleasant business for an erstwhile school teacher, who had earned a salary that had not gone before marriage, as did her butter and eggs and chickens afterwards, for groceries, and to pay taxes or keep up the wear and tear of horseshoeing, plow-sharpening and harness-mending. My recreation during those monotonous years was wearing out my wedding clothes, or making over for my cherished babies the bridal outfit I had earned as a school teacher.

My good husband was not idle; he was making a farm in the timber and keeping a lot of hired men, for whom I cooked and washed and mended, as part of the duties of a pioneer wife and devoted mother.

As I look back over those weary years, the most lingering of my many regrets is the fact that I was often compelled to neglect my little children, while spending my time in the kitchen, or at the churn or wash tub, doing heavy work for hale and hearty men—work for which I was poorly fitted, chiefly because my faithful mother had worn both me and herself to a frazzle with just such drudgery before I was born.

When our four years' probation on my husband's donation claim expired, he sold the place and bought the farm in Yamhill County, now known as the Millard Lownsdale Apple Ranch, where we lived for five years, until an unexpected incident occurred which changed the whole course of our future lives.

CHAPTER II.

Reminiscences.

P REVIOUS to moving to Lafayette, and while we were still residing on the Yamhill County farm, I had written and published a little book. It was a foolhardy thing for an illiterate and half-bent farmer's wife to undertake, backed with only a few months of the most primitive opportunities for education, gathered chiefly in my childhood, as elsewhere stated, from a little elementary spelling book. I scarcely knew the rudiments of correct English speaking, though my little battered, ink-bespattered journal of those old ox-wagon days speaks eloquently to me now of the crude foreshadowing of the long years yet to come, ere I should find myself at the head of great progressive endeavors, with the prospective Woman's Building of the Oregon State University bearing my name, my children occupying prominent and honorable positions, and myself the writer, over the Governor's signature, of the first Woman Suffrage Proclamation ever written by a woman's hand— an event marking an epoch in the history of woman's enfranchisement which, my friends are saying, is destined to become recognized, long after I am gone, as an instrument as historical and momentous, in its way, as the original Declaration of Independence itself.

My little book before spoken of did for me its unconscious part in paving the way which led me at last into a broader field. My advice to every aspiring tyro who may read these pages is: Do not yield to difficulties, but rise above discouragements. If the divine afflatus is within you, yield thereto and let it shine. The tallow dip was the forerunner of the candle; the oil lamp preceded gas and electricity; the pack train and the canvas-

GROUP OF EQUAL SUFFRAGISTS

JOHN H. MITCHELL
Equal Suffragist. Into Ex-Senator of the
United States, and Pioneer
Equal Suffragist

THE LATE SOLOMON HIRSCH
Former Minister to Turkey. Republican
and Pioneer Suffragist

THE LATE JACOB MAYER
Early and Always an Equal Suffragist and
Wholesale Merchant of Portland.
My First Financial Backer

THE LATE COL. H. W. SCOTT
Famous Editor of The Oregonian, who Opposed the Equal Suffrage Amendment
as "A Short Cut to Prohibition"

THE LATE B. C. DUNIWAY
My Husband and Co-Worker in Equal
Suffrage till Called to the Skies
In 1896

THE LATE JOSEPH N. DOLPH
Former United States Senator and Equal
Suffrage Advocate in Public and
Private Life. Republican

THE LATE WM. S. LADD, Esq.
Banker and Suffragist. Republican Leader
During the Civil War

covered wagon paved the way for the railroad; the steam engine led to the telegraph; the bicycle to the automobile; the airship followed—and nobody knows what is coming next. The rude cabin of the borderer opened the way to the better house, the great skyscraper followed in due season; great bridges, spanning mighty rivers, have superseded the erstwhile canoe, and incandescent lights are hung in clusters along city streets where once we floundered, in lantern-lighted semi-darkness, over fallen logs and through the abounding mud. Everything in its day is the order of creation. Success will seldom come in the ways that one has planned for it; but come it will, sooner or later, to all who are faithful, if not in this brief, mundane existence, then surely, as I verily believe, in the broader realm of opportunity that will open for us in the land of the leal.

That Yamhill County farm was my good husband's pride. The location was beautiful, and with the large capital inherited by its subsequent purchaser, Mr. Millard Lownsdale, who was able to finance it for a long period of years before it brought financial returns, it became the pride of its owner, who developed its natural resources, as we could and would have done with equal, outside financial backing.

My labors on that farm became an added burden as our resources grew. I recall one day which, like hundreds of others, was occupied to the limit. After dishes were washed, beds made, rooms swept, and when dinner was over for the family and hired men; after the week's washing was finished and the churning done, and I was busy in an outside house picking ducks—for those were pioneer days, and even our pillows, like our stockings, were home-made—a man came up from the village to our woodpile, where my husband was at work, and asked him to become surety for a considerable sum, with interest at two per cent per month, to be compounded

semi-annually until paid. The two men parleyed awhile
and then went into the house. It dawned upon me suddenly, as I was picking a duck, that it would ruin us
financially if those notes were signed. I tried hard
to be silent, being a nonentity in law, but my hands trembled, my heart beat hard, and I laid the pinioned duck on
its back and repaired to the living room to investigate.
My husband had already signed two notes, and was in
the act of signing the third, when I leaned over his shoulder and said, tremulously: "My dear, are you quite certain about what you are doing?" The other fellow looked
daggers at me, but said nothing, and my husband answered, as he signed the last note: "Mama, you needn't
worry; you'll always be protected and provided for!"
I wanted to say: "I guess I'll always earn all the protection I get," but I remembered that I was nothing but
a woman; so I bit my lips to keep silent and rushed back
to my work, where for several minutes, I fear that duckflesh suffered, for I didn't pluck the feathers tenderly.
But I cooled down after awhile, and to my credit be
it said, I never alluded to the notes afterwards. But
hard times came, crops failed, my butter and egg money
all went to pay interest and taxes, and the months went
on and on. A great flood swept away the warehouse
on the bank of Yamhill River at holiday time, carrying
off the year's harvest, and the unpaid notes, with accrued
interest, compounded semi-annually at 2 per cent per
month, all fell due at once.

One busy day, when I had added to my other duties
several rapid hurries down the hillside to scare the coyotes
away from the sheep, and just as dusk was coming on—
my husband having been away from home all day—the
sheriff came to the house and served summons on me for
those notes! Now, observe that, when that obligation
was made, I was my husband's silent partner—a legal
nonentity—with no voice or power for self-protection

under the sun; but, when penalty accrued, I was his legal representative. I took the warrant smilingly from the sheriff's hand, and said: "It is all right. Won't you walk in?" He excused himself and went to a neighbor's house, nearly a mile distant, and served a wife with another paper. I afterwards learned that the good wife had, as the sheriff expressed it, "blowed him up," and he said to her, as he turned away: "You'd better go and see Mrs. Duniway and learn a lesson in politeness."

When the hired man came in to supper I was as entertaining as I knew how to be. I told them of some cute sayings of the children, and strove in many ways to conceal the fact that I had been sued. I had yet to learn that the right to sue and be sued was the inalienable right of an American citizen.

As the night came down my husband came home, and, after he had eaten his supper, and while he was playing with the children, the hired men having gone to their quarters, I confess I felt a little secret satisfaction when I served those papers on him. I had framed up a little "spiel," which I meant to practice on him when I should serve the papers, but he turned so pale and looked so care-worn I couldn't even say, "I told you so!"

The lawsuit was not alluded to again until the next morning, when my husband informed me that he was going to town after breakfast to get that trouble settled out of court. Just what sort of a deal he made I do not now remember, but it resulted in the sale of the farm for just about enough to pay those security notes and interest, leaving us in possession of a little piece of town property in Lafayette, where I had often said I wished we were poor enough so we might be able to live in such a place, that I might have a chance to keep a few boarders, or take in washing for a livelihood; then I thought I might not only make a living more easily, but might have control of a little money that I could call my own, with which to clothe my children properly.

We had hardly become settled in our new quarters when an accident with a runaway team befell my husband, which, though he lived for many years thereafter, incapacitated him for physical labor on a farm, and threw the financial, as well as domestic, responsibility of our family upon my almost unaided self. His serious accident aroused the keenest sympathies of my being. He had become so deeply depressed by reverses for which he blamed himself, that I endeavord in every way to encourage him in negotiations he was making for another farm, by opening a private school. But this accident upset all of our plans. Our cottage was a one and a half story frame building, with the upper part merely enclosed and roofed. This enclosure I lined and ceiled with unbleached muslin; and by working at it outside of school and kitchen hours, I soon had a neat and comfortable dormitory for the accommodation of young lady boarders, whom I added to my burdened household. Finding hired help unattainable, as the marriage of girls in their early teens was at that time universal, and Chinese servants had not yet penetrated our village, I would arise from my bed at 3 o'clock in Summer and 4 o'clock in Winter, to do a day's work before school time. Then, repairing to my school room I would teach the primer classes while resting at my desk. For two hours afterwards I would occupy the time with the older students, often hearing recitations from text books I had never studied, over which, so keyed to thought was I from sheer necessity, that I caught the inspiration of every problem as I came to it, and never stumbled over any lesson, or let my pupils see that it was new to me.

I would prepare the table for luncheon in the dining room before repairing to the school room; and, returning to lessons at 1 o'clock P. M., would resume school work until 4 o'clock, before taking up my household duties again in the home. And yet, notwithstanding all this effort, I led an easier life than I had known on a pioneer farm. My work was rest for both mind and body. Health improved and hope revived. The evenings were recreative, musical, intellectual and thoroughly enjoyable; but how I got through with all of this physical work, and kept ahead of my constantly improving classes, as the weeks and months and years went on, I do not know. I had never had an opportunity to study English grammar, higher arithmetic or algebra; but I never failed, as a teacher, to impart any required knowledge at any recitation. I could never even find time to look at any lesson until my classes were called. I would then call a student to the blackboard, where he or she would stand with chalk in hand till, after reading the problem for the first time myself, I would ask the pupil to state it according to formula. If the class had mastered the lesson, the rest was easy. But if, as sometimes happened, the solution was not comprehended at all, I had to think like lightning to catch the inspiration myself. So I would say: "Suppose we analyze it." Taking for example, articles in the room, such as the stove, doors, windows, sashes or panes, desks, seams in the floor, etc., and by grouping, analyzing and amalgamation, adapting such articles to the solution of the problem before us, we would all begin to see through it at once; and the pupil at the board would begin with a hurried, nervous movement, to transcribe his thoughts in characters, figures, letters or diagrams; and the lesson would be mastered in fine shape—no student imagining that I had been catching the inspiration of it myself as we went along.

* * *

The town of Albany had sprung up in the interior of the Willamette Valley, and we sold out our little posses-

GROUP OF EQUAL SUFFRAGISTS

COL. ROBERT A. MILLER
Prominent Equal Suffragist and a Democratic Leader in Politics

U. S. SEN. GEORGE E. CHAMBERLAIN
Author of the U. S. Senate Amendment for Equal Suffrage. Democrat

JONATHAN BOURNE, JR.
Ex-United States Senator. Leading Advocate of Equal Suffrage in Oregon, and in the U. S. Senate. Republican

EX-SENATOR CHARLES W. FULTON
Who Introduced an Equal Suffrage Amendment in the Oregon Legislature in 1902. Leading Republican

HIS EXCELLENCY, OSWALD WEST
Governor of Oregon. Democrat. Leading Advocate of Equal Suffrage

JOHN BARRETT
of Oregon. Ex-U. S. Minister to Colombia, and President of American Republics. Republican and Suffragist

W. M. DAVIS, Esq.
Prominent Attorney. President Oregon Men's Equal Suffrage League

sions in Lafayette and moved to this wider field, where
I again engaged in teaching until I thought I had money
enough to go into trade. By the time I had moved my
school house to Broadalbin street and converted it into
a store, with counters, shelves and showcases, and had
bought out a partner and was ready to start up with
millinery and notions, I had left on hand, after paying
expenses to Portland and return, just thirty dollars.

The late Jacob Mayer, Esq., the original wholesale dealer in such goods as I wanted, was doing a good
business in the lines I was seeking, and I went to him,
introduced myself and stated my need, explaining the
state of my finances. "Won't some of your friends go
security for you?" he asked, with a businesslike air that
sent a chill to my heart. "My husband went broke by
going security," I replied, with a shake of my head, "and
I vowed long ago that I would never copy his mistake."
"How much of a stock do you want?" he asked, in a
tone that reassured me a little. "About a hundred dollars will do for the beginning," I said tremulously. "Nonsense!" was the hearty response of the experienced merchant. "You could carry home a hundred dollars' worth
of millinery in a silk apron. Let me select you a stock
of goods!" To my surprise the bill amounted to twelve
hundred dollars. "I'm afraid to risk it," I said anxiously,
as I produced my little wad of thirty dollars to offer in
payment. "Never mind," he said, "you'll need that money
to get some articles at Van Fridagh's retail store. Take
this stock home and do the best you can with it. Then
come back and get some more."

* * *

I was back in three weeks and paid the debt in full.
My next account was for three thousand dollars; and
from that day to this, I have not known extreme poverty;
though I am not wealthy and never can be. I have earned

and expended over forty-two thousand dollars in my long-drawn struggle for Equal Rights for Women, which if I had used in trade, or invested in real estate, would have made me several times a millionaire.

CHAPTER III.

Experiences in Business.

MY MILLINERY business flourished reasonably well in a financial way, but the lessons it taught, that brought me before the world as an evangel of Equal Rights for Women, were of far greater value than dollars and cents. One day, as I was standing behind the counter, making a twenty-dollar bonnet for a fashionable member of one of our leading churches, I had open before me a copy of the "State's Rights Democrat," when my eye fell upon a paragraph announcing that a certain well-to-do farmer had recently purchased a valuable race horse. I was musing over the investment, as I worked on the bonnet, and wondering how much the outlay would mean to his wife and children, when the family drove up in a two-horse wagon, in charge of a hired man. The day was gloomy and disagreeable, and I led the family into my work room, where there was a cheerful fire. After the mother and children had become apparently comfortable, I asked what I could do for them. The mother looked at me hesitatingly and said: "I came to see if I couldn't get some plain sewing to do. I am obliged to earn some money." Instantly I thought of her husband, riding into town and leading that beautiful horse, which he had covered with a brown Holland "polonaise." The high-spirited animal was stepping proudly, as if conscious of the admiration of the men and boys that followed in its wake, while the owner couldn't have sat more erect on the pony at his side if he had swallowed a yard stick. "I am sorry," I said to the expectant woman, with a baby at her breast, "but I am giving out all the work

I can spare from the store to women who are helping their husbands to pay house rent, or lift widows' mortgages to stop interest on their little homes." I wish I could forget the disappointment in the woman's face, as I added: "You don't look able to bear another burden of any sort. But I'll sell you what you and your children need, and charge the bill to your husband." The woman gave a hollow cough, as if to clear her throat, and said: "I am not strong any more, and I don't care what becomes of me, but I promised these girls (apparently 12 and 14 years of age) that if they would work hard and make lots of butter, I'd buy them water-proof suits to wear to Sunday school. But (and her voice filled with sobs) *he* used the 'butter money' to help pay for his race horse, and the girls took on so about their water-proof suits that I've got to earn the money for them some way, or go crazy." "I'll sell you the goods and charge the bill to your husband," I replied, huskily. She shook her head and said: "John doesn't allow me to go in debt." "If John confiscates your butter and cuts off your credit you are out of luck!" I said sharply. But I couldn't sell her the goods, though I offered to cut and fit the suits without extra charge. She went her way sorrowing, and I never saw her again. The next Summer, I think it was in the following August, a funeral procession went through Albany—the bells tolled solemnly, and the mortal remains of that wife and mother, after having bequeathed another baby to the care of its over-burdened maternal grandmother, was laid away in the churchyard. The clergy of several churches alluded to the burial in the next Sunday's pulpits, offering condolence to the bereaved husband; but I, who had had a glimpse behind the scenes, pondered long and deeply over that "butter money," the defrauded children, the deceased wife, and that thoroughbred race horse.

On another occasion, a woman came to me in great

distress, telling me between her sobs that her husband had sold their household furniture and disappeared, and she was left destitute, with five little children. We had, in those days, no mother's pension, no Boys' and Girls' Aid Society, no Woman's Sole Trader Bill and no rights, under the law, for any wife, which any husband was bound to respect—an amazing proof of the fact that the vast majority of men have been so much better to wives, through all the centuries, than the inherited laws of the receding barbaric ages from which we are slowly emerging, that we hear only now and then of a husband and father who is heartless enough to act toward his family as the law permits.

The woman of whom I was speaking dropped upon a chair and said: "There is a family on a central street that is going away. I could rent their house and keep my family together by taking in boarders; but I haven't any furniture. If I could borrow six hundred dollars on the furniture, I could pay for it in installments, and I thought you might assist me." I had more obligations of my own than I could carry comfortably, and had to send her away weeping. While I was racking my brain for some way to help her out, a neighbor called on some errand, to whom I related the woman's story. "I'll lend her the money and take a mortgage on her furniture," said my friend, who, though not rich, was known as a benevolent man. As soon as I could leave the store, I sought the woman in her deserted home, where nothing was left but the weeping children, the family's scanty clothing and a few battered chairs and dishes. To make matters worse, the rent would be due in a few days and the payment would take her last dollar. The memory of the look of relief that came into her face as I related my errand has amply repaid me for every slur or snub and slight that came to me afterwards in pursuit of my public mission. The transfer was soon made; the woman and her children took possession of the furnished home, and a half dozen boarders were installed, creating an income out of which she could supply her table and general operating expenses. Things were going well with her when her husband returned and took legal possession of everything. He repudiated the mortgage, which the wife had had no legal right to contract, and there was nothing left for her but the divorce courts. The family was scattered, my philanthropic neighbor lost his money, except what had been paid in two little installments, and the little religious world of Albany went on sighing over the degeneracy of the times that was making divorces easy. In looking backward, it seems strange to me now that I didn't sooner see the need of votes for women.

* * *

One day, in the following Spring, after I had returned from Portland and San Francisco, with a stock of millinery and notions, when the weather was fine and everything seemed bright for a good season of trade, a well-to-do farmer drove up to the store in a handsome family carriage, drawn by a pair of spirited dapple grays. His wife and four little daughters accompanied him, and I felt sure of a good forenoon's business. The wife asked for some hats for the little girls. I took from the shelves a pretty bandbox and uncovered a line of misses' hats made of a then fashionable stuff, called "Neapolitan." They were prettily trimmed and not expensive, and while the mother was making her selections, I kept up a running conversation with the father, largely because I always enjoy conversing with a sensible man, but more especially, in this case, to give his wife a chance to complete her choice of hats without suggestions from myself. The husband turned to her at last, with a matter-of-fact air, and said: "Have you made your selections?" She nodded assent, and he turned to me with a smile, and said, in the familiar vernacular of the pioneer: "What's the damage?" I noticed that he hadn't smiled when he looked at his wife, causing me to recall the familiar fact that men were oftener in the habit of smiling when talking to other people's wives than their own. I smiled back at the husband as I said: "Four hats, at three dollars each, will be twelve dollars." The custodian of the family purse turned to the woman and said impatiently: "That's more money than I can spare for children's hats!" Then he accosted me with another smile, and said: "Haven't you got something cheaper?" I then handed down a lot of hats made of the woven fiber of the inner bark of the horse chestnut, which I kept for sale for the convenience of Indian berry pickers for "six bits" each. The profit to me on those hats was better than the Dutchman's one per cent; that is, when an article was bought for one penny, I would sell it for two. My customer didn't look at the hats, but he said: "They'll do. Put up four of 'em in a box so they won't get jolted out of shape on a rough road." The children all looked disappointed, and one of them said: "He thinks silver-mounted harness isn't a bit too good for his horses, though!" They were all facing me, standing in front of the counter, and the woman turned to her children with the shake of her head and an admonishing look, which silenced their objections without another word. Then the wife looked up at the husband with a smile; something, no doubt, like the smiles she had bestowed upon him in their courting days. "Are you tired?" she asked, in a voice of solicitude. "No," he replied bluntly. "What have I been doing to tire me?" "I left a butter firkin at Barrow's store. I forgot it. Won't you please go and get it?" asked the wife, sweetly. The man started off willingly, believing himself to be the head of his family. As soon as he was gone, the real head of the close corporation said to me: "Put up those four

Neapolitan hats—two trimmed in straw-color for the brunettes, and two in blue for the little blondes." As I was boxing her purchases for safe transportation, I said: "Won't your husband notice the difference when he sees the hats?" "No!" she replied sharply. "He doesn't know any more about a hat than I do about a horse collar! When he comes in he'll pay you three dollars—all he meant to allow me to spend." Then she put her hand in her pocket and drew out some half-dollar pieces. "Here," she said, "are four dollars and a half. That's all I have with me today. I'll still owe you the balance— four dollars and a half. When I come to town again I'll bring you the rest of the money." The husband returned, threw down three dollars on the counter with a jingle, and off they went, apparently at peace with all the world, while I felt almost as guilty as if I had been compounding a felony. A few days afterward I was in a neighboring store, and I asked the merchant if he thought I'd ever see that balance of four dollars and a half. "Of course!" was his emphatic reply. "We merchants couldn't make any profit on fancy goods if it wasn't for what the women steal from their husbands."

* * *

Years passed. I had crossed the Rubicon and burned my bridges behind me. I was lecturing in an Eastern Oregon town, on the need of Equal Rights for mothers, where I related the foregoing incident, and pointed its moral. The churches were not open for women speakers at that time, except in rarest intervals, so my work was handicapped by hall rent—always hard to collect. But I explained as best I could the fundamental, and now rarely disputed, fact that children inherit their tendencies for good or evil largely from the environment of their mothers. "Give them the fruit of their hands," I cried, in closing. "Make women free financially, and let their own works praise them in the gates!" After the close of the lecture, and while people were crowding about me for handshaking and introductions, a nice-looking young man came up and introduced himself. I did not recall the name he gave me, so he related, as briefly as possible, the incident detailed above. "But I don't think I ever met you before," I said in surprise; "I thought all the children of the family were girls." "Oh," he replied, with a shrug, "things didn't go right with me and the Gov, and I skipped. I came up into Eastern Oregon and—they say—I stole a horse! So I served time in Salem; but the time's out now, and I am going back to make a new start." "Were you really guilty?" I asked earnestly. He did not reply, but passed on through the crowd and I never saw him again.

Will the reader please remember the physiological and psychological fact that "When the parents eat sour grapes the children's teeth are set on edge"?

CHAPTER IV.

Starts a Newspaper.

I ATTRIBUTE what I was pleased to call, in later years, my third and latest birth, to my experiences in my before-mentioned millinery store. My mother, my sisters and myself had not been burdened with dissipated or cruel husbands; we had had no reason for hating men, and we believed it was our religious duty to accept our lot as we found it. We were all proud of our skill as cooks and housewives. As mothers we were devoted to our many children, though, as a rule, we cherished ambitions for them which our border husbands did not share.

I recall a St. Valentine's day, which brought me an overpowering humiliation, over which I smile in this evening of my life, as I pause to record it here. My husband came to our hillside home that memorable day, bringing the mail, among which was a large envelope addressed to me. I was standing near the fireplace, tugging with all my might at the dasher of an old-fashioned churn, which formed an important part of my almost daily duties. Every farmer's wife of my acquaintance was doing likewise, and some of them had husbands who would go on occasional sprees, and spend the wives' "butter money" for whiskey and tobacco, which my husband was spending chiefly, at that time, for taxes and that awful interest at two per cent per month on another man's debt, as recorded elsewhere, "compounded semi-annually until paid." As soon as the butter had "come," I carried the heavy churn to the kitchen, lifted out the butter into a wooden bowl, and returning, seated myself to nurse the baby and read the mail. On opening the big envelope, I discovered a gaily-covered, poster-like

Valentine. Seated on a chair was pictured a typical hen-pecked husband, trembling as if in terror. Clambering over him were a lot of squalling children, and above his cowering form stood an irate, illy-clad, toothless, straggling-haired woman, brandishing a broom. Under this delectable picture were the following lines:

> "Fiend, devil's imp, or what you will,
> You surely your poor man will kill,
> With luckless days and sleepless nights,
> Haranguing him with Woman's Rights!"

I gave the screed to my husband and said, through falling tears: "Did I ever give you, or anybody else, a reason for attacking me with a thing like this?" "No," he replied impatiently, as I interrupted his frolic with the children, "it was sent to you by some fool as a joke. If I had known what it was, or that you would care a rap about it, I wouldn't have brought it home."

Years after, when my public career had become established, I was presiding at a suffrage meeting in the opera house at Salem. Again it was St. Valentine's day, and a page brought a large envelope to the platform, which I opened curiously, drawing therefrom a gaudy, poster-like picture, which carried me back to what seemed another epoch. I advanced smilingly to the front of the platform. Before my mental vision came the old-fashioned churn, my life of hopeless toil, amid uncongenial surroundings, and that first comic valentine. I smoothed out the folds of the gaudy sheet and stooping above the footlights, exhibited it before the audience. "The author of this exquisite piece of art didn't give his name, but he has sent along his picture," I said, as the audience roared. "You see," I continued, "that it represents a henpecked husband. He is lying helpless on his back, on the floor, a picture of terror. Over him stands his wife—half hen and half woman. Her beak is clutching a few straggling hairs on the top of his head. I know the

poor artist doesn't intend to represent my husband, for
he isn't bald-headed." The memory of that incident
and the merriment that followed, are haunting me as
I write. "Don't you see, ladies," I said, turning to the
crowded platform, and relating the older scene before
described, "that all we have to do, when we meet the
nettle of ridicule, is to grasp it tightly, and then it cannot
sting us much?"

I have never had another comic valentine.

In transcribing these foregoing incidents, I am re-
minded of another that calls for insertion here, though
I see that I am still wandering from my opening text.

Another year had passed, and the Equal Suffrage
Association was again holding a mass meeting in the
Salem opera house.

A peculiar character, well known among Oregon
pioneers at that time, was the late Mr. Elisha Applegate,
a younger brother of Jesse Applegate, the prominent
borderer, of whom I shall speak in another chapter.
Among the speakers on the platform were seated Dr.
Mary P. Sawtelle, Hon. W. C. Johnson, Josephine De
Vore Johnson. John Minto, Sr., and his gifted wife,
whom we afterwards lovingly called our "Musket Member." This name was accorded her in honor of a pleasing
reply she had once made to a speaker who had said: "If
women vote they must fight." "I am willing to carry
a musket at any time in defense of my liberties," said
the gentle little woman, who was radiant with smiles.
Then, addressing the speaker, she had said: "Are you,
sir, willing to shoulder a musket in defense of my
rights?" while her bright eyes were sparkling with merriment. But he didn't reply, and the audience was convulsed with laughter as he took his seat.

To return to Mr. Applegate. "You must confine
yourself to fifteen minutes," I said, aside, before announcing him as the next speaker. I kept close tab on his

"time" till it was up, but he paid no heed to the limit, and kept on talking in his familiar, drawling way, repeating his lecture on "Bagdad" till the audience grew restless, and I sensed the approaching stampede he was evidently expecting, so I seized Mrs. Johnson's fan—a large and pretty one—and standing close to the speaker, began a vigorous use of it before his eyes. To my delight, and the amusement of the audience, he collapsed utterly, and took his seat amid much hand-clapping and laughter. "You didn't even give me a chance for my peroration," he said to me afterwards, in recalling the incident, over which everybody was happy but his dear little wife, who didn't like it a little bit.

At the time of our removal to Portland, in 1871, the village contained about eight thousand pioneers, who were nestled in primitive homes, among fallen trees and blackened stumps. The ambitious little city-to-be boasted one principal street, along which stood flourishing double rows of dry goods stores, groceries, meat markets, a primitive hotel or two, and once in a while a Chinese laundry. An occasional saloon peeped out on the Willamette River, with now and then a wooden building rising to obstruct the view, to the disgust of older occupants, across the street.

I had no acquaintances in the little city besides my good brother, Harvey W. Scott, and his little family, except Jacob Mayer, proprietor of the wholesale establishment which had supplied me with goods in the millinery line. As elsewhere stated, I was wholly ignorant of the publishing business, into which I was stumbling blindly, but I hired a foreman at twenty-five dollars per week, who placed my type and galleys in shape, using two upper bedrooms of a two-story frame house, at the corner of Third and Washington streets, which I had hired at forty dollars per month. The foreman taught my growing sons the printer's art, and "The New Northwest" soon became a household visitor throughout my chosen bailiwick of Oregon, Washington and Idaho.

My good brother, Mr. Harvey W. Scott, whom I had not ventured to consult at all while I was preparing to issue my initial paper, and who, knowing my limitations, was naturally uncertain of the result, called upon me, for the first time after the publication was out, and was extremely cordial. "You have made a capital paper," he said, as he surveyed my little "plant," his eyes gleaming with pleasure and surprise.

Forty-two years have been folded away into the irrevocable past since that memorable day. My foreman, my father, my daughter, my husband, two of my sisters and my first born son have solved the eternal mystery; and here I sit in the lengthening shadows unavailingly evoking the unseen shades of departed dear ones, as my aging hand records the facts that memory portrays with a vividness which is as ineffaceable as the love of God.

Our next caller, after the first paper was issued from the press, was my beloved, honored and Christian friend, Rev. T. L. Eliot, founder of the First Unitarian Church of Portland, now minister emeritus, whose able son is now the pastor of the church the father builded. A halo of well-earned glory is shining around the senior minister's whitened head; and I honor him beyond power of words to express, as one who has ever been faithful to my strenuous endeavors, who has always forgiven my blunders and commended whatsoever of well-doing I have been capable.

The next clergyman whose voice and visage I recall, was the late Dr. A. L. Lindsley, a Presbyterian minister of the old school, who was as non-committal before the public, about votes for women, as President Wilson now is. He was as unable to control his emotion, when we met, as our distinguished president was on an-

other occasion, when women asked him to advocate Equal
Rights before Congress. During a previous pastoral
call, I had related some of the personal experiences that
had inspired my mission, and he had said he would be
glad to aid me, if permitted by his church. His memory
recalls one special incident as I write, well worthy of
recording here. Our family was seated at the breakfast
table on a Sunday morning when Willis, who had brought
in a weekly paper, unfolded it, and on glancing at the
editorial page, turned very pale. He passed the paper
to his brother Hubert, who read the paragraph, and
the two, without a word, arose from the table and left
the dining room, taking the paper with them. I instinctively felt that something was wrong and followed the
boys to the door, where I begged them to do nothing
rashly. They did not reply, but hurried away; the next
I heard from them, they had been arrested for assault
and battery and released on bail, which was placed at
ten thousand dollars, offered by Mr. D. W. Prentice,
a prominent dealer in musical instruments. Judge J. F.
Caples, the prosecuting attorney, told me afterwards that
he risked his official standing by saying, aside: "Stay
with it, boys. You did exactly right!"

The offending paper was not allowed to go in the
mail, and the only copy I saw of it afterwards showed
why. The next morning's Oregonian gave a blistering
editorial in defense of myself and sons, hotly excoriating
any paper that tried to slur or slander the good name
of a faithful mother. The next morning as I was going
to my office I met Rev. Mr. Lindsley, who said, seeing
me in tears: "Never mind. The world has always cruci-
fied its Saviors, stoned its Stephens and imprisoned its
Galileos. No lesser lights, who follow at a greater distance, need expect to escape unscathed if they are doing
any good." As I reached the crowded street, which was
fairly black with an excited multitude of men, discussing

the affair, Mr. J. N. Dolph, afterwards United States Senator, crossed the street with his hat lifted and offered me his hand, when, suddenly, every man in the crowd, as if moved by a common impulse, removed his hat and remained uncovered as I went weeping by.

The next clergyman whose espousal of an unpopular cause to which Providence had called me was the late Rev. E. R. Geary, whom I met one day on the train between Salem and Albany. When I had last met him, he was a probate judge in Linn County, where he made a useful record, adding to his slender pay, as a Presbyterian minister, the official duties of an honorable dispenser of man-made laws. Our train had halted at Gervais, and Mr. Geary came to my seat and extended his hand as he stood in the aisle, reminding me of some old Roman senator of whom I had read, and said: "I believe you are going to win, and it seems to me the wisest course for us men to pursue is to wrap our robes about us, like Caesar, and die as gracefully as possible." I replied: "I don't want you to die, Mr. Geary; such men should live to declare the works of the Lord."

I close my eyes, as I pause in writing, and can see a tall, commanding, white-haired figure, cultured, elegant, assuming, grand! Of such are the reformers of earth.

Now comes before my eyes of memory, the venerable figure of my reverend friend, Father Spencer, a clergyman of the olden time, a leader in the Methodist Episcopal Church, who often favored me with words of cheer in the days when I needed them most. He lived, with his devoted family, for many years on a donation claim among the blue heights of beautiful Yamhill, in a lonely but ideal spot, where his descendants yet reside, among them his gifted son-in-law, Rev. G. H. Greer, who, assisted by the loving counsels of his devoted wife, became a Unitarian minister, and is the only one of the clericals

I have named who came first to my assistance, except Rev. Dr. Eliot, who is lingering in the body at the time of this recital.

Then, there was my uncle by marriage, the Rev. Neil Johnson, a Cumberland Presbyterian minister, a pioneer of 1851, who, like most of his forerunners and co-workers of border pulpits, worked at manual labor, between Sundays, to support a large family, while converting neighbors and improving his land. He and his devoted wife have long since joined the great majority, and the remnant of their large family, who still live to honor their names, are filling useful positions in other than clerical callings. The great orchard my uncle planted and tended is a monument to his memory, which, in addition to his work as a preacher, remains to this day a mute, yet eloquent, forerunner of the great orchard industry that, in these later years, has placed Oregon on the maps of the world.

I also recall, with loving memory, the Rev. Thomas Condon, whom I first met at The Dalles, who afterwards became known as state geologist in the University of Oregon.

Rev. J. H. D. Henderson was one of my standbys in Eugene, at whose home I was entertained in the early '70s, when few women besides his faithful wife had openly dared to espouse my mission. The late Revs. Atkinson, Cruzan and Marvin were Congregational ministers of Portland, who often aided me. If I make little mention of the wives of the clergymen named in this recital, it is because I seldom met them. They were, for the most part, mothers of little children, supported and protected at hard labor in an economical fashion by husbands who permitted them to feel that they "had all the rights they wanted." One notable exception was the wife of Rev. Dr. Hall, of Salem, daughter of Rev. Father Waller, a Methodist minister of the early '40s.

Mrs. Hall sometimes entertained me in her home, when other women had no ambition to do so.

Now, as I write, I close my eyes and see the late Rev. Isaac Dillon, whilom editor of the Pacific Christian Advocate, whose memory, friendship and moral support I still highly prize, though he couldn't help deploring, in the columns of his newspaper, that I had outgrown belief in a literal lake of eternally burning brimstone, about which, in my childhood days, I had been so often scared. Brother Dillon passed to his reward many years ago. Though he rests from his labors, his good work follows him.

And now ariseth before my eyes of faith and memory, the last, but by no means least, of my risen coadjutors of the pulpit, Rev. W. R. Bishop, who reminds me as I write of Edward Eggleston's noted character, "The Hoosier School Master," who believed in "The Church of the Big Licks." I had known Mr. Bishop in my childhood's home in Illinois, and while we did not meet for many years after coming to the far distant West, I always remembered him as the one minister whose piety never frightened me. His preaching, though largely of the lachrymose or emotional type, never made him dolorous or disagreeable in our home. As a pioneer educator he was a success. He lived for many years in the town of Brownsville, Oregon, where he built up an excellent school, which still lives as his monument. In after years he removed to Portland, where he spent his declining life in peace, retirement and plenty, revered by all who knew him. One of his last evenings in public was spent as a speaker and co-worker at an Equal Suffrage meeting in our Chamber of Commerce in 1905. Peace to his ashes.

CHAPTER V.

Brings Miss Anthony to Oregon.

AMONG the many incidents I recall, which led me into the Equal Suffrage movement and crowd upon my memory as I write, was one which calls for special mention, and ought not to be omitted here. I had grown dispirited over an accumulation of petty annoyances in the store, when a woman entered suddenly, and throwing back a heavy green berage veil, said: "Mrs. Duniway, I want you to go with me to the court house!" I replied rather curtly, I fear: "The court house is a place for men." The visitor, whose eyes were red with weeping, explained that the county court had refused to accept the terms of her annual settlement, as administratrix of her husband's estate. But her lawyer had told her to get some merchant to accompany her to the court house, to bear testimony to the manner of settling her accounts. "Can't you get some man to go with you?" I asked, with growing sympathy. "I have asked several, but they all say they are too busy," was her tearful response. A sudden impulse seized me, and, calling one of the girls from the work room to wait upon customers, I started with the widow to the court house, feeling half ashamed, as I walked the street, to meet any one who might guess my errand. The woman kept up a running conversation as we proceeded, her words often interrupted by sobs. "Only think!" she cried, in a broken voice, "my husband—if he had lived and I had died— could have spent every dollar we had earned in twenty years of married life, and nobody would have cared what became of my children. I wasn't supposed to have any children. My girls and I have sold butter, eggs, poultry, cord wood, vegetables, grain and hay—almost enough to

GROUP OF EQUAL SUFFRAGISTS

JUDGE WM. GALLOWAY
A Leading Democratic Office Holder
McMinnville, Oregon

HENRY WALDO COE M. D.
National Committeeman of the Progressive
Party and Leading Suffragist

ATTORNEY D. SOLIS COHEN
A Leading Equal Suffragist Republican

HON. BEN SELLING
Prominent Republican and Leading Equal
Suffragist A State Senator

GEORGE H. HIMES
Curator of Oregon Historical Society Sec'y
of State Pioneer Association and
Active Suffragist

MR. W. S. U'REN
Author of the Initiative and Referendum.
Independent in Politics A
Single Taxer

DR. HARRY LANE
United States Senator-Elect from Oregon,
January 20, 1913. Successor to
Jonathan Bourne Jr.

pay taxes and meet all of our bills, but after I've earned the means to pay expenses I can't even buy a pair of shoe-strings without being lectured by the court for my extravagance!" By this time I was so deeply interested that I shouldn't have cared if all the world knew I was going to the court house. I felt a good deal as the man must have felt "who whipped another man for saying his sister was cross-eyed." When arraigned for misconduct before the court he said: "Your Honor, my sister isn't cross-eyed. I haven't any sister. It was the principle of the thing that stirred me up!"

The court had adjourned for recess as I entered the room, and I felt much relieved, as I knew the officers and didn't feel afraid to meet them when off duty. The urbane judge, who was still occupying his revolving chair, leaned back and listened to my story. When I had finished, he put his thumbs in the armholes of his vest and said, with a patronizing air: "Of course, Mrs. Duniway, as you are a lady, you are not expected to understand the intricacies of the law." "But we are expected to know enough to foot the bills, though," I retorted, with more force than elegance. The widow's lawyer beckoned us to him and said, with a merry twinkle in his eye: "I guess there won't be any more trouble with the county court, or the commissioners this year." As we were returning to the store the widow said: "I have to pay that lawyer enough every year to meet all my taxes, if I wasn't compelled to administer on my husband's estate."

In relating this incident to my husband at night, I added: "One-half of the women are dolls, the rest of them are drudges, and we're all fools!" He placed his hand on my head, as I sat on the floor beside his couch, and said: "Don't you know it will never be any better for women until they have the right to vote?" "What good would that do?" I asked, as a new light began to break across my mental vision. "Can't you see," he said earnestly, "that women do half of the work of the world? And don't you know that if women were voters there would soon be law-makers among them? And don't you see that, as women do half the work of the world, besides bearing all the children, they ought to control fully half of the pay?" The light permeated my very marrow bones, filling me with such hope, courage and determination as no obstacle could conquer and nothing but death could overcome.

* * *

Early in the month of November, in the year 1870, shortly after many such practical experiences as related above, which led me to determine to remove from Albany to Portland, to begin the publication of my weekly newspaper, "The New Northwest," I met one day at the home of my estimable neighbor, the late Mrs. Martha J. Foster, and our mutual friend, Mrs. Martha A. Dalton, of Portland, to whom I announced my intention. My friends heartily agreed with my idea as to Equal Rights for Women, but expressed their doubts as to the financial success of the proposed newspaper enterprise. After much discussion and finding my determination to begin the work unshaken, the three of us met at my home and decided to form the nucleus of a State Equal Suffrage Association.

A little local Equal Suffrage Society had previously been organized in Salem, with Colonel C. A. Reed as president and Judge G. W. Lawson as secretary. I at once communicated with these gentlemen, stating our purpose, and, as I was going to San Francisco on business in the approaching holidays, I was favored by them with credentials as a delegate to the California Woman Suffrage convention, to meet in Sacramento the following Spring. No record of our preliminary meeting to form the State Society of Oregon Suffragists was preserved of which Mrs. Dalton or myself had knowledge. The minutes were left with Mrs. Foster, who, like Colonel Reed and Judge Lawson, long ago passed to the higher life. But I promised Mrs. Dalton, who visited me at this writing, in October, 1913, and has since passed away, to make special mention of that initial meeting in these pages, little dreaming that ere this history should see the light, she would have preceded me to the unseen world, leaving me the sole survivor of our compact of 1870.

Mrs. Dalton became one of the charter members of the State Equal Suffrage Association at the time of its permanent organization in Portland, in 1873, and continued a member of its executive committee up to the time of her death. While she was not a public speaker, and was not given to writing essays, she was always ready to attend to any kind of detail work, such as other and less enterprising women might easily be tempted to shirk. Her occupation, as a successful music teacher, afforded her extensive acquaintance among the leading people of Portland, many of whom confided their family or personal grievances to her, to whom she was always a sympathetic friend. As I pause to drop a sympathetic tear to her memory as I add this paragraph, I feel comforted, because I know that in the course of nature I, too, shall join the great majority in the rapidly approaching bye and bye.

* * *

The first number of "The New Northwest" was issued on the 5th of May, 1871. As I look backward over the receded years, and recall the incidents of this venture, in the management of which I had had no previous training, I cannot but wonder at my own audacity, which can be compared to the spirit of adventure which led the early pioneers to cross, or try to cross, the unknown plains, with helpless families in covered wagons, drawn by teams of oxen. It is true that I did not encounter the diseases and deaths of the desert, in making that venture, nor meet attacks from wild beasts and wilder savages, but I did encounter ridicule, ostracism and financial obstacles, over which I fain would draw the veil of forgetfulness. While I did not regret meeting insults and misrepresentation on my own account, I did suffer deeply because of my budding family, who naturally resented the slander and downright abuse I suffered from ambitious editors, to all of whose attacks I replied in my own paper, in such a way as to bring to my defense the wiser comments of successful men, among whom I number many of our most prominent citizens of today; while among my detractors, I cannot recall a single one who has placed on record a single important deed redounding to his public or private credit.

Of the many men and women, who have honestly differed from me in the past, I have no word of censure. To my good brother, the late Mr. Harvey W. Scott, three years my junior, editor of the "Oregonian," then a rising journalist, universally honored in his later years, I owe a debt of lasting gratitude, for much assistance, editorial and otherwise, during the stormy years of my early efforts to secure a footing in my inexperienced attempts at journalism. It was through his influence and that of his honored partner, Mr. H. L. Pittock, that I was favored often with railway transportation across the Continent; and, although my brother did not editorially espouse my mission, as I believe he would have done if I had not been his sister, he many a time gladdened my heart by copying incidents of woman's hardships from my "New Northwest" into his own columns, thus indirectly championing, or at least commending, my initial efforts to secure Equal Rights for women.

To my faithful, invalid husband, the late Mr. Ben C. Duniway, but for whose sterling character as a man I could not have left our growing family in the home while I was away, struggling for a livelihood and the support of my newspaper, nor could I have reached the broader field, which now crowns my life with the success for which I toiled in my early itinerancy, I owe undying gratitude.

To the 61,265 affirmative votes cast for the Equal Suffrage Amendment, at the November election of 1912, and the more than an equal number of women, who rejoice with me over the culmination of my life's endeavors, I turn with words and thoughts of love and thankfulness. Many will live to see the beneficent results of their patriotism and foresight, long after I shall have joined the silent majority. Others may see their cherished ambitions fade, and will lay their failure to their discovery that all women cannot be made to vote or think according to their dictation, any more than all men can be so made, or led or driven.

* * *

First and foremost, among my many Eastern coworkers, who had come to San Francisco on a lecture tour with Elizabeth Cady Stanton in the spring of 1871 (shortly after I had launched my newspaper), I am proud to mention Susan B. Anthony. This wonderful woman had up to that time been an object of almost universal ridicule, being caricatured as a "cross, cranky old maid," an avowed "man-hater" and a "dangerous agitator." I was seriously disappointed when Miss Anthony came alone, by steamer, to Oregon, as I had arranged for, and hoped much from, a visit by Mrs. Stanton as an offset to the caricatures that Miss Anthony's visit had previously occasioned elsewhere. Messrs. Mitchell and Dolph, prominent young attorneys of Portland—both afterwards United States Senators—had obligingly provided me with steamer passes for both ladies; but when

Miss Anthony came alone, and I called upon her at her hotel in the early morning, after her arrival at midnight. I was delighted to find her a most womanly woman, gentle voiced, logical, full of business, and so fertile in expedients as to disarm all apprehension as to the financial results of her visit. She decided, at once, that I must become her business manager during her sojourn of two months or more, in Oregon and Washington; that I must preside, and make introductory speeches at all of her meetings, advertise her thoroughly through "The New Northwest," and print and circulate numerous "dodgers" in her behalf, securing meanwhile such favorable recognition from the general press as I could obtain in our wanderings.

How vividly I recall my first experience before a Portland audience! No church was open to us anywhere, and the old Orofino Theatre was our only refuge. I went in fear and trembling before a cold, curious and critical crowd, half bent with weariness resulting from long, continuous mental and physical overwork, and said in a faltering voice, "The movement that arose in the East nearly twenty years ago, to demand Equal Rights for Women, and appeared, at first, as a shadow not larger than a woman's hand, has grown and spread from the Atlantic Coast, till it pauses tonight in farthest Oregon, almost in hearing of the Pacific Ocean. Keeping ahead of that shadow is the illustrious visitor, who illuminates it wherever she goes with the freedom spirit of her devotion. This distinguished visitor is my world renowned coadjutor, Susan B. Anthony of Everywhere, who will now address you."

Nobody was more astonished over the effect of that little impromptu speech than myself, and from that time to this I have never been without more invitations to lecture than I could fill.

Miss Anthony spoke as one inspired, and many who

came to scoff remained to praise. Her assistance in increasing the circulation of "The New Northwest" was wonderful. The newspapers were filled with generous words of approval of ourselves and of our work, wherever we went, and "The New Northwest" gave Miss Anthony many whole pages of free advertisement for many weeks.

From Portland we went to Salem, Albany and other Willamette Valley towns, meeting success everywhere. Returning, we visited Olympia and addressed the Territorial Legislature of Washington, which was then in session, and were accorded a most gracious hearing. We had had similar success in Seattle and Port Townsend, but were ordered from the home of a Port Gamble citizen, whose wife had invited us to the house in the absence of her husband, who, returning unexpectedly, treated us as tramps. I wanted to stay it out and conquer the head of the family with a little womanly tact, but Miss Anthony hurried me off with her to the hotel. We spoke in the evening to a crowded house, making no allusion to the incident, which had spread through the milling town like wild fire.

We continued finding friends wherever we went, and remained long enough in Seattle to organize a Woman Suffrage Association with a staff of influential officers. No official record of this organization is obtainable, but I copy from the editorial correspondence of "The New Northwest" the names of H. L. Yesler, Mayor of Seattle; Mrs. Yesler, Reverend and Mrs. John F. Damon, Mrs. Mary Olney Brown, Reverend and Mrs. Daniel Bagley and Mr. and Mrs. Amos Brown. A Suffrage Society was also formed in Olympia, under the leadership of Mrs. A. H. H. Stuart, Mrs. C. P. Hale, Hon. Elwood Evans, Mrs. Clara E. Sylvester and Mr. J. M. Murphy, editor of "The Washington Standard."

When we returned to Portland, the winter rains were

deluging the earth. The stage carrying us from Olympia to the Columbia River at Kalama, led us through the blackness of darkness in the night time, giving Miss Anthony a taste of pioneering under difficulties that remained with her as a memory to her dying day.

We had previously visited Walla Walla, enjoying the hospitality of Captain J. C. Ainsworth's Company of Columbia River Steamers, and stopping at The Dalles, where my personal friends, Mr. and Mrs. Joseph Wilson and Mrs. C. C. Donnell, secured the Congregational Church for our meeting, much to the disgust of the pastor, to whom our supposed-to-be-inferior sex was his only audible objection.

The steamer stopped for an hour at Umatilla, where Miss Anthony happened to meet the son of an old lady friend of Rochester, New York, an humble bar keeper of the village, whose only way to exhibit his hospitality was to offer her a drink of white wine of which she politely took a sip and gave him back the glass with a gentle "Thank you." The news of this trivial incident preceded us to Walla Walla, and was made the excuse by the preachers for denying us the use of any pulpit in the little city; and we were compelled to speak in a little room in the rear of a saloon, the Pixley Sisters having previously engaged the only theatre. The next Sunday, the preachers who had closed the churches against us, solemnly denounced the Equal Suffrage Movement, giving as one of their reasons therefor, the fact that we had lectured in the dance hall, but failing to tell the other side of the story.

No suffrage organization was effected in Walla Walla, but the interest our visit created was much enhanced by the prohibitory action of the clergy. Many influential families entertained us in their homes. "If you want any cause to prosper, just persecute it," said Miss Anthony—and she was right.

When the Annual State Fair of Oregon convened at Salem, Miss Anthony camped with my family on the grounds, her first experience at camping out. There was no assembly hall at that time on the Fair Grounds, and we held an open-air meeting in the shade of the pavilion, where the shrieking of whistles and blare of drums and brass instruments, combined with the spieling of side-show promoters, compelled us to speak with a screeching accent, but brought us much commendation from a large and intelligent audience, and secured us many subscriptions to "The New Northwest."

The autumn rains were in their glory in Portland before Miss Anthony finally left us, going by stage to Sacramento, and lecturing at stopover stations along the way. She informed me regularly of the incidents of her journey by letter, and I particularly recall her favorable mention of Dr. Barthenia Owens, of Roseburg (now Dr. Owens-Adair), who arranged a successful meeting for her at the Douglas County Court House and entertained her in her home. The Doctor is now a retired physician, and like Dr. Mary A. Thompson, of Portland, the original, though only "irregular" path-breaker for women practitioners, is honored now by the medical profession, which formerly denounced and ridiculed all such women as "freaks."

* * *

Many important occurrences, well worthy of record, have doubtless escaped my memory through the passing years. But one of these was brought to my recollection recently by a call from a lady formerly of Gervais, Oregon, which I will stop to transcribe, before I again forget it. Shortly after the close of Miss Anthony's successful tour with me in the summer and fall of 1871, a committee of gentlemen, of which the late Dr. Magers was chairman, invited me to visit their town and deliver some lectures on the "Woman Question." I had tried hard to heed Miss Anthony's parting injunction, that I must never attempt to speak in public without careful preparation and committing to memory everything I should want to say. But I was running a millinery store, attending to the needs of my family and editing a newspaper, and I never found any time to obey her instructions. I found myself at an early hour in the morning, on my way to my appointment buttoning my gloves and adjusting my wraps as I ran to catch the train. Dr. Magers and his committee met me at the station on arrival, and informed me that a young lawyer, in Gervais, was very anxious to debate the Suffrage Question with me; but, they said that, as I had been invited to lecture and not to debate, he would be ruled out if I said so. But I said, "By all means let us have a debate!" I had never debated in my life, but I thought this was a good opportunity for practice, so I wasn't much frightened at the prospect. But I did feel a little relieved when Dr. Magers, acting as moderator, put the question to the packed audience at my request, and the debate was voted down.

I recall very little of what I attempted to say at that meeting. The argument was, doubtless, more florid and perfervid than I would attempt to make it now, but I was new at the business, and being new, and the great audience being in a receptive mood, the lecture went off well. At its close, I said I didn't want to be dispensing any false doctrines, and, if I had poisoned the minds of any of the young ladies in the "Amen Corner," I hoped they would call out the young lawyer aforesaid, and we would have the debate. Applause gave consent and the young man arose and moved with some difficulty through the crowd to the pulpit, where I managed, by hitching my chair aside, to make room for him to stand between myself and the Moderator. The young man made a clever speech. His Irish wit convulsed us all with laughter at times, and occasionally evoked vehement applause. He said he was at a disadvantage, because the speaker had followed a different line of argument from that he had anticipated. Then, as is the habit of opposing counsels in almost any case at court, he tried hard to make it appear that I had said things I didn't say, and meant things I didn't mean. He drew a lurid picture of what he said I had called "the good time coming," when he declared that women would desert their homes for lawyers' offices and judges' seats, leaving the deserted men to quiet the babies, as best they could, with rubber substitutes. After entertaining the crowd along similar lines of stock arguments for more than half an hour, he folded his arms in dramatic fashion, elevated his shoulders and chin and said: "In conclusion, gentlemen, allow me to say that I have often known a hen to try to crow, but I've never known one to succeed at it yet!" He took his seat amidst a storm of laughter and applause, in which I joined as heartily as the rest. In reply, I said that I hadn't needed the information conveyed to me by the worthy Moderator, who had told me that the speaker was a bachelor, whose sweetheart was chuckling in the "Amen Corner," but, I added that I hoped some one of the handsome young ladies present would some day be kind enough to initiate him into the mysteries of matrimony and maternity and cure him of his present agony of fear, lest women would neglect the babies if enfranchised. I begged leave to inform the gentleman that women would never dare to neglect their babies; for if they did, we'd never have any more bachelors. The audience tittered, the young orator blushed, and I passed on to other remarks. He had apologized for some of the crudities of his speech by explaining that, unlike the speaker of the evening, he was a manual laborer, and evidently the lecturer knew nothing about the roughening influences of physical toil. To this I replied, that as a farmer's wife, I had milked milk enough with my two hands to float the Great Eastern (the largest steamer at that time afloat) and had made butter enough for market with the propelling power of my hands at an old-fashioned churn, during nine previous years of my life on a farm, to grease the axles of creation. The audience roared and I felt sorry for my opponent, though not yet sorry enough to quit; so I said, "Friends, I am almost ashamed to notice the last clause of my friend's argument, but I must not forget that I am here to demolish, if I can, the sort of opposition that has been set up. The gentleman has said (and I folded my arms and imitated his intonation) that he has often known a hen to try to crow, but he has never known one to succeed at it yet!" A half-suppressed chuckle went through the house, followed by a moment's waiting of quiet expectancy. Then I said, "I am free to confess that the gentleman is right; I have myself discovered the same peculiarity in hens." Again there was an expectant silence, and I added, "But in the poultry yard of my friend, Colonel D. M. Thompson, in Albany, I once saw a rooster try to set, and he made a failure too." The house fairly vibrated with enthusiasm, and my opponent got away as soon as he could.

That was forty-two years ago and I have never seen the gentleman since; but I am told by those who know him, that to this day he has never entered a hall or church where a woman was to be the speaker, and he considers debates on the "Woman Question" nothing else but "vanity and vexation of spirit."

CHAPTER VI.

First Anniversary Meeting.

AT THE first anniversary meeting of the Oregon State Equal Suffrage Association, of which mention was made in a foregoing chapter, we were unable to secure but one gentleman (Colonel C. A. Reed) to occupy the platform with us as a steady coadjutor, but we were favored with a fine address by Reverend T. L. Eliot, and received excellent reports in "The Oregonian," "The New Northwest" and other leading newspapers throughout the state. Following Colonel Reed and Reverend Mr. Eliot were addresses by Miss Virginia Olds, Mrs. Josephine DeVore Johnson, Mrs. Beatty (colored) and the writer. The celebrated McGibeny family furnished popular music, and valuable aid was contributed by the late Mr. and Mrs. D. H. Hendee, the late Mr. and Mrs. J. W. Peters, the late Mrs. M. J. Foster and the late Mrs. G. W. Brown.

Meanwhile, for the whole year thereafter, the movement went on through my work in the lecture field and the weekly issues of "The New Northwest." Our strength became much increased in 1884, by the able assistance of the late Mrs. H. A. Laughary, who suddenly took her place in the front ranks as a platform speaker. "The New Northwest" received a valuable auxiliary this year, in the person of my sister, the late Mrs. Catherine A. Coburn, a lady of rare journalistic ability, who held her position for five years, when my three eldest sons, the late W. S. Duniway, Hubert R. Duniway and W. C. Duniway, having completed their school duties and attained their majority, were admitted to the partnership, and Mrs. Coburn, after serving as editor of "The Evening Bee" and "The Evening Telegram," accepted an editorial posi-

tion on "The Oregonian," which she held for twelve
useful years, until called to the higher life.

* * *

Beginning my travels in 1871, shortly after the departure of Susan B. Anthony to other fields, as related
elsewhere, I kept up my journeying with almost continuous regularity, carrying the gospel of equal rights into
all parts of Oregon, Washington and Idaho, making converts everywhere, especially among the men, whom I
could more easily reach in their stores and offices than
their wives in their homes and kitchens, never forgetting
that one convert with a vote was worth a hundred who
possessed the secondary and almost negligible power of
"influence." It was no small task to travel, often by
night, over the terrible roads of the Pacific Northwest,
lecturing from three to five evenings every week, writing
serial stories for "The New Northwest," illustrative, always, of various phases of my theme, and furnishing editorial correspondence often covering a full page of the
paper. Added to all this was my necessary work of canvassing for the paper, meeting all sorts of social activities, "talking shop," at retail, with the women in their
homes, ministers in their studies and judges in their court
rooms, often departing by stage, at night, after a lecture,
for the next way station to make preliminary arrangements for another series of meetings and repeating the
same process at every settlement large enough to warrant
a stopover. Occasionally, especially in towns and villages
near the railroad, I would gather the women together in
a Suffrage Society, leaving their dues with their local
secretary as the nucleus for future campaign work; but
on the whole, I did not find my time thus spent at all
profitable. Some traveling lecturer, usually an almost
unknown hobby rider, would often come along, and, after
lecturing before the little local Suffrage Society of a dozen

members, would receive the contents of the treasury as a contribution for her services, leaving the association to disband, or "ravel out" for lack of funds.

These experiences finally led me to give up organizing suffrage societies, as I learned that lecturing, writing serial stories and editorial correspondence, and canvassing for subscribers to "The New Northwest" afforded a more rational means of spreading the light. But I always left a state officer in charge at every county seat, so she might be ready to hold the fort and confer with headquarters after a faithful few of us had succeeded in securing the submission of a Suffrage Constitutional Amendment for adoption or rejection by the voters at large. And now, in this year of grace 1914, after the lapse of forty-two strenuous years, as I look backward and note the difference between our progress in the Pacific Coast States in pursuit of the ballot and that of our co-workers in the farthest East, I am more strongly encrusted than ever in my conviction that the only time for active, general organization in any state is after a few devoted workers have succeeded in using the press for getting our movement as a square issue before the voters in the shape of a proposed Equal Suffrage Amendment to a State Constitution. Every state thus added to our galaxy of free states is a powerful factor to induce favorable action before Congress as a National movement.

I was absent at the Centennial Exposition in the autumn of 1876, where I had gone in the summer in response to an invitation from the National Equal Suffrage Association to come over into "Macedonia" and help. "The New Northwest" continued its labors under the capable management of Mrs. Coburn and my faithful family, and the work for Equal Suffrage made favorable headway in the Legislature of Oregon of that year, through the influence of a convention held at Salem, under the able leadership of Mrs. A. J. Laughary, assisted by Dr. Mary A. Thompson.

* * *

The speeding years went by and the time for assembling the Washington Territorial Legislature of 1883 was at hand. Meanwhile, the Woman's Christian Temperance Union had been born, and gave promise of becoming a lusty infant. Its cry of "No quarter for the liquor traffic" had awakened a new idea among the preachers, who decided to use it as fuel for their pulpits, and alarmed the majority of the voters everywhere. While clergymen of eminence had learned to favor votes for women, preachers of small caliber, who had fought to prohibit the Equal Suffrage movement at every step, grasped at the new prohibition movement, whose "Christian" attachment attracted their notice, and, seeing in its use a possible opportunity to stimulate their flagging business, many of them were induced to become its excited adherents.

Pettifogging politicians saw their opportunity and began to roar. The need of a common-sense temperance movement was lost sight of. The legitimate business of selling liquors, under proper regulation, to the majority of men who wanted to buy, was overlooked, and "No quarter for the liquor traffic" became the war cry of political demagogues. Men with rum-blossomed noses and loaded breaths, whose gifts of voluble utterance were only equaled by the lachrymose emotions of unthinking multitudes, were easily entrapped by conscientious but inexperienced women, who had just begun to look for liberty for themselves as a cure for their financial limitations as servants without wages in the home; and such women were caught in the current of the new deluge.

When I reached Olympia, I was visited by members of the Legislature, who had become frightened over a new current of affairs, and urged me to abandon my work. But there were wise men and women who saw through the situation and urged me to remain at the helm, as correspondent for the weekly issues of "The New Northwest" and "The Daily Oregonian."

The Suffrage Bill, which had been prepared by Professor William H. Roberts, had passed the House by a safe majority, early in the session. I, who had become almost worn out with work and watching, was induced to remain at my post, awaiting the action of the Council, by such women as Mary Olney Brown, mother of the first movement for Equal Suffrage ever inaugurated in the Territory (See Vol. 3 of the National History of Woman Suffrage, page 779), and by Abby H. H. Stuart, who was afterwards noted as the mother and founder of the Woman's Club Movement in the Pacific Northwest. I was entertained during the entire session at the hospitable home of Mrs. Clara E. Sylvester, wife of the founder of Olympia, and was ably assisted by John Miller Murphy, founder and editor of "The Washington Standard."

The Suffrage Bill came up for final passage in the Council on November 15, 1883, when only three women besides myself were present. The death-like stillness of the Council Chamber was broken only by the clerk's call of the roll and the firm responses of the "ayes" and "noes." I kept the tally with a nervous hand, and my heart fairly stood still when the fateful movement came that gave us the deciding majority of one. Then I arose, and without exchanging words with anybody, rushed to the telegraph office, half a mile distant. Judge J. W. Range, at that time President of an Equal Suffrage Society at Cheney, overtook me on the way, going on the same errand. He spoke, and I felt as if called back to earth with the painful reminder that I was mortal. A few minutes more and my message was on its way to

"The New Northwest." It was publication day and the paper had gone to press, but my jubilant and faithful sons opened the forms and inserted the news; and in less than half an hour, the newsboys were crying the fact through the streets of Portland, making our Equal Suffrage newspaper, which had fought the fight, and led the work to the point where legislation could give a victory, the very first newspaper in the nation to carry the tidings to the world. (See National History of Woman Suffrage, Vol. 3, page 776.)

The bill was signed November 22, by Governor William A. Newell, with a gold pen presented him for the purpose by women whom he had thus made free.

An immense ratification meeting was held in the evening of the same day in the City Hall, where speeches were made by Governor Newell, Judge Orange Jacobs, Mrs. Pamela Hale, Judge B. F. Dennison, Mr. W. S. Duniway of Portland, Hon. P. D. Moore, Captain William Smallwood, the writer, and a large number of the members of the Legislature.

It has always been the habit of politicians and preachers of small mental caliber to oppose my humble mission in the cause of equal rights; but they have never scrupled to seize votes for women when achieved in spite of them, to advance some other hobby, causing me to recall with gratitude the memory of those brave and kindly men and women who, in the words of Richard Realf:

> "Did not wait till freedom had become
>   The willing shibboleth of the Courtier's lips,
> But spoke for her when God, himself, seemed dumb
>   And all the arching skies were in eclipse."

CHAPTER VII.

Oregon Equal Suffrage Association Organized.

A FTER Miss Anthony and I had completed our campaign in Washington Territory and British Columbia, we returned to Portland and called a mass meeting to complete the initial and permanent organization of the State Equal Suffrage Association, with Mrs. Harriet W. Williams, a venerated octogenarian, as President. This estimable woman had been one of the earliest leaders of the Woman Suffrage Movement in New York, and her installation, at the head of our association in Oregon, was the source of general satisfaction to the friends of the cause in the new state of her adoption. Subsequently, Mrs. Williams was compelled to resign on account of the infirmities of age, but her wise counsels remained with us long after she was called to unseen shores.

Among those enrolled as early co-workers, who have since been called to the higher life, are such honored names as Mr. Josiah Failing, Mr. D. W. Williams, Mr. and Mrs. W. T. Shanahan, Mr. and Mrs. G. W. Brown, Mr. Ben C. Duniway, Mr. J. H. and Mrs. M. J. Foster, Colonel C. A. Reed, Judge G. W. Lawson, Mr. and Mrs. D. M. Thompson, Mrs. M. A. Dalton, Mr. and Mrs. J. W. Peters, Mr. and Mrs. D. H. Hendee, Mr. and Mrs. A. R. Burbank, Mr. and Mrs. Ashby Pierce, Mr. E. F. Heroy, Judge John F. Caples, Mrs. Nancy Hembree, Mr. and Mrs. Elijah Strong, Dr. J. C. Hawthorne, Mr. Elijah Williams, Mrs. Clara Duniway Stearns, Mr. John M. Bacon, Dr. J. G. Glenn, Mr. D. W. Prentice, Editors H. W. Scott and Paul Crandall, Mr. W. Carey Johnson, Mr. F. O. McCown, Mr. and Mrs. H. A. Laughary, Mrs. S. M. Kelty, Mrs. C. A. Coburn, Mr. W. S. Dun-

GROUP OF EQUAL SUFFRAGISTS

FRANCES WILLARD MUNDS
President Arizona. Vice-President
National Council of Women
Voters

MARTHA A DALTON
December, 1870. Albany, Oregon. One of
the Founders of Oregon State Equal
Suffrage Society in 1870

COLONEL C. E. S. WOOD
An Effective Equal Suffrage Leader and
Well Known Attorney-at-Law
of Oregon

WM. HANLEY
A Leader for Votes for Women. Champion
of The Progressive Party in State
and Nation

SARA BARD FIELD EHRGOTT
A Leading Platform Advocate of Votes
for Women. A Gifted Orator

MRS M. J. MAYORN
Pioneer Suffrage Leader of Vancouver,
Washington, from Territorial Days
to Statehood

ADA CORNISH HERTSHE
Active Equal Suffragist of Oregon. A Mem-
ber of Executive Committee of State
Association

iway, Mr. W. S. Ladd, Mr. and Mrs. Jesse Applegate,
U. S. Senator John H. Mitchell, U. S. Senator and Mrs.
J. N. Dolph, Hon. Solomon Hirsch, Mr. and Mrs. Joseph
Gaston, Mr. and Mrs. J. C. Trullinger, Captain J. C.
Ainsworth, Sr., Mr. and Mrs. Simeon Reed (founders of
Reed College), Hon. D. P. Thompson, Hon. and Mrs. Lee
Laughlin and—Oh! the list is too long to continue, but it
is not yet full.

Dr. Mary A. Thompson, Reverend P. S. Knight,
Reverend Dr. Eliot, Mrs. Mary F. Cooke, Mrs. C. C.
Donnell, and the near-octogenarian who pens these chron-
icles, alone remain to bear testimony to the work we did
in laying the foundation for the Equal Rights of the
millions of men and women who shall reap as we have
sown.

* * *

I went to Salem in September, 1872, to visit the
Legislature, which met annually at that time in the
autumn, in a little brick building, across the street from
the Chemeketa, now known as the Willamette Hotel. As
no woman prior to that time had visited the Legislature,
except occasionally with others, on some social occasion
in honor of the success of some political aspirant, I found
it difficult to prevail upon a woman to accompany me. As
the etiquette of those times demanded that I must have
a chaperone, I spent two whole days in canvassing the
city in quest of a friend who would dare to escort me.
The first woman in Oregon to undertake a mission so far
out of the ordinary, was Dr. Mary P. Sawtelle, who was
being widely criticized at that time, as the first Oregon
woman to dare to graduate from any medical institution,
and receive her diploma as a regular physician. This doctor, who had failed to pass "exams" as a "regular" at
home, had but recently returned from an Eastern Medical
Institute, fully equipped with the accessories of a phy-

sician's degree; and, being known as an active rebel
against an early and most unfortunate domestic relation,
which had married her off at the age of fifteen and compelled her to bear four children before she was twenty,
was objected to, afterwards, as my chaperone, for the
alleged reason that I should have selected a woman of
whom their husbands, or a regular masculine doctor, had
no cause to be jealous, or afraid. But Dr. Sawtelle's
sad domestic experiences appealed to me, from the first,
as the principal reason why I should defend her openly.
She was then happily remarried, and was the pioneer path-
breaker among the great army of divorced women—servants without wages—whom District Judges, good and
true, are now rescuing from legalized prostitution,
through the machinery of the divorce court. When I
last heard of her, she was engaged in a lucrative practice in San Francisco, loved and honored by all who
knew her.

* * *

When Dr. Sawtelle and I entered the legislative hall
my heart thumped audibly, as I realized that I was entering a domain considered sacred to the aristocracy of sex.
We took our seats in the lobby of the House of Representatives, where for a full minute I felt in danger of
fainting and creating a scene. But Hon. Joseph Engle,
perceiving the situation and knowing me personally,
arose to his feet, and, after a complimentary speech, in
which he was pleased to recognize my position as a farmer's wife, mother, home-maker, teacher and now as journalist, moved that I be invited to a seat within the bar
and provided with table and stationery, as were the other
members of the newspaper profession. The motion carried, with only two or three dissenting votes; and the
way was open, from that time forward, for women to
compete with men, on equal terms, for all minor posi-

tions in both branches of the Legislature—a privilege of
which they have not been slow to take advantage, scores
of them thronging the Capitol in these later years and
holding valuable clerkships, many of them sneering the
while at the efforts of those who had opened the way for
them to be there at all. (See History of Woman Suffrage, Vol. III, page 770.)

The late Hon. Samuel Corwin introduced a Woman
Suffrage Bill in the House, early in the session; and
while it was pending, I was invited to make an appeal in
its behalf, of which I remember very little, so frightened
and astonished was I, except that I once, inadvertently,
alluded to a gentleman by his name, instead of his county,
whereupon, being rapped to order, I blushed and begged
pardon, but put myself at ease by informing the members that in all the bygone years, while they had been
studying parliamentary rules, I had been rocking the
cradle. One member who had made a vehement speech
against the bill, in which he declared that no respectable
woman in his county desired the elective franchise, became particularly incensed, as was natural, upon my
exhibiting a woman suffrage petition from his county,
signed by the women whom he had misrepresented, and
headed by his own wife.

* * *

The Senate, the House concurring, passed a Married
Woman's Property Bill in 1874, under the able leadership
of Hon. J. N. Dolph, who afterwards distinguished himself in the Senate of the United States. This enactment has ever since enabled any woman, engaged in business on her own account, to register the fact in the office
of her County Clerk and thereby secure her tools, furniture or stock in trade against a liability of seizure by
her husband's creditors. (Ibid, p. 771.)

* * *

The State Temperance Alliance had met at Salem in February of the preceding year, to which a number of delegates were sent, bearing credentials from the State Woman Suffrage Association. I had become interested in the temperance question in childhood; and when the Temperance Alliance was organized had become one of its charter members, and had written most of its constitution. The prohibition question had not, at that time, been considered seriously; and I, like most of my acquaintances, looked upon temperance in everything as a question of moral and individual responsibility, instead of depending upon such temporary expedients as the legal enactments that have since become fashionable, and are keeping the state in continual turmoil.

Every attempt of men to prohibit economic rights for women has ever since increased my feeling of opposition to any sort of prohibition which would destroy the moral responsibility, or individual right to self-control in any man or woman. This fact became known to a few cheap politicians early in my career, and such men, being prohibitionists on general principles, decided to prohibit admitting the delegates of the Woman Suffrage Association to the Alliance by ignoring us altogether. We sat there, dumb with amazement, when somebody placed my name in nomination as chairman of an important committee. The presiding officer was seized with a sudden deafness when my name was called, and the men in attendance were convulsed with merriment. Ladies left their seats and buzzed about me, urging me to resent the insult in the name of womanhood. As no other woman was at that time known in the Northwest as a public speaker, I felt obliged to arise and speak for my sex. "Mr. President!" I exclaimed, as I stood in the aisle, "by what right do you refuse to recognize the women, when their names are called? Are men the only lawful members of this Alliance? And if so, is it not

better for the women delegates to go home?" "Mr.
President," shouted an excited voter, "all committees are
now full!" Somebody, doubtless in ridicule, then placed
me in nomination as Vice-President at Large, which was
carried amid uproarious laughter. I took my seat, half
frightened and wholly indignant, and the deliberations
of the sovereign voters were undisturbed thereafter for
several hours by word or sign from women. At last
somebody offered a motion that set the Alliance to discussing a bill for a prohibitory liquor law. During the
excitement a note was carried to the presiding officer,
who read it smilingly, colored, and on rising said, "We're
hearing nothing from the ladies, and yet they constitute a
majority of this Alliance. Mrs. Duniway, will you not
favor us with a speech?" By the time I was sufficiently
recovered from surprise to be fully aware of what I was
saying, I exclaimed in part,—"Give women the legal and
financial power to combat intemperance in their homes
and they will soon prove that they do not like drunken
husbands any better than men like drunken wives. Make
women *free!* Give them the power the ballot gives to you,
and the control of their own earnings, which rightfully
belong to them—whether married or single—and every
woman will soon be able to settle this prohibition business in her own home and on her own account. Men
will not tolerate drunkenness in wives, and women will
not tolerate it in husbands, unless compelled to do it
through their servitude without salaries!"

A prominent clergyman (Reverend I. D. Driver)
arose and said: "Mr. President, I charge the sins of the
world upon the mothers of men. There are twenty thousand fallen women in New York—two millions of them
in America—we cannot afford to let this element vote!"
Before I was aware of what I was doing I was on my feet
again. Shaking my finger at the clergyman, I said: "How
dare you make such charges against the mothers of men!

You tell us of two millions of fallen women, who, you say, would vote for drunkenness; but what say you, sir, to the twenty millions of fallen men—and all voters—whose patronage alone enables fallen women to live? Would you disfranchise them, sir? I pronounce your charge a libel on womanhood, and I know that if we were voters, you would not dare to utter it!"

A gentleman from Michigan—a Mr. Curtis—called me to order, saying, "Prohibition is the question before the house. The lady should confine herself to the question." "That is what I am doing, sir. I am talking about prohibition in the home—the only way possible to make any sort of prohibition succeed."

Over forty years have passed since that memorable occasion; and to this day, I have found no better argument against the politico-prohibition movement, now agitating the public mind, than my inexperienced impromptu utterances which are still quoted in the public prints. (See History of Woman Suffrage, Vol. III, page 772.)

* * *

A year passed and the Temperance Alliance was again in session. The first anniversary convention of the State Equal Suffrage Association, of which mention is made elsewhere, had met in Portland, on February 9, 1873. Delegates were again chosen to attend the Alliance, beginning February 20th, and a dozen women attended bearing credentials. It was evident from the first that trouble was brewing. The enemies of Equal Suffrage had had a whole year to prepare an ambuscade, of which our delegates had no knowledge. A committee on credentials was appointed, with instructions to rule the Equal Suffrage delegation out of the Alliance, as a "disturbing element." The late Hon. J. Quinn Thornton was chairman of that committee. In his report he declared all delegations to be satisfactory (including those from the

Penitentiary) except women, whom he styled "setting hens," "belligerent females," etc., after which he subsided with pompous gravity. "Mr. President," I exclaimed, as soon as I could get the floor, "I move to so amend the report of the committee as to admit the Suffrage delegation." The motion was seconded by half a dozen voices. Then followed a scene which beggars description. It was pandemonium broken loose. When I again arose to address the Chair, that worthy ordered my arrest by the sergeant-at-arms, saying, "Take that crazy woman out of the house and take care of her." The officer came forward in discharge of his duty, but he quailed before my uplifted pencil, as several gentlemen stepped into the aisle and began taking off their coats to defend me, among them the late Reverend J. L. Parrish, a veteran minister of the Gospel. All that day and evening, and until one o'clock the following afternoon, a noisy rabble of self-styled temperance men sought to prohibit bringing the question to a square and honorable vote. But Major George Williams, a brave man who had lost a limb in fighting for his country, at last succeeded in bringing the chairman to a semblance of duty, and the vote was ordered. The result was a triumph for the advocates of Equal Suffrage. A recess followed, during which my hand was so often and enthusiastically shaken that my shoulder was severely lamed.

Upon re-assembling for duty, I offered a fair and unequivocal Equal Suffrage resolution, which was triumphantly carried. The disappointed prohibitionists then seceded from the Alliance, and set up a "Union" for themselves; but their confederacy did not live long, and its few followers finally returned to their Alma Mater and gave us no further trouble, except in collusion with the liquor elements, with which they often worked, openly and in secret, to prohibit women from achieving recognition of their right to vote.

For further particulars concerning these stormy times, when Equal Rights for the mothers of the race were in the throes of early gestation, the reader is referred to Vol. III, Chap. 4, of the National History of Woman Suffrage, by Susan B. Anthony, Elizabeth Cady Stanton and Matilda Joselyn Gage.

CHAPTER VIII.

*Meets With California Suffragists—An Experience and
a Temperance Meeting.*

(Through an oversight, resulting from my handicap in later
years as a rheumatic "shut in," the following chapter, which was
written and should have been printed in the first edition as
Chapter VIII, was overlooked. The reader is asked to turn to
pages 57 and 58 and read it in as an imaginary insert.)

MY FIRST connection with any Equal Suffrage
organization outside of the Pacific Northwest
was begun in California during the holidays of
1870 and 1871, as the result of credentials introducing me
as a delegate from the initial Suffrage Association of
Salem, Oregon, spoken of elsewhere. My memory of that
first meeting with California Suffragists is vivid. I met
in San Francisco, as one of its many results, with the late
Colonel John A. Collins and his gifted wife, at whose home
I was a delighted guest. I had known almost nothing,
previously, of the parliamentary proceedings of organized
bodies, with which subsequent experiences have made me
familiar. The late Laura DeForce Gordon, whose acquaintance I had made in Oregon on a previous occasion, was
at that time president of the California State Woman
Suffrage Association. But this gifted orator, writer and
path breaker for the cause was being side-tracked, as I
was many years after in the Pacific Northwest, by Eastern invaders; and I was made acquainted, early in my
public career, with the "ways that are dark and tricks
that are vain" which are by no means "peculiar" to
professional politicians of either sex, or of both of the
sexes. But the State Executive Committee, with headquarters in San Francisco, was composed of both men
and women, as all such organizations ought always to

be; and by working together in apparent harmony with opposing factions, managed to keep the movement before the people in peaceable shape; and the press, always ready for news items, did its part with vigilance, if not always with fairness.

I recall many pleasant associations with such early workers in California as the late Mrs. Caroline M. Severance, Mrs. Ellen E. Sargent, Nellie Holbrook Blinn, Mrs. Sarah B. Cooper, Mrs. Sarah Knox Goodrich, Dr. Alida C. Avery, and such survivors as Mrs. Mary E. Sperry, Mrs. Mary Wood Swift, Sarah M. Severance and Alice Moore McComas. But by no means least among these co-workers is Clara Shortridge Foltz, formerly of Salem, Oregon, later of San Francisco, and now a prominent lawyer residing in Los Angeles.

My first set speech, outside of an Oregon school room, was made in a public hall in San Francisco on the New Year's Eve of 1871, and was so favorably reported by the press that I at once became the recipient of invitations to lecture in many adjacent towns and cities, for which I was offered a stated salary. Instead of accepting the offer at once, and binding the bargain, I wrote, as was a faithful married woman's habit, to my semi-invalid husband, asking permission to accept the position, which would include the salary, much-needed between seasons in the millinery business in Oregon. It was before the era of Oregon railroads; and, just as the weekly steamer was about to sail, I received a telegram saying "come home immediately; business requires it." As I had left a good housekeeper in the home and a capable manager in the store, I could think of no real cause for the telegram, except possible illness in the family; so I canceled all engagements and sailed for home, where I found no visible need of anything but the salary. I had relinquished in blind obedience to what I considered an unreasonable mandate.

With the outbreak of the temperance crusade among
the women of Ohio, came a general uprising of women in
almost every state; and many women, myself among them,
who were at first disposed to look upon this unnatural
uprising as a means for accelerating the Equal Suffrage
movement among the self-centered women of the
churches, met our first organized opposition to votes for
women in the ranks of the Prohibitionists.

* * *

I was recalled to California in the midst of this excitement, to do what I could to take advantage of the
intemperate and so-called temperance awakening of the
times, only to find pastors and the women of their flocks
so determined to prohibit votes for women that I returned to Portland in the hope to find a better opportunity
for spreading the gospel of liberty among the women of
the churches. But I soon learned that the spirit of bigotry and intolerance was permeating my original bailiwick,
prohibiting me from bringing into the churches the spirit
of free speech whose humble servant I have always been.

A great temperance movement, so-called, had been
organized in my absence, with headquarters in the base-
ment of the dear old historic Taylor-street church. I
united at once with this society, only to encounter worse
opposition to equal rights for the mother-sex than I had
met in the churches of San Francisco and Sacramento.
A little choir of hostile women was organized to sing
me down whenever I arose to speak; and, at a signal
from Rev. Mr. Izer, pastor of the flock, the women would
obey his uplifted hand and begin to sing. As it would
have been as impossible to out-speak a choir as to out-
shriek a brass band, I would demurely take my seat;
but only to rise again when the singing ended, and resume
my plea for equal rights for the mother-sex, speaking for
half a minute before the choir would again be ready to
drown my voice.

On one such occasion I found room to say that every attempt of women and the clergy to enforce obedience to their man-made edicts upon the outside of human nature would come to naught; that human nature was of the spirit; that it was ordained by our Heavenly Father and could only be destroyed by shutting off human life; that every attempt of the few to enforce obedience against its will upon the self-willed, animated handiwork of God was like trying to stop a cat-hole with a stove pipe; and I added, before the choir would sing me down, "You can't kill an evil by driving it into hiding! If you want anything on earth to prosper, just persecute it!" This was too big a dose for the preacher to swallow; so he said, "As pastor of this church, I prohibit Mrs. Duniway from speaking in it again."

The choir had by this time found its pages, and the sacred tune of Old Hundred rose upon the air, the singers pretending to "Praise God, from Whom all blessings flow."

The benediction was next in order, but it could not stop the rush of hand-shaking with which I was greeted by the astonished multitude, of whom a very few were sympathizing with the pastor. I was called upon the next day at my home by a committee of clergymen who wanted to know what I intended doing next. I replied that I should wait, Quaker fashion, till the spirit moved me. "But," I added, "gentlemen, it was really mean of you to call for the Doxology and benediction without allowing me to reply; don't you think so?" "What would you have said?" asked Rev. Dr. Atkinson, the spokesman of the committee. I answered that I would have said: "Are we living under the walls of the Vatican? And do we hear the edict of His Holiness the Pope?" The committee laughed, and the chairman said, "I am glad you didn't get a chance to make that speech."

My husband wanted me to stay away from the meetings after that, but he saw that I was determined to go, so he reluctantly accompanied me the next evening; but he stopped near the door as we entered, and I went alone to our usual seats directly in front of the choir. There were a few animated speeches and several fiery ones between songs; but there came a lull about the middle of the exercises, when a sudden inspiration seized me and I arose, raised my hand, closed my eyes and said, reverently, "Let us pray."

I was afterwards told that I prayed for twenty minutes, though I took no note of the time. But the words and sentiments of that prayer are ringing through my memory as I write. I besought our Heavenly Father to absolve us from all vainglory, animosity and self-righteousness. I asked that the spirit of harmony might abide among us, bringing us protection from the bigotry and tyranny of the pulpit as well as the vice and tyranny of the saloon. I asked that in all of our deliberations we might be illuminated by the loving spirit of the living Christ, Who came into the world and suffered an ignominious death on the cross, that He might break every yoke and let the oppressed go free. I prayed that in all things our human judgment might be tempered with mercy; that press, people and pulpit might alike be inspired and led to understand that absolute freedom for the mother-sex was the fundamental need of our slowly-awakening people; that the substitution of righteous economic conditions might permeate every home, enabling mothers everywhere to do better work than raising and releasing to the world a progeny addicted to drunkenness, vice and crime. I prayed that the purveyors of immorality might be led by the spirit of Christian love into the ways of righteousness and peace; and especially, as a means to this end, that the mothers of the race might be freed from the servitude without wages that now so often makes it impossible for them to release children to the world who are not robbed of their birthright of self-control and sobriety before they are born.

When I was able to cease praying and open my eyes I beheld a silent, astonished multitude, in front of which, facing myself and choir, sat the pastor, his elbows on his knees, his open hands clasping his jaws, his eyes staring at vacancy. The crowd slowly arose and began surging forward to clasp my hands. The preacher and choir joined in the Doxology, after which they slipped silently away through a side door.

The meetings, thereafter, soon ceased to draw crowds and raveled out for lack of patronage. But votes for women began to permeate the air; and churches, no longer able to prohibit the progress of the spirit of Liberty, though still determined to prohibit something, or somebody besides themselves, have turned their attention to the prohibition of the personal responsibility and self-control of all the people over self-organized Committees of One Hundred—more or less—who are thanking God that they are not as other people, and are driving into apparent hiding the temptations with which God has endowed human nature, bidding His moral agents to resist them or take the consequences, all such committees or organizations to the contrary notwithstanding.

CHAPTER IX.

Goes as Delegate to National Convention.

I WAS chosen in May, 1872, as delegate to the Annual Convention of the National Woman Suffrage Association, to be held in New York the following month.

I stopped over in San Francisco, visiting at the home of the late Mr. and Mrs. John A. Collins, where I met many faithful coadjutors of the Equal Suffrage Movement, most of whom, at this writing, have joined the great majority. During this visit, I repaired, one early April morning, to Laurel Hill, or Lone Mountain Cemetery, where I began to write the following Ode, while sitting on the concrete curb surrounding the grave of General Edward Dickinson Baker, who had fallen in battle at Ball's Bluff, and was the first famous victim of the Civil War. He was a United States Senator from Oregon at the time of his death, and his last and greatest speech was delivered in Congress, in reply to Judah P. Benjamin, who had attempted a defense of the alleged right of secession by the people of the Southern States. I completed the Ode on the 7th of June following, at the tomb of Abraham Lincoln, while sitting on the stone steps of the open, iron grated portal, inside of which the great martyr's remains are resting. It is inserted here at a request of many friends. I called it

"OUR FALLEN HEROES."

Beside the vernal sloping shores
    That hem the broad Pacific's billows,
I sat and gazed toward the sea
    From underneath the weeping willows;
And listening to the monotone
    Of singing, surging, murmuring waters,
I closed my eyes, as if entranced,
    Scarce heeding gay Columbia's daughters,

Who, chatting lightly, as they sped
  From shrub to tomb, from tree to marble,
Made discord with the melody
  Of whispering winds and wild birds' warble;
Then, turning from the giddy throng,
  In silence—lest from sleep I'd wake her—
I passed an infant's new-made mound,
  And stopped beside the grave of Baker.

A low stone wall, and marble slab,
  Of name and date of birth gave token,
And briefly spoke his greatest deeds,
  And when his thread of life was broken;
While overhead the moving clouds,
  And underfoot the grasses vernal,
And all around, the flowers and trees
  Spoke to me of the grand Eternal,
In words so plain I could not fail
  To heed and understand their voices,
As when immortal spirits sing,
  And my tried soul with bliss rejoices.

"Forever!" sang the cooing winds;
  "Forever!" spake the surging ocean;
"Forever!" said my answering heart,
  "Shall live the works he put in motion."
And while, alas, ungrateful man,
  Regarding his great deeds too lightly,
Rears no meet monument to mark
  His wondrous words and works, which rightly
Live in the hearts, all leal and true,
  Of those who knew him but to love him,
Fair California's arching skies
  In smiling beauty bend above him,
And perfumes, from the balmy breath
  Of breezy-laden plants exotic,
Fill all the air with redolence,
  And rouse me from my thoughts chaotic.
No more shall mortals hear his voice,
  But thousands spread in song and story,
Meet praises of his noble life,
  And martial deeds and well-earned glory.

* * * * * * *

I turn me to the distant East,

  And ponder o'er the din of battle,
Which called our brave and good to face
  The cannon's roar and musket's rattle.

Again I sing, and now my theme
  Is not of surging, murmuring billows,
Nor yet of flowers, and ladies fair,
  Nor yet of waving. weeping willows.
My lyre I tune, and now, once more,
  I sweep the chords with trembling fingers,
And strike a dirge, all grand and deep,
  Which in my sad soul fondly lingers.

And from the vernal, sloping shore,
  Where I stand rapt in meditation,
My memory notes the troubled clouds
  Which shrouded once our suffering Nation,
When, yielding to his country's call,
  In her dark hour of tribulation,
(Sing softly, Muse, and do not wake her,
  The infant under yon earth-mound)
Up sprang to arms, met death and fell,
  Our gallant, glorious, Colonel Baker.

The winds went sighing through the trees,
  And white sails decked the foam-capped ocean,
And San Francisco's busy hum
  Was heard above the waves' commotion,
And sea gulls in the craggy clefts,
  Against whose feet wild waves were dashing,
Cooed to their mates, who sought their food
  Where breakers 'mong the rocks were crashing;
And in my soul a quiet peace,
  Composed of joy and pain and sorrow,
Awoke me to the toil of life
  And its demanding, stern to-morrow.

I turned, and sped me through the vales,
  And o'er the frowning, snow-clad mountains,
Through broken wilds and desert plains,
  O'er arid wastes, past gurgling fountains.

Lone Mountain still slept by the sea,
  While on I sped from hill-side Rincon,
Till, past Oak Ridge's welcome gates,
  I stopped, beside the tomb of Lincoln.
The circumambient air was still;
  The warm, spring day with Peace was laden,
And trees and birds and flowers and bees
  Sang welcome to their blissful Aidenn.

I stood beside the monument
  And gazed, enrapt, into the portal,
Where rests, all that belongs to earth,
  Of proud Columbia's son immortal;

And as I mused upon his life,
    And on his dreadful death-scene pondered,
Methought he from the vault emerged
    And stood before me as I wondered.
His fine, expressive countenance
    With thought and joy and peace was beaming,
And "welcome" spake his kindly voice,
    While his glad eye with love was gleaming.

I stood transfixed, and while I gazed,
    The misty, dream-like vision vanished,
And for a moment time and place
    Were from my 'wildered senses banished.
But reason rallied to my aid,
    And memory quickly reassured me,
And back upon life's real plane,
    Their joint endeavors gently lured me;
And then I mused upon his life,
    When firm he held our helm of Nation,
And on his tragic, martyr death,
    And his loved country's lamentation,
When the quick telegraphic wires
    Flashed forth, without a second's warning,
Mute tidings of his fearful fate,
    And all the land was draped in mourning.

Oh, why, brave hearts of fallen friends,
    Come ever to the heart of woman
The thoughts that stir and words that burn,
    With fires divine, on altars human,
If to her thirsty, waiting soul
    No privilege or hope is given,
To tread with man earth's path to fame,
    And like him walk high roads to heaven?

Why, brothers, circumscribe her sphere?
    Why hedge, with human legislation,
Her soul, which, like yours, should be free
    To seek its chosen destination?

What we admire let's emulate,
    Dear sisters mine, as on life's highways
We travel with the good and great,
    While shedding light along life's by-ways

The twilight falls; you know I sped
    Past far Pacific's hill-side Rincon,
From Baker's grave, where sea-gulls wed,
    And stopped beside the tomb of Lincoln.

Horace Greeley, the immortal founder of the New York Tribune, had received the nomination for the Presidency at the National Liberal Republican Convention, while I was on the way; and when I reached New York, I at first used what influence I had in the Suffrage Association in favor of the election of the great editor; but Miss Anthony, who knew Mr. Greeley better than I did, caused me to be appointed as chairman of a committee to interview the editorial statesman and officially report the result at the meeting of the evening session. Miss Anthony, of New York, and Mrs. Jane Graham Jones, of Chicago, were the other members of this committee. We obtained the desired interview without difficulty. Mr. Greeley received us cordially at first (having been previously informed of my speech of the morning in his favor), but he was seized with a sudden chilliness of demeanor when I spoke of our errand. He brushed the fringe of his white whiskers under his smoothly shaven chin, and, speaking in a voice as hard as hail stones, said, "I don't want women to be men!" "Neither do I," I said, rising to my feet to end the interview. "I wouldn't be a man if I could! And now, Mr. Greeley, mark my words; you'll never be President! You will find that women can tear down, if they are not permitted to build up."

I was a novice in those days or I would have been more diplomatic. An older, more experienced woman would have sought to placate the great compromise candidate for the Presidency of the United States, by a little flattery, instead of increasing his prejudices by a prediction for which he was wholly unprepared. Cartoons, burlesquing men and measures, were just beginning to come into vogue, and Horace Greeley became one of the first and worst great victims of the innovation. I can see him now, as portrayed in the public prints, with a card carrying the name of B. Gratz Brown, candidate for the Vice-Presidency, attached, on every cartoon, to the tail of his coat. It is little wonder that he didn't long survive his defeat. Like every great genius, he was morbidly sensitive to either praise or blame. If he were with us in his body today, he would have ample opportunity to see, in these Pacific Coast States, that enfranchised women are in no danger of becoming men.

I returned to the Suffrage Convention and revoked my little speech of the morning. Horace Greeley had reason afterwards to consider my humble prediction as a prophecy.

He failed to become President, but he died a wiser man.

* * *

In the autumn of 1876, I was absent at the Centennial Exposition, whither I had gone in response to an invitation from Susan B. Anthony, recognized leader of the National Woman Suffrage Association, to assist in the important experiences of that memorable year. I recall, in this heart-to-heart talk, some of the incidents of crossing the Plains on that memorable journey in 1852, as I contrast the difference between travel then and now.

I remember starting on my journey to the Centennial with just twenty-five dollars in my pocket. Women were not salaried for special occasions on those days; but I had a pass as far as Wallula, up the Columbia, and an abounding faith in the ultimate success of my mission. In gathering subscriptions for "The New Northwest," in the ladies' cabin of the river steamer, I mentioned the state of my finances to an elderly woman of Klickitat County, Washington, who conferred with the captain of the boat, and obtained permission for her to gather the passengers of the boat, to enable me to lecture in the larger cabin, assigned to men. It was an inspiring scene! Our upward way, on the bosom of the broad Columbia, with vast, unsettled sage brush plains spreading away on either side, with mountains in the hazy distance, gave little

promise of the future prosperity of those once thought
to be nothing but desert wastes. At the close of the
lecture, my friend proposed a collection, which brought
me eighty-seven dollars. When I reached Wallula, I
returned half of this contribution to the office of "The
New Northwest." The steamer was tied up for the night
at the village, where I lectured in the evening to the
citizens of the place, and received another contribution.
The next morning at Wallula I received a pass from
Dr. D. S. Baker to Walla Walla. The doctor was at that
time building a narrow-gauge railroad from Wallula to
Walla Walla and had laid temporary rails for the transportation of construction cars. Border men were fighting
the doctor's enterprise on every mile of the road, pioneer
ranchers prophesying the destruction of the stage industry. We found dead cattle placed across the way in
several places. The doctor had trained a little dog to go
ahead of the construction work; and the faithful animal,
with wonderful intelligence, never failed to give us warning in time to avoid a wreck. We reached Walla Walla in
the afternoon, where I engaged a hall for an evening
meeting. But, when time came to open for the lecture,
the key was stolen, and our crowd repaired to the parlors
of the Stein House, where another collection sent me on
my way rejoicing. From Walla Walla, I went by stage,
through Idaho and Nevada, to Kelton, enjoying a seat
over the "boot" on every occasion, beside the obliging
driver, above the abounding dust. One day as we were
nearing Winnemucca, I told the driver that I was getting
tired of fried chicken, which had been furnished me at
every meal on the route. The accommodating driver
said, as he was brandishing his whip and handling his
reins, that the first driver out from Walla Walla had
passed the word along to all the drivers, telling them
that I was coming, and was fond of fried chicken.

At one way station where we stopped for dinner, a

lone station-keeper was keeping vigil over the body of her little babe that had died a few hours previously. She was waiting for the stage to carry the tidings to her husband, a dozen miles away, who was at work on railroad construction. Never shall I forget the hopeless sadness of that bereaved and lonely woman! I told the driver, when we mounted the stage to resume our journey, that when I got to Heaven, I intended to ask St. Peter to let me be usher, so I might conduct pioneer housewives and sturdy stage drivers to the highest seats.

I stopped at Winnemucca, Kelton and other points in places where evenings were cool so I could call meetings. But after reaching the Union Pacific train at Kelton, I made no halts till I got to central Illinois, where the heat was so oppressive as to compel the cessation of further travel or meetings for several days.

On reaching Philadelphia, I was met by the Oregon Commissioner of the Centennial Exposition, Hon. A. J. Dufur, who introduced me to the original Committee of Thirteen Commissioners, who accorded me every courtesy. I needn't go into any particulars about the Centennial Exposition, further than to say that after a long and interesting investigation of its wonders we reached the closing day. Having an hour to spare, I visited the Woman's Pavilion, where woman's handiwork was on display. Compared to the great exhibits displayed elsewhere, in honor of the genus masculine, the women's "show" was too meager to be otherwise than pitiful. After examining some dresses, sacred to royalty, and a few relics from the days of John Adams, Sr., including the baby cap worn by John Quincy Adams, Jr., when he was a week old, I wandered around to the end of the building, near which were stationed the different implements of warfare used by different nations. There were gatling guns, mounted howitzers, modern cannons, Columbiads and other implements of destruction I cannot name, all with their muzzles pointed toward that Woman's Pavilion.

Across the area was a great temporary platform on which were seated the President of the United States and all the other dignitaries of the occasion. A heavy rain began pouring down, and while the ceremonies proceeded, a woman raised a window over the heads of the performers, and held out, at half mast, over the head of President Grant, a tattered flag, a relic of the Revolutionary War. A lady standing at my elbow said, "I do not wonder that a disfranchised woman is weeping with the weeping Heavens. We are under the aristocracy of sex."

* * *

I had about completed the foregoing Chapter, when a friend of my earlier pioneer days came to me, bringing the following poem, and requested its re-publication in this narrative, saying it so accurately related her own experience, in path-breaking days, that it deserved a place in these pages. The little woman is bent with toil and hardship. Her hair is white. Her face is wrinkled and her chest is sunken. But she is one of God's elect, for whose sake I am glad to heed her request.

HEROINES OF OREGON.
By Mrs. Abigail Scott Duniway.
Read at Champoeg, Oregon, May 2, 1901, in commemoration of the organization of the Provisional Government of Oregon, May 2, 1843.

No braver crew e'er manned a Ship of State
Than those whose peaceful deeds we celebrate
On this historic day. A patriot band
Were they who saved this goodly land
From the encroaching grasp of monarchy,
And raised, in noble pride, the banner of the free.

No clash of arms, no glittering array
Of crested helmets, no vibrant display
Of martial music, stirred the listening air;
But rose o'er all, instead, the earnest prayer
Of border statesmen, met in days agone,
To frame the laws, provisional, for Oregon.

As here we gather on this hallowed ground,
Where silence, sympathetic and profound,
For eight and fifty years has reigned supreme,
The deeds of these heroic men our theme,
Be mine the pleasing task to chant a lay
In humble memory of the heroines of that day.

No chiseled lines their strenuous lives proclaim,
No marble shaft records their names; no fame
Accrues to them,—in solitude they strove,
In primitive pursuits, their worth to prove;
And toiling on in their allotted way,
Oft held wild beasts and wilder savages at bay.

Thus bravely did they bear their part, and we
Who ripe fruition of their work may see,
Will not forget to keep their memory green,
Whene'er we meet on this historic scene,
In honor of the sturdy zeal that won
For thee, Columbia, for thee, the State of Oregon!

* * *

I returned to Oregon in the Spring of 1887, after
a long siege of campaigning in Washington and Idaho, to
find the work for Equal Rights had made favorable headway through the steadily increasing circulation of "The
New Northwest" and the popular influence of a convention held at Salem, under the able leadership of the late
Mrs. H. A. Laughary, at that time President of the State
Association, assisted by Dr. Mary A. Thompson. It is
well to say of Dr. Thompson, who at this writing is in
her ninetieth year, that she made a permanent impression
on the medical profession of Oregon, in pioneer days,
by opening the way for other women physicians of the
state, but few of whom realize the importance of her work
as a path-breaker. She was a political prohibitionist and
had different ideas from my own as to the conduct of the
Equal Suffrage movement. She argued that I stood in
her way; that she could carry the movement to success
if she were chosen at its head. Shortly afterwards another doctor—B. A. Owens-Adair, a regular physician,
whose son I had given a home while she was studying
medicine in Europe—said, substantially, the same thing:

and I thought, "Maybe these ladies are right; maybe, if I should get out of their way the work would be more successful." So I left the cause in Oregon, and went again to Idaho and Washington, where I proselyted intermittently for ten years, and returned again to Oregon in 1894 to find that not a single meeting had been called, and no steps of any kind had been taken for advancing the movement; so I was compelled to begin where I had left off, after the defeat of a previous decade.

When I attempted to rehabilitate the movement in 1894 I found the press, at first, determined to ignore the movement altogether. My brother, Mr. Harvey W. Scott, was out of the City, and the managing editor of "The Oregonian" refused to publish the call for our first meeting, thus disarranging our plans until after Mr. Scott returned. I then laid the case before him and another date was set. The call was printed, the meetings began, and the press treated us so fairly that the movement was forged ahead with gratifying regularity for six consecutive years, till our next campaign came on, in 1900, of which fuller details are given in another chapter.

* * *

I found to my dismay, at the beginning of our new dispensation, under management of the national officers in 1905-06, when I began to write this history, that the official records of our work from the beginning, which had been placed in the hands of our valued co-worker and recording secretary, the late Mary Schaffer Ward, for revision and compilation for future reference, had been lost; and Mrs. Ward, having died in a San Francisco hospital, her residence in Portland was broken up, and her husband, Judge Ward, had returned to his Eastern home, where he, too, had died. Therefore, we, as a State Association, have no official record available for this narrative, and I am compelled to depend upon such material as I can gather from memory, from volumes of "The New Northwest," from the files of "The Oregonian," the memory of friends and the National History of Woman Suffrage, before referred to in these pages. To make the situation still more difficult, the voluminous records preserved by Mrs. Ward since 1894, were turned over to a new administration created to sidetrack my work in 1905, and were never heard of afterwards.

The new administration, chosen in 1905, under direction of our National officers, ignored all of the previous work and workers of thirty-four strenuous years, and the new management, thus chosen, took legal possession of the books, placing them out of my reach.

My friend and co-worker, Dr. Annice Jeffreys-Myers, who was Vice-President at Large throughout that disastrous campaign (to be fully described hereafter), was seized with a fatal illness at the close of our national defeat; or we should, doubtless, now be able to get some light as to the fate of the lost records.

But, I am happy to say that we have preserved all records since the parting of ways in the autumn of 1906 (See Chapters 24 and 25); that our faithful Executive Committee has prepared and kept them intact; and any member in regular standing, desiring to look them over, may find them in possession of our Recording Secretary, Miss Elma Buckman, No. 42 East 18th Street North, Portland, Oregon, with whom they are filed for safe keeping.

* * *

I went to Southern Oregon in 1879, and while sojourning in Jacksonville, was assailed with a shower of eggs—since known as "Jacksonville arguments." The leading men of Jacksonville, or those posing as such, were mostly old miners, or refugees from the bush-whacking regions of Missouri, whence they had been driven by exigencies growing out of the Civil War. This egg-throwing incident created great excitement, for which I was partly to blame, since, in writing up the incidents of the journey in my editorial correspondence, I had not hesitated to retort, with humorous details, over which I had been burlesqued.

To make a long story as brief as possible, I will state that while awaiting the result of my write-up, due the following week, I lectured in adjacent towns and villages and returned in care of the sheriff, who found the town in an uproar, which he quelled to some extent with a posse of deputies. After the close of my last lecture, which no resident woman of Jacksonville was allowed to attend, I shook the dust of the town from my feet and departed in a closed carriage, for the home of a friend, four miles away, where I slept an excited sleep, till the stage came along the next day and carried me to a different degree of civilization. But, in justice to the town of Jacksonville, I wish to add that, in these later years, the town has become the center of a large degree of Equal Suffrage sentiment, and there is no place in the Pacific Northwest where I am better received or feel more at home than within its beautiful environments. Jacksonville has always polled a splendid vote for the Equal Suffrage Movement. Ashland, Medford, Phoenix, Goldhill and other towns are nestled among its fruit-laden hills and verdant vales, and no more beautiful surroundings can be found within all the confines of beautiful Oregon. No more whole-souled men and hospitable women abound anywhere; and, what to me is more worthy of record, from the days of my first and last uncomfortable experience in Jacksonville I have never been met with insults or missiles of any kind in any of my travels throughout my entire bailiwick.

CHAPTER X.

Convention at Walla Walla and Incidents of Travel.

A CONSTITUTIONAL convention had met in Walla Walla, Washington Territory, in June, 1878. It was composed of a delegation of fifteen gentlemen, and its business, as is usual in such deliberative bodies, was the creation of an initiative constitution, to be ratified, or rejected, by a referendum vote of the legal electorate. Acting upon the invitations of Hon. and Mrs. H. P. Isaacs, Hon. and Mrs. Philip Ritz, Judge and Mrs. Thomas H. Brents, Judge and Mrs. Mix and others, I visited the convention and was permitted to present a memorial in person, praying that the word "male" be omitted from the fundamental law of the incubating state. But my plea (like that of Abigail Adams on a like occasion on the other side of the continent a century before) failed of acceptance at the polls; though through a close vote—it stood eight to seven—and men went on as before, saying as they did in the beginning of our struggle, "Women do not wish to vote; if they want the ballot let them ask for it." (See National History of Woman Suffrage, Vol. III, p. 777.)

* * *

Invitations to lecture in various parts of Washington and Idaho Territories came to me so frequently, after the foregoing experience, that I was kept engaged constantly for many months in visiting various towns, some of which were in the formative period, with no place to lecture but a barn, or the skeleton frame of a future school house, store, stable, saloon, hotel or blacksmith shop; and there was often no place for entertainment at night but a hospitable shanty of a single room, where I was often glad to get the corner bed, with two or more children as sleeping companions. Where the people came from to attend the meetings was a mystery. They came in wagons, on horseback, in buck-boards or afoot; and never in the crowded cities of our Eastern border have I met more open-hearted or progressive men and women. I remember meeting, at one of these rural centers, with several federal officers, whose names I have forgotten, one of whom said, "Madam, you are carrying your mission to the right spots, and among the right people. You are sowing the seeds of liberty in virgin soil; and you'll succeed in getting the ballot for women in this new Western country before our Eastern people can see how it was done."

One incident, or rather, several of them, occurred at different times, that seem well worth the telling. I had gone to the town of Palouse, in the famous fertile and beautiful region of Idaho known as the Palouse Country. The frame work of a primitive hotel was up, floored and enclosed, and the rather spacious dining room was placed at my disposal for a meeting in the midst of which the floor fell into the cellar, precipitating the crowd to the bottom, in a bunch, leaving me and a few friends standing near a wall that had not collapsed. "Don't hurry, friends!" I called at the top of my voice. "Remain perfectly quiet, and there will be no danger." Luckily, the kerosene lamps were in brackets on the wall, and there was no threat of fire. The crowd instinctively obeyed the warning, and in less than half an hour we were collected in another room, where, on motion of some big-hearted man with a voice like a Stentor's, the crowd voted for the lecture to go on.

* * *

Several years thereafter, I was passing that way again. The town had grown surprisingly, the hotel had

GROUP OF EQUAL SUFFRAGISTS

MRS. CLARA E. SYLVESTER
Leading Washington Suffragist in Territorial Days of 1885, whose Home was My Headquarters

THE LATE MRS. S. M. KELTY
Leading Worker for Equal Suffrage for Twenty-Five Years in Yamhill County, Oregon

MRS. H. L. PALMER
Leading Worker for Equal Suffrage Since 1871 in Oregon and Washington

MRS. DUNIWAY'S DAUGHTER
The Late Mrs. Clara Duniway Stearns, Member of Grand Jury, Clark County, Washington Ty., in 1879

ATT'Y CLARA SHORTRIDGE FOLTZ
Prominent Lawyer of California and Early Oregon Suffrage Leader. Noted Co-Worker of Mrs. Duniway's Since 1871

THE LATE MRS. C. A. COBURN
Suffragist and Writer for New Northwest and Oregonian. From Photograph Taken in 1880

THE LATE SUSAN B. ANTHONY
National Equal Suffrage Leader. From Photograph Taken in 1871, while Lecturing in Oregon

changed hands, and I stopped over to give a few talks to the people and catch up with my writing for the paper. The people were friendly, the hotel was comfortable, and I remained for five days. As I was to leave on the stage, on the last evening after the remaining lecture, I called at the office to pay my bill. The landlord said the charge was ten dollars. I paid the bill and added, as he signed a receipt, "I saw on the printed directions in my room that your rates are $7.00 a week." "So they are," he said, coloring, "but my rates are $2.00 a day." "Very well," I replied, without hesitation, "suppose you give me back $3.00, and I'll stay with you the rest of the week."

Several men who were sitting in the lobby overheard the remark and spread it over town, greatly to the amusement of the audience I met in the evening, and somewhat to the embarrassment of the landlord, who didn't exactly enjoy the joke.

On another occasion, late in the season, I was journeying through Eastern Washington, on my way from Goldendale to Yakima and Ellensburg. A light snow was falling, the day was cold, the wind was biting, the night was coming down, and I was glad when a bend in the river, along which our winding roadway ran, displayed in the distance the gleaming lights of Yakima. As the day waned, and the sun sank low, I saw the men on seats behind myself and the driver passing a bottle, which I pretended as usual, not to notice. Finally, one of them, who had evidently become more mellow than the rest, accosted me, saying, "Madam! you ought to be at home, enjoying yourself, like my wife is doing. I want to bear all the hardship of life myself, and let her sit by the fire, toasting her footsies." I didn't answer and nobody else said anything. It was almost dark when we reached the town, and the obliging driver went out of his way to leave this fellow-passenger at his own door yard, where we found his protected wife, busy with an ax, chopping away at a pile of snow-covered cord wood. "I see, my friend, that your wife is toasting her footsies! Good-bye," I said at parting; and I afterwards heard that the men who saw the incident nicknamed the husband "Old footsie toaster."

* * *

When the Legislative Assembly met, in Salem, in the autumn of 1880, it was decided by the State Equal Suffrage Association that we could better encourage the prosecution of our work by making an attempt, with the aid of well-known lawyers, so to amend the State Constitution as to eliminate the word "male" from its chapter on "Privileges and Elections." Pursuant to this decision, a resolution to that effect was offered in the Senate by Hon. C. W. Fulton, of Clatsop, and in the House by Hon. Lee Laughlin, of Yamhill. I was graciously invited to participate in a discussion on the floor of both houses; and our joint resolution was passed by the requisite two-thirds majority. A grand ratification meeting was held in the Opera House in honor of the event, and resolutions of thanks to the lawmakers were passed, accompanied by many expressions of faith in the legislation of the future. But the resolution was vetoed because of some technicality known to lawmakers, and was declared "unconstitutional."

* * *

In the meantime, the work was going steadily but quietly forward in Washington Territory, my own labors being distributed about equally between the different sections of the Pacific Northwest, now known as Oregon, Washington and Idaho.

* * *

During most of the following season, I was engaged in the pursuit of my calling in different counties of Oregon. On one occasion, after I had been lecturing at McMinnville, North Yamhill, LaFayette and Dayton, everywhere meeting much encouragement and adding long lists to the subscription rolls of "The New Northwest," my lectures had been concluded and the little river steamer, on which I was to return to Portland, left Dayton at an early hour. My friend, the late Captain Bas Miller, master, for many years, of river craft, placed in my care for consignment to the Children's Home in Portland a quartet of half-clad, mangy little waifs, rescued from some hovel by the proper authorities. I secured them a charity breakfast, through the kindness of the steward, and after warning them against falling overboard, became absorbed in my writing. I noticed, after awhile, that several women, occupying a corner of the cabin, were eyeing me furtively, and I could feel that they were discussing me, though I pretended to pay no attention. Finally, one of them approached me and said, with a severe look on her expressive face, "Mrs. Duniway! Don't you think you had better spend a little time in taking care of your children?" I looked up from my work in surprise, and she added: "Can't you see that you are wasting your time, advocating women's rights, when your children need proper care?" I didn't catch her meaning at first, but when the poor little waifs came romping through the cabin, quarreling over some childish dispute, it dawned upon me to say, above the din, "Do you think those children belong to me?" "Why certainly," she said; "they are in your care. Who else could they belong to?" I wanted to call the Captain to my defense, but we were approaching some rapids, and he was upstairs at the wheel; so I drew from my satchel a portfolio of photographs and said "Here are my six children." Then, rising to my feet and speaking to all the women who had been discussing me, I told them, to their evident surprise, that my children were all engaged, after school hours, in setting type for the Equal Rights newspaper, "The New Northwest;" and we were all hoping to see the day when all mothers could be as successful with their children as I had been with mine. I distributed copies of my newspaper among them, and, after trying in vain to quell the noisy waifs in the cabin, returned to my writing, too badly perturbed for many minutes to catch the thread of my theme. One of those women offered to subscribe for my newspaper before the boat landed, but, being married, and a servant without wages, she couldn't pay for it.

The foregoing story seems like a far-off dream, as I sit in the gloaming and ponder over the present day activities of the Child Welfare League, the Parent-Teachers' Association and the Boys' and Girls' Aid Society, of which the Children's Home in South Portland was the forerunner; though it is well to add that its promoters found, after they had secured the location, and gathered funds for the building and its maintenance, that they could not form a corporation to perpetuate their philanthropy, because they were married women; so they incorporated under the names of prominent men, most of whom are now numbered among the dead, though all of them, but one, afterwards became Equal Suffragists.

On another occasion, after I had given a Fourth of July address at Camas, in Washington Territory, I was returning to Portland on a river steamer, when, as I happened to be standing at a window overlooking the blue hills of Washington, I spoke to a lady tourist at my right, in praise of the territory wherein women were voters, and added that I was glad to call Washington "The Land of the Free and the Home of the Brave." The lady said, as we further discussed the question, that she would be a Suffragist if the cause had the right kind of leaders; and she named Elizabeth Cady Stanton and Susan B. Anthony as particularly objectionable, because of their alleged "coarse manners and unwomanly conversation"; but she admitted, in response to my query, that she didn't know them, except by general report. "And, in Oregon," she said, "I am told that you have that horrid woman, a Mrs. Duniway, who drinks, and smokes and swears like a man." "Do you know this to be true?" I asked, as I gave a warning glance at other women, to impose silence. But one of them attracted the lady's attention to something on the other side of the boat and led her away; though she said to me at parting, "The purser told me about her, on The Dalles boat." I did not see the tourist again, as she retreated in confusion to a stateroom, but I was told that the purser she had quoted had told her this to "jolly" her, though with no idea that she would take him seriously. I have often met with other incidents, equally unbelievable, that were told by prominent men to create a laugh at my expense, among crowds of hearers, who would relate them to their wives at home, as facts, many of which would not be admissible in print. Taking such reminiscences into consideration, it is little wonder that women were slow in coming to the front as suffragists. The wonder is that anyone should have been endowed with sufficient courage to endure them, and persevere in her demand for woman's enfranchisement.

CHAPTER XI.

Discusses Prohibition and Meets an Accuser.

DURING the meetings of the session of the year 1879, much discussion had come up in the Legislative Assembly of Oregon over a resolution proposing the prohibition of the liquor traffic. After a more or less heated fight over the question, pro and con, which became state-wide as the controversy proceeded, the Equal Suffrage Movement was steadily gaining ground, mainly through my personal efforts in the lecture field, added to the constantly extending influence of "The New Northwest." Controversies over the liquor traffic came up between voters in almost every county. Many farmers were interested in hops, barley, rye, cherries, apples, berries and peaches, cultivation of which had increased many fold. Illicit distilling had become an art in many remote places. Breweries had multiplied, saloons, of more or less questionable character, were rapidly increasing, and the alarming consumption of intoxicants, per capita, was paraded in official statistics. The work for voluntary progress in the temperance movement was overshadowed. In the meantime, the late Judge John F. Caples, a prominent man in political circles, who afterwards became Minister Plenipotentiary to Chili, had proposed to me the formation of an open temperance movement, which soon became very popular. Judge Caples, as President, and I, as Vice-President, held the boards for several successive years. Our Saturday evening meetings were held in the old Y. M. C. A. Hall, on First street, which was too small to accommodate the crowds. We were not advocating prohibition, or anything else but temperance in all things. Caples had a great book, containing a pledge against the use of intoxicants as a beverage, in which, he said, were recorded over four thousand names. Whether the book is now in existence or not, I do not know. One day Caples called on me and said that the new fad of prohibition which was springing up in the land was assuming big proportions. He said it would get into politics; and the real temperance reform we had at heart would be lost sight of till this craze, spreading like the measles, had run its course. The Woman's Christian Temperance Union was not yet active on the Coast, but Caples said it was going to be taken up by the churches, and he thought we had better quit while our credit was good. I consulted my husband, who said that Caples was right, and the meetings were discontinued.

As population increased, the advocates of prohibition of the liquor traffic grew more aggressive, its opponents became correspondingly more alert in their endeavors to defend their own financial interests, as was only natural, and might have been expected everywhere, when financial interests are in jeopardy.

As Caples had predicted, prohibition got into politics; and I, who had for years been advocating the liberty, as well as the duty of every individual to govern himself, having no faith at all in the new movement, was no longer a member of the Temperance Alliance, which met again in Salem,—this time in the commodious Methodist Episcopal Church.

I had business before the Legislature, at that time in session, and during an interval, desiring to meet old friends in the Alliance, I entered the church, where I was accosted on every side by friendly greetings. A young lady friend, who had been holding a whispered conversation with a *vis a vis,* informed me that a prominent clergyman had been openly accusing me from the platform of being in the habit of meeting men in my rooms at the hotels, and drinking intoxicants. I immediately scribbled a few lines and sent them to the preacher, demanding an explanation. It was interesting to note the result. The offender's face and pate turned scarlet. He mopped his head and forehead with a red bandana handkerchief as he exhibited my note to a fellow prohibitionist, an import from California, who hurriedly scribbled a resolution to prohibit any person from speaking on the platform. unless invited by the program committee. The resolution passed without comment, nobody outside of the managers paying any attention to it but myself.

I spent an agreeable recess hour, getting subscribers to my newspaper, gathering an encouraging amount of shekels from patrons new and old. To all questions as to what I had in contemplation, I gave noncommittal or evasive replies. The attendance in the evening was large. The singing was good, and several women, who had by this time learned to speak in public, made pleasing remarks. Things went on swimmingly until there came a break in the program. Two state senators, whose names were announced as speakers, dodged the issue and stayed away. While the chairman was gathering his wits together over some sort of a new deal, I advanced to the platform and began some running remarks of a congratulatory nature, over the songs and speeches of the evening. I got along splendidly for a few minutes, when the chairman, seizing the cane of the clergyman who had slandered me, thumped it on the floor, till I turned and said: "What is it?" "Did you hear the resolution passed this afternoon to the effect that nobody was to be allowed to speak unless invited by the Committee on Program?" "Yes, sir." "Don't you know you are out of order?" "Yes, sir." "Then you must take your seat!" "I was only showing you some prohibition that couldn't prohibit," I said laughing. "But, sir!" and I had grown emphatic, "I rise to a question of privilege!" "State your question of privilege." "Sir!" I said, and I felt myself growing taller, "I am not a delegate to this convention, because I am not in sympathy with its present methods and I have had no intention of antagonizing yours. But my question of privilege is this: I was informed, on entering the church this afternoon, as a visitor, that Reverend I. D. Driver had been accusing me of indulging in Bacchanalian revelries with men in my room at hotels. I demand his authority for such an accusation, and shall hold him responsible until he names it." My accuser gave the name of a man who, he said, kept a hotel in Port Townsend; but he spoke in a voice so low and tremulous that he couldn't be heard from the platform, so I said, aloud: "He says the man's name is Sayles!" Reverend Harvey K. Hines, addressing me aside, said in an undertone, "That man Sayles has been dead for five years, and he was always such a liar nobody believed what he said about anything!" I repeated what was said to the audience, and added: "I don't pretend to be a saint. I've done a good many mean, little things I'm ashamed of, in my life, but nobody knows about them but myself, and I won't tell. But," I continued, "suppose it were true that I had done the dreadful things of which Mr. Driver has accused me, and nobody knows better than my assailant that they are not true! But suppose they were true! There are probably a hundred men in this assembly who have been drinking intoxicants today. Why doesn't he bring their names before this body? Suppose that I, when appearing before an Equal Suffrage Convention, imagining that Mr. Driver was absent, had dragged his name before the assembly, and repeated the often circulated scandal, falsely accusing him of killing four of his deceased wives!" I then sat down, and the audience departed in profound silence a few minutes after. Though, again, as on a former occasion, many years before, my hand was so often enthusiastically shaken that my shoulder was severely lamed.

The Alliance died in a year or two, of inanition, and

was never born again. But before I leave this subject, I wish to say a good word for the late Brother Driver, whom I forgave. He was a man of large intellect and quick impulses, much given to controversy, and when angry was always ready for a fight, physical as well as wordy. I remember, with thanks, that he opened his church for me once, for a series of suffrage meetings in Eugene, after a custodian had locked me out of the Court House; and I doubt not that I shall meet him again on some future harmonious occasion, in the happy land of souls.

Requiescat in pace!

* * *

I herewith insert the following incident, illustrative of the style of opposition I have often encountered in unexpected places:

I was on my way to Washington in 1910, as a representative of Governor Benson, to attend a National Conference of Governors, when our train was held up for a few hours by a snow blockade. I had asked a porter to make up my berth as soon as the night came down, so I could read by my electric light. Just as he had let down the berth above my head, a very pretty little white-haired woman, neatly dressed, came in from a way-station, and asked me to request the porter to make up her berth first, as she was going to leave the train early the next morning. I said, "Certainly," and made room in my seat for her and her bundles. Pretty soon a waiter came through with a tray, bearing a couple of foaming steins, headed for the men's smoking room at the farthest end of the car. "It won't be but a very few years until that curse of curses will be driven from the land," said the little lady; "Don't you think so?" "That depends on whether men will stop manufacturing, buying or drinking stimulants," I said, feeling sorry I couldn't avoid her question. "Don't you believe in prohibition?"

was her next rejoinder. "I believe we can protect ourselves from all the elements. We are protected from this
snow-storm, but we can't prohibit it. God has put it
among the elements of nature. There is only one Power
that is capable of prohibiting snow-storms or alcohol, and
He doesn't seem ready to act." The dear little lady with
hands as bony as bird's claws, clutched my arm nervously,
and said: "Do you mean to say that God is the author of
alcohol?" "Certainly! The Bible tells us that God
makes everything." She clasped my arm as tightly as
she was able, and rising, said: "I don't want anything
to do with your kind of a God!" She then flounced away
and retreated to the farther end of the car, as near the
men's smoking and drinking room as the partition would
allow, and stood there to avoid further contamination
from my blasphemous self. When her berth was ready,
she gathered up her belongings from my compartment
and rushed behind her curtain, without stopping to thank
me or say good-night. When I awoke the next morning,
she was gone. I asked a lady across the aisle who she
was, and was informed that she was a "White Ribboner,"
who was advocating Equal Suffrage as a "short-cut to
prohibition." "Do you wonder that wise men hesitate
to give such women the ballot?" asked a business man at
the lady's side. "Such women are as wise as the men
who are harping on the same string," I couldn't help re-
torting, as I arose to leave my seat, in response to a
waiter's "Last call for breakfast in the dining car!"

* * *

On one occasion, while I was campaigning in Idaho
in 1889, I stopped over in a railroad town to deliver two
lectures. Churches were no longer closed against me
anywhere; but I had learned that only a small fraction
of the men, and but few women, would attend a lecture
in a small town in any other church but their own; so I

went to the chairman of the committee having charge of the one public hall in the place, who agreed to let me have it at a reasonable price, if I were not a member of the Woman's Christian Temperance Union, against which he seemed to have a grievance. I had a good audience, before which I read a note from the Circuit Judge, tendering me the Court House for the next evening's meeting, at which there was an augmented crowd. In reply to a question from some one in the audience, I was forced to state my views on the temperance problem. As prohibition had recently become a live political issue, and I was trying to steer clear of it, at least till women would get the right to vote, I complied with reluctance; but I never was successful as a dodger, so I said, in substance: "With all due deference to everybody's opinion, whether coinciding with my own or not, I will say, frankly, that I am opposed to two kinds of prohibition. One of these would prohibit woman from the use of her right to vote, and the other would prohibit a man's right to sell a sober man a drink of liquor if he should want to buy. If one of you were to call a physician to prescribe for an abscess in the side, and the doctor should order the abscess to be overspread with a rigid prohibition plaster, big enough to cover both the diameter and the circumference of the entire ulcer, a ten-year-old boy who was having the benefit of the common schools, and understood something about the circulation of the blood, could tell you that your doctor was a quack. He would know, if you didn't, that the virus thus confined would burrow deeper and yet deeper into the body of the man, and would ultimately rot him to death. The abscess in the Nation's side is drunkenness. It is a disease of the Nation's blood; you cannot cure it by sumptuary laws. You must treat it openly, with the sanitary usages of common sense. The large majority of men who use intoxicants are not drunkards; yet there are men who fall victims to the disease of drunkenness, just as there are men who are victims of gluttony. We should have laws to quarantine and cure the drunkard; and we should fine or imprison any man, or set of men, who would supply a drunkard with intoxicants. But you would not think of compelling every man to walk with crutches because now and then some man walks lame; nor would you think of prohibiting the existence of all women because a man is sometimes guilty of coveting his neighbor's wife."

The necessary little exercise of taking the collection was then in order, and I was keeping up a running fire of little jokes during the performance, when a man who had been sitting in a corner at my left, arose and said: "I was formerly opposed to women's rights; but I had begun to believe in 'em, because I thought women would be sure to vote for prohibition. But," and his voice reached a high key as he exclaimed, "I don't want any woman to vote unless they'll all vote for prohibition!" To this I replied: "The gentleman reminds me of Brigham Young, who at one time advocated Equal Rights for the women of Utah, in the firm belief that all women would vote for polygamy. In like manner the gentleman who has just spoken, has been led to advocate Equal Rights for women, but only because he has thought that all women would vote his ticket. And, like Brigham Young, my friend will in due time discover his mistake. He'll find that there is but one thing in the world a little stronger than a woman's will, and that is—her won't. Of what good would the ballot be to women, if my friend here could have control of barbed hooks fastened in their jaws, with strings attached and himself clothed with arbitrary power to yank every string?" The house laughed and applauded, and I added: "Would you compel every man to go into quarantine because some man gets the smallpox? I know the argument my friend will use in reply to this. He'll say, 'We prohibit the spread of smallpox. Wouldn't *you?*" My reply was easy. I said: "Everybody wants to avoid smallpox. Can't my hearers see the point? If the Snake River flowed intoxicants, and pure water was prohibited to flow at all, unless held in licensed leash, like liquor, the secret demand for the water would increase to the law-breaking point. Then, children would learn to shun intoxicants and hunt for water, just as calves and colts, and lambs and pigs hunt for it, just as they instinctively shun the alkali puddles of the desert." The gentleman looked the chagrin and disappointment he felt, and I got a little sorry for him, so I added, "I know, good friends, that my opponent here isn't half as narrow as he thinks he is. There is only one streak of tyranny in him, and, of course, there is a cause for that, somewhere. A man is what his mother makes him; and somebody must have sinned against this man's mother, or he wouldn't have that one streak of tyranny in his mental makeup."

The house roared, and a comely little woman came laughingly forward, as the discomfited speaker escaped through a side door. Laying a half dollar on the desk, the lady said, "The collection missed me, and this discussion is worth half a dollar." The general laughter continued until after the close of the meeting; and on my way back to the hotel, I said to the landlady at my side, "I can't see what everybody is laughing about. I surely didn't say anything cute enough to arouse so much merriment." "That man," said the lady in reply, "is the alleged illegitimate son of a Southern governor. We all knew you didn't know about it, so nobody blamed you; and that pleasant little woman, who laid that half dollar on the desk, is his wife." I was afterwards informed that my opponent was in reality a good husband, whose streak of tyranny—though only a streak—was excusable under the circumstances.

* * *

Before leaving this chapter, I ask the reader to go with me to another point of observation, when I was campaigning in Benton County, Oregon. I was the guest of some friends near the college town of Philomath, where I held several evening meetings under their pleasant auspices. To show the difficulties of my position as a pioneer pathbreaker in the cause of human rights, I will here insert one of the many stories put in circulation by men for the purpose of making their wives contented with their lot. I was told by an eye-witness that a party of women out on a blackberrying excursion, came to a cabin built over a gulch, from which half a dozen half-naked, tow-headed, half-frightened children were peeping. One of the ladies suggested calling at the cabin to ask for a drink of water. They found two families huddled in the shack, with no furniture visible but a few three-legged stools, and no beds but some rough bunks in the corners, filled with loose straw and some not very inviting bedding. One of the women, pale, weak, and freckled, sat on a stool, holding a very young infant, while by her side, on the puncheon floor, lay a year-old baby not yet able to walk. My friend and hostess, who is a very practical woman, said, addressing the mother, "My good woman, don't you know that you have too many children? Don't you see that you have more babies than you can properly care for?" "Yes," replied the woman languidly, "it does seem like I have too many; but I couldn't give 'em away, like that old Mrs. Duniway does hers!" "Do you know this to be true?" said my friend in response. "Yes; I know it must be so," was the firm rejoinder, "for he" (of course meaning her husband by the use of that omnipotent word "he") "heard men saying so in the saloons and livery stables in Corvallis."

Is it any wonder that many women, in the lower, ignorant and povery-stricken walks of life, have been slow to accept a movement having for its object the ultimate amelioration of their condition? My friend assured me that, although she could not convince the woman that she was not a better mother than "old Mrs. Duniway," she did set two women to thinking that they had been altogether mistaken about one item of saloon and livery stable gossip—also that men of a certain grade, who get their news in the livery stable and the saloon, were causing women on their lowly plane to oppose their own emancipation from lives of sexual and financial degradation by slandering women better off than themselves.

I cannot at this writing think of anything of my own to say, on this unpleasant theme, that equals the following poem by Edward W. Sanborn, clipped from the "New York Sun." It illustrates another phase of the subjugation of women and was cut from the "Oregonian" while Edwin Markham's "Man With the Hoe" was being universally quoted by the press. "The Woman of the Shack" of whom I have been speaking, is infinitely better off, having no house to clean, than "The Woman with the Broom," who inspired Mr. Sanborn's muse, as he said, "after seeing a farmer's wife cleaning house":

Bowed by the cares of cleaning house, she leans
Upon her broom, and gazes through the dust,
A wilderness of wrinkles on her face,
And on her head a knob of wispy hair.
Who made her slave to sweeping and to soap,
A thing that smiles not and that never rests,
Stanchioned in a stall, a sister to the cow?
Who loosened and made shrill this angled jaw?
Who dower'd this narrowed chest for blowing up
Of sluggish men-folk, and their morning fire?

Is this the thing you made a bride and brought
To have dominion over hearth and home?
To scour the stairs and search the bin for flour?
To bear the burdens of maternity?
Is this the wife they wove, who framed our law,
And pillared a bright land on smiling homes?
Down all the stretch of street to the last house,
There is no shape more angular than hers,
More tongued with gabble of her neighbors' deeds,
More filled with ever-aching and rheumatic twinge,
More fraught with menace of the frying-pan.

O, lords and masters in our happy land,
How with this woman will you make account?
How answer her shrill question in that hour
When whirlwinds of such women shake the polls,
Heedless of every precedent and creed,
Straight in hysteric haste to right all wrongs?
How will it be with cant of politics,
With king of trade and legislative boss,
With cobwebs of hypocrisy and greed,
When she shall take the ballot for her broom
And sweep away the dust of centuries?

I am happy to say, in concluding this chapter, that a better day has dawned for many women of the farm. Many of them, except in remotest districts, now enjoy the benefits of art, invention, music, literature, the telegraph, rural post delivery, creameries, bakeries, canneries, laundries, etc., of which their progenitors never dreamed. Men, as well as women, are learning that the most important asset of any generation is its children. Men learned this long ago, when raising the lower animals, and both the men and women of the farms are not only learning it now, but are also teaching their sons and daughters valuable lessons concerning the fundamental laws of life, which their own parents were compelled to learn by cruel experience.

CHAPTER XII.

Congress of Women—Woman's Club Movement.

As written for and partly published in Ida Husted Harper's "Life and Work of Susan B. Anthony." Vol. IV—pp. 891-897 (complete in four volumes).

By Abigail Scott Duniway.

AFTER the defeat of our Equal Suffrage Amendment in 1884, and especially after the subsequent overthrow of women's right to vote in the incoming State of Washington in 1887, all of which came upon us as the reflex action of the prohibition movement, which had made the Pacific Northwest its storm center, the leaders of the cause in Oregon were compelled to remain apparently quiescent for a term of years, waiting for the animosities to die out which had been engendered by the efforts of a few women who were not suffragists, to establish an arbitrary government over the inalienable rights of men, to which the average voter quite naturally objects, even as self-respecting women object to the efforts of men to legislate for them as to what they shall eat, or drink, "or wherewithal they shall be clothed."

I returned to Oregon in the summer of 1894, after ten years' work in Idaho, and called a meeting to revise our work and resume our regular labors, although, even then, so necessary had our work of conciliating voters become, as the result of their combined opposition to measures to which women were supposed to be pledged *en masse,* that we have never since deemed it wise to pursue "National" tactics as to agitation and organization. But we worked actively, if quietly, disseminating peace-making sentiments among the lawmakers of the state; and when the Legislative Assembly convened in 1895, its leading members, appreciating our long-continued efforts to hold the Equal Suffrage Movement aloof from all side issues, decided to again submit our constitutional amendment to a referendum vote. So skillfully had we kept our work for the cause free from public agitation of an aggressive character, since our defeat of 1884, that there was little opposition to overcome; and, with the tactful co-operation of the late Dr. Annice F. Jeffreys, our influential Vice-President-at-Large, there was no trouble in securing the necessary majority to start the proposed amendment on its way to ratification by the succeeding biennial assembly. As I was absent for more than half of the year 1894, disseminating suffrage sentiment in Idaho, as I had previously done at intervals for many years in the whole Pacific Northwest, including Northern California, and was away from my Oregon field altogether during the Legislative Assembly of 1895, I cannot relate the proceedings from the standpoint of an eyewitness; but I have since learned, from many sources, that great credit was due to Dr. Jeffreys for her agency in securing the start of our movement through the legislative straits of 1895, and on through a succeeding assembly, through which it had to pass before launching it, fully equipped, upon the sea of one-sexed decision at the ballot box.

Early in 1896, our State Executive Committee, having learned that our greatest difficulty lay in holding down such agitation between the biennial sessions of the Legislature as would, if not attracted to activity in another direction, arouse the enemy to defeat us, decided to organize a Woman's Congress and secure the affiliation of all branches of women's patriotic, philanthropic and literary effort, under its banner, to be officered and managed by the State Equal Suffrage Association.

It was voted, at our first executive session after or-

GROUP OF EQUAL SUFFRAGISTS

MRS. EUGENIE DE SPAIN
First President of Equal Suffrage Association in Eastern Oregon. Prohibitionist

MRS. S. L. KLINE
An Active Suffragist of Oregon

MRS. E. H. COLEMAN
A Noted Oregon Suffragist

SUSAN B. ANTHONY
In 1905

MRS. HARRIET JANE HENDERSHOTT
Prominent Suffragist and Charter Member of O. S. E. S. A.

JOSEPHINE DE VORE JOHNSON
Past President of Oregon State Equal Suffrage Association

ADA B. MILLICAN
A Prominent Worker for Equal Suffrage in Oregon

ganization of the Woman's Congress was completed, to secure, if possible, the attendance of Miss Anthony at our first biennial meeting.

(The officers chosen were Abigail Scott Duniway, Honorary President; Dr. Frances A. Cady, President; Ada Cornish Hertsche, Treasurer; Maria C. DeLashmutt, Corresponding Secretary; Jennie C. Pritchard, Recording Secretary.)

(Our state officers at that time were: Abigail Scott Duniway, President; Ada Cornish Hertsche, Vice-President; Frances E. Gotshall, Corresponding Secretary; Mary Schaffer Ward, Recording Secretary; Jennie C. Pritchard, Treasurer; Annice F. Jeffreys, Vice-President-at-Large.)

Susan B. Anthony, our venerable and venerated national leader, was then sojourning in San Francisco, assisting the women of California in their heroic endeavor to secure the adoption of an Equal Suffrage amendment which had been submitted to the electors by the previous Legislative Assembly, and was to be voted up or down in that state at the coming November election.

Never has a more successful public function transpired in Oregon than our Congress of Women, which was held in June, 1896, with Miss Anthony as its bright particular star. The love of the people for our great leader was spontaneously expressed in every phase of our social as well as public life. Our Congress was enlivened by topics from leading women, representing all lines of woman's work, embracing every organized variety of effort, including education, art, science, medicine, sanitation, literature, the duties of motherhood, the care and training of children, etc., but excluding for the sake of harmony in its deliberations all sectarian gospels, partisan politics and political revolutions. Miss Anthony, who was present at every meeting of the Congress, which was continued through three consecutive days and evenings of three sessions each, was delighted to note the clever manner in which almost all the speakers sandwiched their speeches and papers with suffrage sentiment, and also the heightened applause which followed every allusion to our proposed Equal Suffrage amendment, from audiences that packed the spacious and popular Taylor Street Church from pulpit to doors, multitudes often being turned away for lack of standing room. Sarah B. Cooper, the noted San Francisco philanthropist, whose tragic death the Nation was shortly after called to mourn, was also a star attraction, who made many converts to the Equal Suffrage movement during her brief sojourn with us.

Most of our leading men, who had deserted our movement, like sailors deserting a sinking ship, during the prohibition excitement of 1886-7, have been willing to espouse our cause again since the first biennial meeting of our Woman's Congress; but we have been careful at all times, and especially when any of our friends have been candidates for office, to abstain from parading their (to us) greatest political virtue, lest, having no votes of our own with which to sustain them at the polls, we should jeopardize their chances of election to the only positions wherein they might officially aid us, and thus defeat and disgruntle our most valued allies.

A commodious headquarters of the Equal Suffrage Association was maintained at the Willamette Valley Chautauqua Assembly in July of 1896, for ten consecutive days, under the supervision of our tireless Recording Secretary, Mrs. Mary Schaffer Ward. Our "Anna Shaw Day" (managed by myself) was the most successful day of the Assembly. Dr. Shaw spoke as one inspired; and the reception held in her honor at headquarters would have done honor to a President of the United States.

The meeting of the Legislative Assembly of 1897 found us ready and waiting for the ratification of our Suffrage Amendment; but our Solons of the non-emotional sex fell to quarreling among themselves over the

United States Senatorial plum, and, being unable to agree as to a choice of candidates, refused to organize for any kind of business; so our Suffrage leaders were compelled to enforce another biennial period of masterly public inactivity upon our impatient co-workers, such as is always harder for officers and soldiers to endure than the privations of a campaign in the open field.

But the Woman's Club movement, that had by this time assumed important proportions, had become our safety valve. This movement, while it was yet new to Oregon, had been sprung among our society women by the tactful management of our staunch pioneer co-worker in the Equal Suffrage Movement, Mrs. A. H. H. Stuart of Olympia, Washington. Mrs. Stuart, despairing of all hope to secure and hold the ballot through recognized channels of effort, had so cleverly organized her own state through the club movement that her co-workers were enjoying a State Federation of Women's Clubs before the women of Oregon had hardly begun to organize clubs at all. The extension of Mrs. Stuart's club work into Oregon was a stroke of wise statesmanship. Our Equal Suffrage Association, realizing the impetus the club movement would bring to the Suffrage cause if we would tacitly humor the winds and waves of public sentiment in other directions for a while, thus giving our work a chance to grow spontaneously along new lines, joined heartily in the new organization, in which it was for a long time our chief public diversion to call club women to order whenever they would, inadvertently, break the rules by offering some motion, tending in our direction, from the floor.

At our annual meeting of the State Equal Suffrage Association for the year 1897,* a regular system of

* (Our state officers were re-elected without change until 1898, when Mrs. W. H. Games was chosen Recording Secretary, and Mrs. H. W. Coe, Treasurer. In 1899, Mrs. Games, being unable to continue her work, Mrs. M. C. Athey was made Assistant Secretary, and re-elected in 1900.)

private correspondence was arranged for, and many hundreds of prominent men and women who were not openly allied with our movement became, through this means, our silent helpers.

ᶠ The year 1898 was a season of much quiet but persistent work for our devoted leaders. The business was all transacted in executive sessions, but the indirect work went on openly, gaining strength steadily. The Woman's Club movement continued, in spite of its non-political character, to broaden and deepen our channels and strengthen the current of public opinion in behalf of the proposed amendment; and the Oregon Emergency Corps and Red Cross Society became a tacitly acknowledged auxiliary. "The Oregonian" of November 2nd, 1900, says of the good work of this society in aid of the Oregon Volunteers: "This work has been far-reaching and has made for Oregon a name to be loved and remembered by the thousands who have been assisted and cheered on their way through the united service of its Red Cross Society. What the future has in store cannot be known, but in time of calamity or distress, the women who have contributed to membership will be found ready for action," thus proving that the heart of its great editor was right in the abstract even on the Woman Question. But more of him further on. The Oregon Pioneer Association approved the amendment by unanimous resolutions, and the State Grange and Grand Army of the Republic became our recognized allies.

The Legislature convened in January, 1899, and with it came our long-delayed opportunity. But we encountered one serious obstacle. The Woman's Christian Temperance Union, having grown discouraged over our long period of apparent inactivity, seized the legislative helm and struggled hard with the Solons, till the term was nearly half expired. Then, finding their efforts futile, they abandoned the field, and Dr. Jeffreys, the lone

watcher on our political walls at the Capitol, summoned
me to her aid at the State House. Upon entering the
atmosphere of the Solons we were at once recognized
by leading members and admitted by vote to the privileges of the floor of each House, where, rapidly as the
term was waning, we schooled ourselves to patience.
To all attempts to draw us into discussion of the amendment, we returned evasive answers, but we were at all
times ready to chat upon other topics. Then, the Solons
finding no cause to be afraid of us, we ventured to ask
State Senator C. W. Fulton, who had distinguished himself as the champion of our amendment in 1880 and
1882 (and has borne more manfully than most men the
political eclipse he has suffered subsequently) to once
more carry our banner to victory. Mr. Fulton assured
us that he was personally willing to aid us, but he feared
our mission was futile; that so many bills, upon all sorts
of side issues to which the majority of the Legislators
objected, had been offered and insisted upon by women,
that members were not in a mood to listen to any more
propositions of a legislative character from persons who
had no votes.

We did not press the matter that day, nor the next,
but repaired to Dr. Jeffreys' office, where we prepared
short, pithy letters for the Salem papers, explaining that
women in large majority believed, as the Legislature did,
that men had the same inalienable right to rule themselves that belonged, with equal justice, to their mothers
and sons; that as Equal Suffragists we were opposed
to every sort of prohibition that interfered in any way
with the inalienable right of every individual of account-
able age to govern either himself or herself, and were
especially opposed to the prohibitory legislation that
prohibits one-half of the people from exercising their
right to a voice in the Government for which they furnish
all the soldiers, at the risk of their lives, for the Govern-

ment which they pay their full quota of taxes to maintain, and to whose laws they, equally with men, are held amenable. In another day's papers we would assert that women were only afflicted with emotional politics because they were allowed no vent for their pentup energy in legitimate channels; that Equal Suffragists did not look upon the Legislature as a reform school to relieve mothers of their responsibility in the home, nor as a means of providing a support for defective men. We also sent an open letter to each member, fully explaining the nature of our plea for Equal Rights, basing it wholly upon the fundamental right of self-government, that inheres in the individual, which the Declaration of Independence and the Constitution of the United States had taught us to revere. In this open letter, we enclosed to every Republican member the leaflets, "Clarkson on Suffrage in Colorado," and Clara Barton's "Appeal to Voters." To every Democrat, we enclosed Clara Barton's "Appeal" and some other document, taking care to keep off of everybody's partisan toes, thus avoiding all political antagonism. Finally, Senators Fulton and Brownell, both recognized leaders in the Upper House, considered the time ripe for calling up our amendment, which was at once sent, in regular order of business, to the Lower House, where it was referred to the Judiciary Committee and—buried. As nothing could be done to resurrect it from that committee till the following week, an anxious interval followed, during which I returned to Portland to reassure our waiting friends at home and try my best to reassure myself. The term was rapidly drawing to a close and no time was to be lost. So I returned to Salem the following week, and repaired at once to the House of Representatives.

The look of illy-concealed triumph with which the chairman of the House Judiciary Committee informed me that there was no time to resurrect the amendment

that term, sent a cold chill to my heart. But Senator
Fulton promptly came to our aid by securing a request
from the Senate that the amendment be returned to that
body for consideration,—a request that could not be
ignored. Then, on motion of Mr. Fulton, seconded by
Mr. Brownell, the final hearing was made a special order
of business for 3 o'clock the same afternoon. When the
fateful hour arrived, the lobby was well filled, many of
the leading women of the Capital City having been notified of the coming event during the noon hour by Dr.
Jeffreys, who had called at their homes on her wheel.
The vote was called for in the midst of a silence that
could be felt. But, before the roll call began, a motion
was offered by Senator Mulkey, seconded by many voices,
that Mrs. Duniway be invited to present the claims of
the women of the state, over half of whom had, through
the officers of the various societies of women, and of men
and women of the state, asked by petition or resolution,
that the amendment be submitted to the voters at the next
general elecion. The invitation to address the Senate
came to me as a complete surprise. No attempt had been
made to secure it, and my response was necessarily spon-
taneous. But I spoke to the amendment for four, or at
most five minutes, stating that we were not at that time
asking for any expression of individual opinion on the
merits of the question from any Senator. All we asked
was a vote to submit the question to the voters, a request that we felt they could not in fairness refuse to
grant. The vote followed without a dissenting voice till it
reached Mr. President, who, though recognized as a
Suffragist, responded with a chuckling "No," which
created much good-natured laughter. The vote stood 25
in our favor to 1 against, and the Senate shortly after
adjourned, having performed a patriotic duty of which
it was proud. The measure at once went to the House,
where, on motion of Representative Hill, seconded by

voices from all parts of the hall, it was made a special order of business for the evening session at 7:30 o'clock.

Although it was the most stormy night of the year, the commodious Hall of Representatives was crowded to the extent of its standing room by an expectant multitude, many being women. Mrs. Duniway, upon invitation of the members, presented the women's side of the question from Speaker Carter's desk, speaking this time for about ten minutes. The amendment then went to a vote, proceeding without interruption, except that two or three members took pains to say, presumably for the gratification of their constituents at home, that they were voting for the submission and not the adoption of the amendment. The vote continued as the roll-call proceeded, interrupted by an occasional "No," till it reached the "W's." Then a member arose and drew from his desk a voluminous array of "anti" documents, such as had been crowding the desks of all the members of both Houses during the entire term, and made a long harangue, of which many of the Solons said afterwards that if it had been offered at the beginning of the roll-call there would have been no dissenting vote, except one. The vote stood 48 "ayes" to 6 "noes," and the child of our hopes was launched, like a venturing ship, upon the troubled seas of anxious expectation.

Then came our tug of war. It was hard to keep our "still hunt" in force before; it was next to impossible now. Within three weeks I received no less than 40 appeals from Eastern women, urging an immediate organization of a "hurrah campaign." Each applicant expected employment at a good salary, expenses included, to be guaranteed by our Executive Committee, not one of whom was receiving or expecting a penny for her long years of devotion to the work which had made a "campaign" possible. But, as there was no money to hire speakers (and none were wanted) I, at least, felt for the first time in my life like saying, "Blessed be poverty."

Just here a word is in place in relation to the "antis" of the East, who sent a bright little schemer to Oregon in October, 1899, on an intended-to-be *sub rosa* mission, to organize an "Association opposed to the Enfranchisement of Women," her salary and expenses being paid, as she alleged, by a society of wealthy women of New York and Massachusetts.

Armed with an abundance of imported "anti" literature, remarkable only for the dullness and verbosity of its platitudes and their general misfit in our local affairs (since the Liquor League of Oregon had discovered, through the example of the four states where women vote that the only cure for the emotional politics of women is their full and free enfranchisement), some eight or nine of our "neglected rich," and a satellite or two, attempted to run the state election, so far as the Equal Suffrage amendment was concerned. Although the strictest secrecy was promised their proceedings by the Eastern "agent" aforesaid, who organized them, the Suffragists were as faithfully informed of their proceedings, from first to last, as were the officers of the Union Army by their interested colored allies in the War of the Rebellion. It was through this means that we smoked the "antis" into the open, compelling them to rush into "The Oregonian" with their "arguments," which became objects of good-natured ridicule everywhere. For several weeks I could not go down town without being offered more of their documents than I could carry home, by business men who said they had no time to open them, much less to read their contents. One woman only remained openly active after the Eastern "agent" had gone, and this woman, a recent import from the East, had received her education in a great affiliated university, only opened to women in recent years, through the long-continued efforts of such eminent Suffragists as Lucretia Mott, Elizabeth Cady Stanton, Mary A. Livermore, Susan B. Anthony, Lucy Stone, Julia Ward Howe and Harriet Beecher Stowe! But enough. I have mentioned the "antis" in this connection merely to open a way to express thanks for the help they gave us when they meant to hinder. When the vote was taken on our suffrage amendment in June, 1884, just sixteen years prior to the last vote, there was no such thing as an "Association Opposed," etc., and, notwithstanding the fact that our population had more than doubled in the cities where the slum vote is naturally the heaviest and always against us, the total increase of the "No" vote of the state was only 226, while in the same time the "Yes" vote had been augmented by a total of 15,032.

As it was our purpose from first to last to make no hurrah campaign, we worked as far as possible with the different political organizations of men, and held no public meetings at all under the auspices of the State Equal Suffrage Association. But Miss M. Lena Morrow, of Illinois, and Mrs. Ida Crouch Hazlett, of Colorado, did some effective work under the auspices of the National American Woman Suffrage Association, Miss Morrow working chiefly among the various labor organizations and other secret and fraternal orders of Portland, and Mrs. Hazlett holding meetings in outside counties, away from the railroads.

Our period of active office work was confined to the two and a half months of the political campaign preceding the June election. During this time, having been reinforced in our treasury by a campaign fund of $100 from the N. A. W. S. A., and $400 from the Massachusetts W. S. A., we were able to send out from headquarters immense quantities of our Campaign Leaflet, with many thousands of pages of other literature to which we added 6,000 personal letters, addressed to leaders and molders of public opinion. We also sent out 1,000 Open Letters, signed by our full State Committee.* · This letter, which was as complete a statement of our case as its space of four pages would allow, was published in all of the 229 papers of the state except nine, and two of the nine explained their inability to publish on account of their columns being engaged to political candidates till after the election. Many journals gave us editorial endorsement, and all was going well until about two weeks before our fateful day of trial at the polls.

Although it was well known that all women of "The Oregonian's" acquaintance who possess an ounce of brains or a shred of patriotism were Suffragists, and all were holding out to it a flag of truce, while, unarmed and utterly defenseless, they awaited the fiat of ignorance, oppression, conservatism and licentiousness, which instinctively combine for imaginary self-defense when the mothers of men are seeking enlargement of rights, duties and responsibilities through the votes of their justice-loving sons, yet, day after day, these devoted women, not one of whom occupies a mediocre position, in pedigree or respectability, were doomed to see themselves insulted, derided, slandered and belittled through the columns of the only paper that treated us unfairly.

"The Oregonian" asserted that its war (at that time) upon Equal Suffrage was not a personal matter. Nevertheless, it is a personal matter to me, and to all women who seek opportunity to do the very best that is in them for themselves and the world; and we, and not a man's newspaper, must be the judges as to what that best shall be. It was a personal matter to Fred Douglas when he made

---

*It is well to add, in this connection, that the "Morning Oregonian" became our chief ally and champion during our victorious campaign of 1912; and the writer hereof accords to it unstinted praise for its timely change of front, without which we might still be struggling for victory.

tracks for the North Star. But it was not a personal
matter to the bloodhounds which pursued him, nor to the
oligarchy of color that urged them on. It was a personal
matter to Dred Scott, and every other colored man or
woman, when Chief Justice Taney decided that a negro
had no rights which a white man was bound to respect;
but it was not a personal matter to the be-gowned and
be-wigged Chief Justice who rendered that infamous
decision.

No man, or set of men, can destroy Liberty. The
"best" women of Oregon, such as have helped their husbands and fathers to create their homes and keep them,
have earned and ought to possess their right to vote. If
there is no hitch in our Legislature of 1901, we will reach
another, and I trust, final vote on our Equal Suffrage
amendment in 1903. By that time I shall be nearing my
70th year; and no man need fear that I will ever rival
him, or any other man, as a candidate for any position of
emolument or power. I do not envy any man his power,
property or position, nor would I pluck from his brow
a single laurel. But I have sought, for thirty years,
to so open the way for the women of the present and
the future that each and all may have the untrammeled
opportunity the ballot alone can give to do their best
and noblest work in the world's highways and byways,
the most important of which is connected with motherhood and home. As the chivalrous, patriotic men
of Oregon gave us 48 per cent of all the votes cast upon
our amendment at the June election of 1900, and two-
thirds of the counties of the state gave us big majorities,
we confidently expect the Legislature to resubmit our
case, while we serenely await their verdict.

We realize that self-respecting men chivalrously resent the mandate of the slums, which by their vote, sustain the Government in holding their wives and mothers

in the political category of idiots, insane persons, criminals, Chinamen not native-born and Indians not taxed. The women of California and Washington are hoping to see themselves enfranchised before we can reach our next opportunity; but Oregon has another fighting chance to become the first of the Pacific Coast states to open her gates to the Orient with all her people free.

CHAPTER XIII.

Oregon Work Resumed.

THE Twenty-fifth Annual Convention of the State Equal Suffrage Association met in Portland, Oregon, in November, 1898. The reports of various committees showed a broadening of the movement through many of the women's organization of the State, of which the Equal Suffrage Association was the first. The Society reported its debts all paid and a small balance in the treasury, which was materially increased by the payment of annual dues. The work of the Woman's Congress, elsewhere more fully recorded, had gathered the representatives of forty-two different societies under colors of red, white, blue and gold. The Chautauqua Assemblies and the Woman's Club Movement had become, whether consciously or not, great recruiting grounds for the Woman Suffrage cause. The Red Cross Society, being wholly non-partisan, was particularly popular because of its patriotic work among the soldiers of the Philippine war. Clara Barton's plea for the political equality of women, who give and preserve life, which men destroy on the field of battle, had been circulated freely by the Equal Suffrage Association, among the voters through the previous year. Woman's Missionary and other reformatory societies, including charities and philanthropies, managed by both men and women, became tacit coadjutors of the Suffrage Association, though it was generally understood, among our Equal Suffrage workers, that we were not to scare any societies away from our principles by openly parading them as allies, till they got ready to so announce themselves.

"Every institution organized for good," the President and chronicler hereof said, in her opening address, "is preparing the way for our common enfranchisement. The voice of duty is calling us, as emphasized recently, by a vote of men in South Dakota in the late election, which was so close as to demand an official count before its adherents would acknowledge even temporary defeat of their Equal Suffrage Constitutional Amendment." "In Washington," the speaker said, "the late November election to re-enfranchise women, though not yet a majority, was more than a third larger than when the last vote was taken, which easily could have been won if allowed to go before the voters on its own merits. But it was everywhere adroitly overloaded by the usual irrepressible prohibition rider, from which the Equal Suffrage Movement must learn to openly separate itself, in all future campaigns, if we would not invite inevitable defeat."

A plan was formulated at this convention for creating a Pacific States Voting Alliance, and a committee was appointed to confer in a semi-official way with leading men and women of Oregon, Washington, California, Utah and Idaho, to assist in selecting a time and place for its first annual meeting. But the materialization of this plan remained incomplete till Mrs. Emma Smith DeVoe appeared upon the scene as a resident of the State of Washington, who succeeded by a series of statesmanlike maneuvers, assisted by a host of co-workers of both sexes, who had succeeded in establishing votes for women at the November election of 1910, of which further mention is made elsewhere.

The following officers were elected as our State Executive Committee to serve for the year 1899:

Abigail Scott Duniway, president; Ada Cornish Hertsche, vice-president; Dr. Annice F. Jeffreys, vice-president and chairman of legislative committee; Frances E. Gotshall, corresponding secretary; Mrs. W. H. Gaines, recording secretary; Mrs. H. W. Coe, treasurer; Miss Sophie Rinehart and Mrs. W. H. Barmore, auditors.

* * *

The following open letter was issued in 1898, by the order of the State Equal Suffrage Association:

"To all members of the Legislative Assembly and all political parties of the State of Oregon, to the Members of the Press and

"To you, Sir, Greeting:

"The many adherents of the Equal Suffrage Movement for which a Constitutional Amendment is now pending, have held their peace for many months, lest they might embarrass you in some way concerning the partisan and personal conflicts in which you have been striving against each other for the mastery. But, now that your nominations are all made, and your plans adjusted for your various campaigns, we desire to place before you our plea for our own enfranchisement. We feel that you cannot justly, or honestly, deprive us of our voice in the administration of the affairs of the government, since we are taxed to maintain its laws, to which, equally with yourselves, we are held amenable. As we provide for the government all its soldiers, at the risk of our lives; and, when you call our sons to battle, we bid them God-speed, even though our hearts be breaking, do we not perform duties, equal with yours, in the maintenance of government?

"In respectfully demanding your affirmative votes upon a question we are not permitted to decide for ourselves, we are not asking for the adoption of any partisan issue, nor for any untried experiment.

"Directly to the East of us are four sovereign states, in which the women are enjoying the free use of the ballot.

"The leading citizens of Wyoming, the pioneer state of this great movement, have from time to time during

the past 30 years, announced, over their own signatures
through her press, her Legislatures, her Governors, Senators, Clergymen, Judges, Representatives and chief educators, that good, and only good, has accrued to the
people and the state, from the enfranchisement of women.
They have often publicly challenged anonymous writers
from other states, who have misrepresented the facts,
to find two men, or women, in all Wyoming, who will
assert over their own names and addresses, that Equal
Suffrage has produced any bad results. It is needless to
say that no such opponent has yet responded. Governor
Campbell, who was in office when the law was passed in
1869, in his message to the Legislature two years later
said, 'It is simple justice to say that the women, entering for the first time upon their new and untried duties,
have conducted themselves in every respect with as much
tact, good judgment and good sense as men.' Similar
testimony has come unsolicited from each succeeding
Governor of Wyoming and from all the highest officials
and educators of both sexes and all parties.

"The very leading men of Colorado, and other states
where women vote, have issued circulars, saying: 'We
believe the greatest good to the home, the state and the
nation is best advanced through the operation of Woman
Suffrage. The evils predicted have not come to pass, the
benefits claimed for it have been secured, or are in process
of development. A very large proportion of Colorado
women have conscientiously accepted their responsibility
as citizens.'

"From Idaho, where women have been voters since
1896, have come to us many testimonials, also unsolicited,
highly endorsing the movement, signed by men and
women of unimpeachable integrity and standing, among
whom are Chief Justice I. N. Sullivan, Associate Justices
Huston and Quarlles, H. E. McElroy of the State Normal
School, Wm. Balderston. editor of the 'Idaho States-

man,' and a great many other prominent men, as well as the women who lead in society, education and philanthropy.

"Everybody knows that the enfranchisement of women is coming, and is inevitable. Oregon, today, is the only State where an Equal Suffrage Amendment is pending. She, and she alone, is in a position to lead the van of progress in this dawn of the new century.

"It is related that the poet Whittier, upon being asked his opinion of a future state of existence, replied by quoting from an epitaph he had read somewhere, as follows:

> "Here lie I, Michael Angelbrod,
> Have mercy on my soul, Lord God,
> As I would do, were I Lord God,
> And you were Michael Angelbrod.

"It was the apt significance of this epitaph that appealed to the solons of the Legislature who submitted the Equal Suffrage Amendment for which we ask your vote. We believe you also will see the point. A word to the wise is sufficient.

"By the order of Oregon State Equal Suffrage Association.

"(Signed) Abigail Scott Duniway, President; Mrs. M. C. Athey, Asst. Secretary; Ada Cornish Hertsche, Vice-President; Mrs. Viola M. Coe, Treasurer; Frances E. Gotshall, Cor. Secretary; Dr. Annice F. Jeffreys, Vice-President-at-Large.

"Chairmen County Committees: Baker, Mrs. Celia B. Olmstead; Benton, Mrs. Clara Zimmerman; Clackamas, Mrs. C. H. Dye; Clatsop, Miss Belle Trullinger; Coos, Mrs. A. E. Lockhart; Crook, Mrs. M. Moore; Columbia, Mrs. James Muckle; Curry, Mrs. J. H. Upton; Douglas, Mrs. S. A. Child; Gilliam, Mrs. R. Pattison; Grant, Mrs. N. Rulison; Harney, Mrs. J. B. Huntington; Jackson, Mrs. M. E. Thompson; Josephine, Mrs. J. W. Virtue; Klamath, Mrs. P. L. Fountain; Lake, Mrs. Bernard Daly;

Lane, Mrs. A. S. Patterson; Lincoln, Mrs. R. A. Bensell; Linn, Mrs. Anna B. Reed; Malheur, Mrs. J. A. Blackaby; Marion, Mrs. J. J. Murphy; Morrow, Mrs. W. R. Ellis; Multnomah, Mrs. C. R. Templeton; Polk, Mrs. Almira Hurley; Sherman, Mrs. Ellen Kinney; Tillamook, Mrs. T. B. Handley; Umatilla, Mrs. Stephen A. Lowell; Union, Mrs. J. B. Eaton; Wallowa, Mrs. Jennie McCully; Wasco, Mrs. E. L. Smith; Washington, Mrs. Col. Thos. Cornelius; Wheeler, Mrs. Thomas Stewart; Yamhill, Mrs. H. A. Laughary; Miss M. Lena Morrow, Mrs. Ida Crouch Hazlett, Representing National Equal Suffrage Association."

* * *

Our campaign of 1899, preceding the June election of 1900, was going quietly forward without apparent obstruction, when the Executive Committee of the State Equal Suffrage Association received the following report of a meeting, and organization of a branch of the Massachusetts Association Opposed to the Further Extension of the Right of Suffrage for Women. The report was submitted to the Suffrage Committee by Mrs. C. A. Coburn, then, and up to the time of her death, a member of the editorial staff of "The Oregonian." The meeting was held in the palatial home of our esteemed fellow townswoman, the late Mrs. W. S. Ladd, widow and legatee of our great pioneer banker, who was, during his life time, one of the best financial backers the Equal Suffrage Movement has ever had. The meeting was intended to be absolutely secret, its chief promoter being a Miss Bissell of Massachusetts, who explained that she was in no way capable of meeting Equal Suffrage leaders in debate. The amusing part of this attempted secrecy lies in the fact that, like perpetual motion, it wouldn't work.

A synopsis of Miss Bissell's attempt at argument is herewith submitted:

1. "Only about four per cent of the women want

to vote, the best women not voting when they have a chance."

2. "Women do not have the time to vote. They already have all they can do in home and church work, charity and philanthropy."

3. "Leaders, including Mrs. Duniway, tell a vast majority of women that they mean to force them to vote."

"Eastern women got tired of this impertinence and organized the Association which I have the honor to represent. Only unhappy, discontented women want to vote. Suffragists are not among the best people. Prominent, representatives women of the East do not care to associate with the women who want the ballot."

4. "Women are to be forced to hold office and sit on juries. This later iniquity had really been perpetrated in Washington Territory, while women had the ballot there."

5. "Woman Suffrage would duplicate the ignorant and vicious vote without having a like effect on the intelligent vote, since the best women would not go to the polls."

Mrs. C. A. Coburn and Mrs. H. W. Scott were present at the meeting. Mrs. Coburn submitted to the State Suffrage Association the following report:

"Appeal was made to the few women present to organize for the purpose of distributing leaflets, 'setting forth these alarming facts among the voters of Oregon.' The literature the lady heralded should be distributed 'absolutely free.' Mrs. Duniway was mentioned as 'a bright, capable, ambitious, dangerous woman, who was not a representative woman of Oregon at all.' To this the lady (Mrs. Cleveland Rockwell), who had been called to preside at the meeting, demurred, declaring that Mrs. Duniway (who was not present) was a woman of whom the whole State of Oregon was proud; that she, herself, was witness to the fact that during the visit of the National Press Associaion in July (1899), her friend, Mrs. Duniway, was more frequently called for by Eastern delegates than all the other women of Oregon put together. To this Miss Bissell made no reply, but adroitly presented other assertions of a like character, by claiming that the distribution of 'anti' literature had defeated the Suffrage Amendment in Washington the previous year. Her literature is of the same character as that which filled the desks of the Oregon legislators the previous winter, when the Suffrage Amendment was submitted to the electors by a practically unanimous vote."

At the meeting of the State Executive Committee of the Equal Suffrage Association, held at headquarters October 30, 1899, it was moved to send the above report of Miss Bissell's "Secret Meeting" to the press; but better counsels prevailed, the Chairman deeming it unjust to ladies, who had been entrapped into implied complicity with the hired emissary of a few meddlesome women of Massachusetts, to annoy them with such humiliation as they do not merit, since it did not dawn upon them at the time that Miss Bissell's intervention was both dishonorable and impertinent. It was, therefore, decided by motion of Dr. Annice F. Jeffreys, Chairman of Campaign Management, to send the above synopsis as part of the foregoing report, to such leading voters throughout the State as we could trust; and I have never doubted that this action had much to do with creating the largely accelerated vote of 1900, as compared to that of 1894, which is elsewhere recorded in these pages.

CHAPTER XIV.

Addresses Idaho Constitutional Convention.

SEEING that progress in my work for Equal Rights had encountered a blockade in Oregon and Washington, I ceased open activities therein and turned my entire attention to Idaho, where my husband and sons had gone, in quest of health and change of climate, and had filed on government lands, and were engaged in the stock business. Entering with them into the formative period of a new enterprise, I was deeply immersed in the pastoral pursuits of a pioneer home-maker, gardener, poultry raiser and general factotem, when the State Constitutional Convention met at Boise, in the summer of 1889. I had given up public work for the nonce, and was waiting for prohibition agitators to "sober off" on the liquor question, when I received a message from my Equal Suffrage co-workers in Boise, urging me to come to them at once. "The Woman's Christian Temperance Union is spoiling everything," the letter said. "They have arranged for a hearing before the convention, in advance of ours, asking for a clause in the new Constitution to prohibit the liquor traffic. They won't get it, of course, but they will prohibit us from getting a Woman Suffrage plank, if you don't come!"

It was a long, hot, rough, dusty ride over the stage road, but I answered the call, and arrived in Boise on time, after taking the train at Blackfoot, eighty miles from our lodge in the wilderness. I found the suffragists in a flutter of trepidation. They had made everything in readiness for me to address the convention, but the Woman's Christian Temperance Union had secured a hearing the night before, and they were afraid I had come too late to accomplish our purpose. But they gave me a copy of the morning "Statesman," containing a full report of the argument of the prohibitionists, which I proceeded to analyze and answer before a packed house at the evening session, July 16th, and was fairly reported in the "Statesman" the morning of the 18th following.

The plea of the Woman's Christian Temperance Union resulted, as was predicted, in the defeat of the Equal Suffrage article in the State Constitution at that time; but the arguments of the suffragists, backed as they are by the great, silent majority of women voters, as was proven by the absence of state-wide prohibition in every enfranchised state, secured an unofficial pledge to me, from members of the Convention, and from the leading statesmen who were present from all parts of the Territory, who agreed to submit the question to the electors in the form of an unrestricted Equal Suffrage Amendment to the proposed state Constitution by act of the first State Legislature whose members should consider the prohibition question sufficiently quiescent to afford a reasonable prospect that such an amendment would be ratified by a majority of the voters at the next general election succeeding such submission. This pledge was honorably fulfilled in February, 1895; and this argument, which had first appeared in the "Idaho Statesman," of July 18, 1889, was reprinted and circulated freely all over the Territory, as a campaign document until 1896, resulting not only in the full and free enfranchisement of the women of Idaho, at the general election of that year, but, as predicted, has opened up such rational avenues of thought and action among women as afford them, as voters, little time or opportunity for the successful agitation of such emotional politics as prevail among states where women are prohibited from using the right to vote.

My argument, which now appeals with equal force to the voters of every state where an equal suffrage

GROUP OF EQUAL SUFFRAGISTS

L. VICTORIA HAMPTON, M.D.
A Leading Oregon Physician, Chemical
Analyst and Suffragist

MRS. N. R. REYNOLDS
An Equal Suffrage Like Wife of Oregon

HELEN W. CRAWFORD
Former Prof. of Education, State Agric'l
College, and Now a Successful Farmer

THE LATE MYRTLE PEASE HATFIELD
Canvasser and Chief Field Worker among Voters in Aid of Enfranchisement of Women
to Time of Her Marriage and Death

MISS ELMA BUCKMAN
Recording Secretary of Oregon Equal
Suffrage Association

CORA TALBOTT, M. D.
Prominent Suffragist

ANNA B. REED, M. D.
One of Oregon's Charter Suffragists

amendment is pending under conditions similar to those at that time prevailing in Idaho, is hereby appended. I had the honor to say, in part:

Mr. President, and Members of the Convention, Gentlemen and Ladies: Although much of what I have to say in your presence tonight will differ materially from the utterances of other women who have been graciously accorded a hearing before your honorable body, I think you will concede, before I have finished, that women are learning to express their differences of opinion in a spirit of tolerance toward one another such as would have been beyond their power to exhibit before they had begun to be imbued with the desire for liberty which now inspires them.

Just as, in the infancy of the government of these United States, the people who lived beyond our Rocky Mountains, and beyond the valleys of the Ohio and Mississippi Rivers, formed newer and broader conceptions of the fundamental principles of a true democracy than had been dreamed of by their ancestors across the Atlantic seas, so in these yet new states of the Pacific Northwest, the people of a new generation are forming broader conceptions of the glorious heritage in store for them and their children than their ancestors ever anticipated.

Although there is a wide diversity of opinion among us upon one question, which women have sought to place before you at a former hearing—I allude to the trite one of prohibition, to which less than two per cent of the women of this territory, or of the nation, adhere—there is a growing unanimity of sentiment in our ranks concerning the justice of our plea for our own enfranchisement.

Women, like men, are rapidly outgrowing the idea that prohibition is a reformatory measure. When the idea was first placed before them by press and pulpit, a good many grasped it as a sort of providential opportunity for a popular compromise between their own long-repressed mentality and their desire to perform some public act for which press, people and pulpit would praise and pat and pet and pay them. These facts, and more especially the last named, have so stimulated the repressed ambition of a few women that it has not been difficult for political cranks and professional agitators, who had previously been kicked out of the old parties, to secure their cat's-paw services in raking chestnuts for themselves from the fires of political controversy.

The stale argument, with which you have recently been regaled, that compares horse-stealing, against which we have prohibitory laws by common and undisputed consent, with liquor selling, using, or buying, about which there are many differences of opinion, is most unfair, since there are no laws against horse-selling, provided the purchaser is ready with the cash and the horse he wants to buy is all its owner claims for it. In like manner is the comparison between the prohibition of liquor-selling and the prohibition of murder unfair, since the sale of ropes, knives, guns and ammunition is not prohibited, except under certain conditions, to which all law-abiding people agree; nor are humanity and horses forbidden to exist because some men are murdered and many horses are stolen.

I frankly confess that if I were the Omnipotent Power with my finite conception of mundane things, I should not hesitate to prohibit everything that I believe to be evil. I should like to prohibit every form of intemperance, including self-righteousness, woe, want, war, poverty, excessive riches, murder, arson, slander, fever, contagion, lust, covetousness, drunkards, gluttony, lying, robbery, cruelty, theft,—everything that debases any element of our humanity; but since I can't, and God in His wisdom plainly teaches me that this is not His plan, I have no desire, nor have the very large majority of women—I mean the self-poised, liberty-loving women whom I have the honor to represent—the remotest desire to run a tilt against Omnipotence.

There were, in the years 1886-7, a few women in the Territory of Washington, who, after they had gotten the ballot, which came to them unawares and unbidden, became unduly intoxicated with their new possession. And these women unwisely yielded to the counsels of a few peripatetic women, non-voters from the East, who, learning that Washington's women had been endowed with ballots, sought them out (on a handsome salary) and induced them to permit idealists and cranks to use their ballots as cat's-paws, in a vain attempt to rake their own chestnuts from the fires of politics. But the majority of even these women long ago discovered, under the humiliation of the great defeat that followed, which logically acted to deprive them, and through them all women of Washington, of their right to vote—which they had just learned to prize—that what women need, for the purification of the race, is not arbitrary laws for the coercion of men, but liberty for themselves, that they may gradually rise above the conditions of subjugation against which their forefathers rebelled, under which, as servants without wages, taxed without representation and governed without consent, so many mothers are compelled to rear a progeny of drunkards.

In Wyoming, where women had been voters long enough to learn a modicum of political wisdom before the prohibition craze became the fashion, better counsels prevailed, and no such innovation exists, to act as a boomerang against their ballots, as destroyed the suffrages of Washington's women. (This is equally true today of Colorado, Utah and Idaho and other Pacific Coast States, where women are voters.)

I am making no remonstrance against prohibition, *per se*. I realize that everybody has a right to ride a pet hobby, provided, of course, that he doesn't strike down other people's liberties with the hoofs of his hobby horse. But I wish I might convince every man in this convention that the majority of women realize, as keenly as you do, the fact that every woman who sits behind the prison bars of her present political environment, lifting her manacled hands to men and saying, "Give us the ballot and we'll put down your whisky," is not only telling a falsehood (since all the force of bullets, to say naught of ballots, could never do it unless men should voluntarily put it down themselves), but actually offers to most men the strongest possible inducement to answer, "Very well! We'll see that you don't get the ballot at all, if you intend to use it as a whip! We don't propose to let women carry a whip hand over us!"

What the great majority of the women of the Pacific Northwest are asking, gentlemen; women who have no time to spend in getting up ice cream festivals to induce men to fill their stomachs with an indigestible compound —for a financial consideration—in the interest of a prohibition fund—festivals that send them to the dramshop for an antidote; what women are asking who study the practical side of every question; women who are not sent out as the paid representatives of any set of men or women, or of any political party, is that you will engraft into the fundamental law of this commonwealth a clause in your chapter on suffrages and elections that, other things being equal, except the right to bear arms, which custom accords to men, and the far more perilous right to bear soldiers as armor-bearers (which nature imposes upon women), there shall be no restrictions placed upon the right of suffrage on account of the incident of sex.

Oh, gentlemen! When you grant us the right of suffrage we shall be so proud of you and of ourselves that we will proclaim the glad tidings of our freedom among all the crowded states and cities of the East, and by so doing we can turn the tide of immigration into Idaho, just as we exultantly turned it into Washington Territory during the three and a half years of her greatest prosperity, when her women were voters; just as we will do some day for Oregon; just as we will do again for Washington, when she again becomes "the land of the free and the home of the brave," as she was known to be before her women's ballots were beaten down by the inevitable recoil of prohibition boomerangs.

Too well I know there is no other attribute of our humanity that dies so hard as tyranny. I know how prone many men are to delude themselves with the fancy that they are "heads of the family." I know how persistently many wives—cunning diplomats—foster this transparent delusion. Men's vanity and self-love are fed upon this sophistry, although they fully understand that it is sophistry. Men are very human. God made them to match the women.

We know every one of our opponents' threadbare arguments against our liberties by heart. You say we "mustn't vote because we cannot fight," forgetting, or pretending to forget, that life's hardest battles, everywhere, are fought by the mothers of men in giving existence to the race. You say, "women do not want to vote," when all the opportunities we have ever had to vote have been as freely utilized by us as by yourselves. You say, "If women want the ballot, let them ask for it," when we have been asking for it, lo, these forty years!

You say, "bad women will vote," when you well know that bad men vote, and claim the ballot for their protection. Why deny protection to one class of human sinners and accord it to another? You say we "must not sit on juries," though ever and anon a woman is to be tried by a jury. May we not look forward, gentlemen, to the day when a woman may be tried by a jury of her peers?

Women who seek the ballot for liberty's sake are not proposing to govern men. We are seeking for an opportunity to govern ourselves. We appeal to your sense of justice, your chivalry, your patriotism, your honor, as we ask you to grant to us, as part of the fundamental law, our free, unquestioned right to a voice in the government which we are taxed to maintain and to whose laws we are held amenable.

The eyes of the world are upon these new states and territories of the Pacific Northwest. The freedom-loving spirit of our Western men is our proudest boast.

Shall we, the women of this border land, who have shared alike your trials and your triumphs—shall we not be permitted to go up to the national capital bearing aloft the banner of our freedom? Shall we not have the proud distinction of proclaiming to the older states of the Union that the chivalry and honor of our fathers, husbands, and sons outrank their own? May we not tell the world that these are the men who scorn to accept any rights for themselves which they would deny to their mothers, sweethearts, wives, sisters and daughters?

I pause just here to read a note, brought to me from the audience a moment ago by a page.

"What do you woman suffragists propose to do with the whisky traffic?" asks the writer, an excellent and earnest little woman, whom I recognize as one who has worked hard for prohibition because she has had no other channel in which to work, and thereby ease the struggling spirit within her which is clamoring for something practical to do. Equal Suffragists answer: "Tax whisky, and all other intoxicants, as heavily as their traffic will bear. Control and regulate that which you cannot destroy." I know all the arguments against the liquor tax by heart. Time was when I supposed it was what men call it, a license. But study of the question long ago convinced me that it is a tax.

Liquors are sold because men demand them, drink them and pay for them. This demand is a perennial fountain, rising in the desires of the consumer. The liquor traffic is like a mighty river that is always flowing. flowing, obedient to a cause. You may change its channels here and there, or drive it into hiding now and then, but you cannot stop its flow.

Near the mouth of the Mississippi there is an immense swamp. So dark and pestilential is it that yellow fever lurks in its murky edges and a green slime crawls upon the top of the stagnant water, among which poisonous reptiles play at hide and seek.

"Prohibit the accursed thing!" cries out the theorist. "Don't tamper, or temporize with it in any way, but put it down! Stop its flow!"

Vain mandate, vain prescription, vain endeavor! You may cover the slum and slime with a prohibition plaster; but, be the plaster ever so strong, the virus will still exude; or, worse still, it will burrow deep and yet deeper into hidden places, marking its track by increased desolation and death.

"Then, what is the final remedy?" is asked by questioning ones, who are not yet willing to be convinced that they can err in judgment.

"Build levees upon the banks of the liquor traffic," says science, and so says common sense. Regulate what you cannot destroy. You build houses to shield yourselves from the cold and heat. You prepare safeguards against fire and flood, and you must protect yourselves against intoxicants by confining their traffic to a margin as narrow as will contain their flow. You must keep the dykes high and in order. This is "high license," falsely so called. It is a levee upon the banks of the stream, of which even those engaged in the traffic, who use the current for financial reasons, can recognize the need; and they will help you to maintain the dykes.

[The foregoing is a declaration that, in the light of recent events, may well be deemed prophetic. For are not liquor men engaged at present in regulating the traffic as never before?]

Give us this levee, gentlemen, and, above everything else. give us the ballot, with which to help you build it high and strong, and we will help you build most loyally.

Our plea is against prohibition of the gravest sort; the prohibition which prohibits us from using our right to vote.

We ask that you remove this disability; to prohibit us from voting no more forever.

We ask nothing but our right to use our voices, as your companions and co-workers, in making the laws under which we, as well as you, must live; laws which we are taxed to maintain, to which we, equally with yourselves, are held amenable.

We could not rule men if we would, and would not if we could. Here, gentlemen, we rest our case, in the serene belief that the first decade of the twentieth century will witness the full and free enfranchisement of every law-abiding woman of this great galaxy of new and vigorous young states of the Pacific Northwest, which need claim no higher distinction than to be forever known as the original Land of the Free and the Home of the Brave.

Hoping that every voter who receives this document will weigh its contents with such care as its importance demands, and feeling that all such will vote "Yes" on every constitutional amendment which comes before them in behalf of human liberty, just as they would wish us to vote for their enfranchisement if the power were ours to withhold or bestow it, and with serene reliance upon the liberty-loving, chivalrous nature of every public-spirited man, I shall now and always appeal for the inalienable right of self-government for every man and

woman who obeys the new Commandment, given to us
by our Elder Brother, "That ye love one another."

* * *

I confess that I was not able for a long time to see
these facts as comprehensively as I see them now. After
the straitest teachings of my religion, I had been raised
a Pharisee. My first nine years of married and maternal
life were spent (as elsewhere related) as a servant without wages and all-around drudge on an unimproved, but
rapidly improving Oregon farm. My good husband, a
farmer and stock man of the olden school, was not addicted to any of the vices of which a comparatively few
men anywhere are reported to be guilty. He had a theory of his own as to the cause and cure of inebriety, under which we raised a large family of sober children, a
theory which I have never seen excelled and have never
known to fail. He said, "We'll give our boys and girls,
at regular hours, all the milk, cream, butter, eggs, sugar,
syrup, fruits, bread, cake and vegetables they can eat, and
all the sleep they want. Then they'll never care for stimulants." I also had a theory of my own, which I began
to put in practice after my public work began. But I
soon saw that few mothers were able to put their boys
upon honor before the public, as I did, because few of
them, in fact none, except myself, were at that time making a demand before the public for equal rights for mothers, a demand which almost everybody was meeting with
ridicule or scorn.

I did not then, nor do I at this writing, expect that
agitation for the state-wide prohibition of the liquor traffic will become a settled issue for many years to come.
Too many men and women are making money, notoriety,
travel and fame, as its proponents, to expect it to be
abandoned without a prolonged and excited struggle.
Too many cases of the abuse of the traffic, by men and
women who have made the sale of intoxicants their busi-

ness but have failed to deal honestly in controlling and exploiting the traffic, and too many cases of cruelty, crime and poverty have been traced to the saloon, to expect this conflict to cease until the saloon shall have reformed itself. Too many well-meaning men and women, who see the evil effect of intoxication in individual cases, but are not able to see beyond the saloon into the personal responsibility, or physical or moral degeneracy of the criminal, are ready to suppress the liquor traffic by votes, vainly expecting thereby to prevent the existence of evils that every well-poised person deplores.

On the other hand, too many men depend upon the production, transportation and sale of wheat, barley, hops, rye, apples, peaches, berries, grapes and cherries, from which intoxicants are made, and too many men are employed in their making and marketing, all of whom depend directly or indirectly upon the traffic; too many men are engaged in transporting these commodities from the farms to the breweries, distilleries and wineries, and thence to the wholesale and retail dealers, and from these to the consumer; too many men and women have capital invested in bottles, in the making of glass, and the bottling industry; too many men are engaged in the manufacture of staves, barrels, kegs, basketry and hoop-iron; too many men are clearing lands in hoop-pole districts, where the hoop-iron industry is not available, and too many men and women sell their goods of the farm to the middle man and to brewers and distillers, to get money to buy farming implements, and livestock; too many men, women and children labor in the grain fields and hop yards to earn clothing, shoes, school books, groceries; too many men are engaged in the hotel and restaurant business, whose most profitable guests are tourists, who demand regular supplies of the stimulants they can buy across the seas, to make prohibition possible.

Many thousands of men and women, who are

neither drunkards nor prohibitionists, and never will be, claim the right to take a stimulant if they choose to buy it, themselves only being the judges as to what they shall, or shall not, eat or drink, or wherewithal they shall be clothed. There are many men and women who own or rent homes, or occupy public and private buildings, who pay taxes to sustain churches, schools, streets, highways, parks, bridges, playgrounds, stores, dwellings, barns, stables, docks, roads, warehouses, hospitals, philanthropies and all sorts of charities; too many men and women are clerks and stenographers, who pay rental for offices, boarding and lodging houses, laundries, fruit canneries, bakeries, blacksmith shops; too many women with dependent families, who have their little all tied up in little mortgaged homes, in little towns, rural districts and hamlets, where they depend upon little gardens, a cow, a pig or two, a few chickens, perhaps a boarder or two, a sewing machine, wash tubs, etc., who see their meager means of livelihood menaced by the professional agitator, who boasts that if the town is "killed by prohibition," he or she will "preach its funeral"; and when to all of these are added the vast array of grocers, bakers, butchers and candle-stick makers, and we turn to the peripatetic, salaried, one-sided orator, who holds a dollar before his eyes so closely that he only beholds the occasional drunkard, or man who whips his wife, or one whose wife supports him while he dallies in the saloon, that there is little wonder that a conflict can be created almost anywhere, that will be compared by observing, level-headed people to a mountain in labor to produce a mouse, or a mythical Jonah, reversing the old tradition by trying to swallow a whale.

Let the blame go to the drunkard, where it belongs; let the drunkard's wife have legal power to protect her home from a husband's debauchery, just as the husband has the power, when so inclined, to protect it now.

CHAPTER XV.

Celebration of Oregon's Fortieth Anniversary.

THE State of Oregon reached its fortieth anniversary of Statehood on the 14th day of January, 1899. The occasion was one of general rejoicing, in which the Legislative Assembly had the leading role. The speakers for the celebration were Governor T. T. Geer, the late ex-Governor W. P. Lord, the late Hon. L. B. Cox, the late Judge George H. Williams, loved and honored as "Oregon's Grand Old Man," and Abigail Scott Duniway, to whom was accorded the place of valedictorian. My theme, chosen by the Assembly for the occasion, follows, by request of many women coadjutors:

WOMEN IN OREGON HISTORY.

The scientific world is slowly but surely returning to the original order of human affairs, in its attempt to re-establish the natural relations between the sexes, in which man and woman are the supplements, the counterparts, but never the opponents of each other. When God saw, in the beginning, "That it was not good for man to be alone," and created woman as his companion, counsellor and co-worker, the influence of our sex in molding the affairs of state and nation began; and no matter how much or how often perverted or hindered, the darkest age has never wholly destroyed it.

The great Author of human destiny understood this fundamental law, when He placed fathers and mothers, brothers and sisters, in the same home and family, and permitted each sex to associate with the other on a plane of governmental, social and domestic equality.

Often, in these later years, when I have been addressing audiences in cities of the Middle West, and in the

East and South, I have been asked why it was that the
Pacific Northwest was so far in advance of the older settled portions of the United States, in its recognition of
the Divine principle of equality of rights between the
sexes, which originated in the human home. To this
query I am always proud to reply, that the territorial domain of Oregon was the first great section of our Federal Union in which woman's equal right to occupy and
possess real estate, in fee simple, and on her own individual account, had ever been recognized or practiced.

All great uprisings of the race, looking to the establishment of a larger liberty for all the people, have first
been generated in new countries, where plastic conditions
adapt themselves to larger growths. It has ever been
man's province to go before, to find the path in the wilderness, and blaze the way for those who are to follow
him. It is man's mission to tunnel the mountains, rivet
the bridges, build the highways, erect the habitations,
navigate the seas, subdue and cultivate the soil. It has
ever been the province of woman to take joint possession,
with him, of the crude homes that he has builded, and
add to the rude beginnings of his border life those femi-
nine endeavors, through which, as the community in-
creases in numbers, a higher civilization asserts itself, till,
as it grows in years and riches, the wilderness is made to
blossom as the rose.

The interests of the sexes can never be identically
the same; but they are always mutual, always interdepen-
dent, and every effort to separate them results, primarily,
in discontent, and ultimately in failure.

When the true history of woman's agency in up-building the State of Oregon, shall have been written, the world
will marvel at the sublimity of the inspiration of the man,
or men, who gave to the seal of the state its enduring motto, *alis volat propriis,* or "she flies with her own wings."

You have heard, on this brilliant and important occa-

Abigail Scott Duniway's Sons

Clyde A. Duniway   Ralph R. Duniway   Willis S. Duniway   Wilkie C. Duniway

Hubert R. Duniway

sion, a great many spirited, time-honored and true rehears-
als of the valiant deeds of Oregon's pioneers and public-
spirited men.   No one reveres or honors more sincerely
than I the noble courage, the sturdy manhood, the spirit
of enterprise displayed by men whose names are insepar-
able from the history of this State's upbuilding.   It required men of brave hearts and firm footsteps to lead the
way in the vast enterprises that have culminated, after all
the weary years that we are here to commemorate, in this
realization of our forty years of statehood.   Their deeds
of daring, danger and endurance have long been chron-
icled in song and story.   Many of their honored effigies
look down upon us today from enduring canvas, upon
these tinted walls.   Their silent images speak to us in
rugged, yet kindly outlines, of bygone days, when, in
their vigorous, ambitious youth, they crossed a barren,
almost trackless continent, encountering roaring rivers
and rock-ribbed mountains, in a country inhabited only by
wild beasts and wilder savages.   They speak to us of the
prophetic vision with which they discerned this goodly
land, long ere their eyes beheld the vernal shore "where
rolls the Oregon."

Other speakers have extolled the spirit of adventure
characteristic of our Anglo-Saxon stock; a spirit which led
men, like these, to hew their way through a perilous,
toilsome pilgrimage, to this summerland of the sun-down
seas.   But many were the women, daily companions of
these men of valor, with lives equal to theirs in rectitude
and energy, whose names, as yet, have found no place
in song and story, who did their part as bravely as did
any man; and their memory remains today enshrined
only in the hearts of rustic neighbors, or of their descendants, who knew and loved them in their obscurity.   Many
and yet, alas, how few, will linger but a few years longer,
to gaze with dimming vision upon the serried ranks of
our annual parades of men, who will march together with

faltering steps, at our regular reunions, until at last, there shall be left no more survivors of our early pioneers.

What further shall we say of the women of Oregon, the wives, mothers and sweethearts of those once mighty men who are soon to vanish from human sight? Have they not as nobly and bravely borne their part as did the men? Were they not as faithful and brave as they in building up this vigorous, young commonwealth of the Pacific Northwest, which today includes the added states of Washington, Montana and Idaho, that, together with this Mother of States, originally comprised the whole of Oregon?

That British Columbia obtained a valuable part of our Pacific Northwest Territory while your humble speaker was yet a child, is a part of our history of which I cannot stop to speak. All of you old Oregonians can still remember that spirited campaign cry of your youth, whose refrain was "Fifty-four forty or fight." The younger Oregonians can read it in school histories.

I have before paid tribute to the bravery and endurance of man in subduing the primeval wilderness. It is now my grateful privilege to recognize woman's part, often more difficult and dangerous, because accompanied by the added terrors of maternity, and always as important as man's in building up a state from its crude beginnings into such fruition as we now behold.

We cannot forget the heroism of the women of the Whitman party, who were both victims and survivors of that horrible and historic massacre. We delight to honor the valor of those intrepid mothers of the mighty men of today, and yesterday, who crossed the untracked continent in ox wagons or on horseback, some of whom have lived to see their native sons and daughters take proper place as living monuments in commemoration of those days that tried men's souls. We cannot forget the faithful bravery of the lone woman in her rough log cabin in the beautiful

hills of Southern Oregon, who, when her husband lay
dead at her feet, from the treacherous aim of a cruel savage, kept the howling despoilers of her home at bay with
her trusty rifle until daylight came, and brought her
succor from the neighboring hills.

But my time is limited, and I cannot linger over
facts already familiar to you all. Let it rather be my
province to speak of those mothers in Oregon, whose
patient endurance of poverty, hardship and toil brought
them naught of public and little of private recompense,
but whose children rise up and call them blessed, and
whose husbands are known in the gates where they sit
among the rulers of the land.

I have spoken of the inspiration that gave to us, and
to posterity, the motto of the state seal of Oregon. But
there was another inspiration, first voiced by Dr. Linn,
of venerable memory, from whom one of our fairest and
richest counties derived its name, and was afterwards put
into practical shape in Congress by Delegate Samuel R.
Thurston. It was an inspiration that placed Oregon as
a star of first magnitude in our great galaxy of states,
causing her to lead in recognizing woman's inalienable
right, as an individual, to the possession and ownership
of the soil, irrespective of gift, devise or inheritance, ante-
nuptial settlement or any sort of handicap, or special
privilege whatsoever. I allude to the donation land law.
A dozen years ago, before my frequent journeyings had
taken me from Oregon (as they have often done in later
years), I became acquainted with hundreds of Oregonians over the State, some of whom are doubtless present at this hour, many of whom have assured me with
pride, and all with gratitude, that, but for this beneficent provision for the protection of home, not only their
wives and children, but themselves also, would have no
homes at all in which to abide.

Woman is the world's home-maker, and she ought

always to be the home-keeper, or at least the privileged and honored keeper of a sufficient area of mother-earth upon which to build and, if necessary, maintain a home. The woman who would neglect her home and family for the allurements of social frivolity, or the emoluments and honors of public life, is not the woman whose name will occupy a place among the annals of the Oregon Pioneers. If Napoleon had said to Madame de Stael that the greatest woman was she who had reared the best, wisest and most patriotic children, his famous answer to her famous query would have been divested of all its coarseness. Men of renown in all the ages have been the sons of public-spirited, patriotic, home-loving women. "All that I am I owe to my mother," said our illustrious Washington; and our martyred Lincoln, in speaking of the deeds of heroism that characterized the women who bore the soldiers, who bore the arms in our civil war, said: "I go for giving the elective franchise to all who bear the burdens of government, by no means excluding women."

I would not have you think for a minute that wise women would lessen paternal responsibility in caring for the home. Man ought to be, and generally is, or is supposed to be, the home-provider. But, that he has often failed to keep his part of the mutual contract, try he how he may, full many a husband can testify, who is living on his wife's half of the donation land claim, which, happily for all concerned, was recognized by law as hers, in the beginning of their married life, and which she has ever since refused to sell, or mortgage, for any consideration whatsoever.

I pray you to indulge me while I say that I have never yet met a husband who has failed to make himself an agreeable and respected companion to the wife of his bosom, the mother of his children, if she possessed, in her own right, the home that sheltered them. Nor have I ever known any woman of Oregon, when so situated, to be compelled to sue for divorce on account of "cruel and inhuman treatment, making life burdensome."

Right here is a pointer for the relief of our overcrowded divorce courts, Mr. Governor.

That the donation land law has its abuses, we all admit. The tracts of land it donated were too large, and the temptations for girl children to marry prematurely to secure land were too great to create, always, the happiest results. But the principle was all right, as to the legality of woman's ownership of a home, and ought, in modified form, to be revived and continued indefinitely, as it surely will, as civilization progresses and enlightenment and liberty increase.

How largely the State of Oregon is indebted to the donation land act for the origin of the spirit of freedom, justice and patriotism that prompted patriotic women to send their sons and grandsons to face death in their heroic endeavor to "avenge the Maine"; how much the State owes, primarily, to that same patriotism for the promptitude of women in forming the Emergency Corps of the State, or becoming auxiliary to the Red Cross Society, for the benefit of our boys in blue, or how far that experience has gone to increase the zeal with which they now come knocking at the gates of state government, for admission within its portals, to take their own position among the electors, where there shall be no more "taxation without representation" to vex the spirits of our lawmakers, with its biennial protest, I am sure I cannot tell you. But I know, and so do you, Mr. Governor of Oregon, and all these honorable gentlemen, that the spirit of liberty and patriotism, like that of necessity and ambition, is in the air. It cannot longer be restricted by the fiat of sex, or suppressed by the fiat of votes. The women of Wyoming, Colorado, Utah and Idaho, today enjoy their full and free enfranchisement; the Governors, the legislatures, the judiciary and the men-voters of all those states, speak as a unit in praise of their women voters. And shall Oregon, the proud Mother of three great states, in the youngest of which the women are voters already—shall she refuse, through her men-voters, to ratify the honorable action of the Legislative Assembly, which has given them the glorious opportunity to celebrate the dawn of the Twentieth Century by making it a year of jubilee for the wives and mothers of the pioneers, to whose influence the up-building of the state is, by their own confession, so largely due? Forbid it, men and brethren! Forbid it, Almighty God!

And now, as I close, I beg leave to present for your edification, the grandest poem that, from the Oregon Woman's standpoint, has ever been written by Oregon's greatest poet, Joaquin Miller, entitled

THE MOTHERS OF MEN.

The bravest battle that ever was fought!
  Shall I tell you where and when?
On the maps of the world you will find it not—
  'Twas fought by the mothers of men.

Nay, not with cannon or battle shot,
  With sword or nobler pen!
Nay, not with eloquent words or thought,
  From mouths of wonderful men!

But, deep in a walled-up woman's heart—
  Of woman who would not yield,
But bravely, silently, bore her part—
  Lo, there is that battlefield!

No marshaling troop, no bivouac song,
  No banners to gleam and wave;
But Oh! these battles, they last so long—
  From babyhood to the grave.

Yet, faithful still, as a bridge of stars
  She fights in her walled-up town—
Fights on and on in the endless war,
  Then, silent, unseen, goes down.

Oh, ye with banners and battleshot,
  And soldiers to shout and praise!
I tell you the kingliest victories fought,
  Were fought in these silent ways.

Oh, spotless woman in a world of shame;
    With splendid and silent scorn,
Go back to God as white as you came—
    The kingliest warrior born.

* * *

The following report appeared in the proceedings of the National Woman Suffrage Association, held at Grand Rapids, Michigan, in May, 1899. The writer, though a prohibitionist and a prominent member of the Woman's Christian Temperance Union, has always contended that the two associations of force and freedom cannot succeed at any political election to amend a State Constitution, except as separate organizations, working each for a single purpose:

Early in the year 1898, our State President and honored leader, Mrs. Abigail Scott Duniway, who, from long and vigilant labor in our cause in the Pacific Northwest, is better prepared to judge the sentiment of our voters than any other of our women workers, decided that all public agitation of our Equal Suffrage Association must cease until the meeting of the Legislative Assembly of 1899. In April of last year our second biennial meeting of the Oregon Congress of Women was held under the auspices of our State Executive Committee of the Equal Suffrage Association, and was participated in by over forty affiliated societies, all of which gladly lent their aid to popularize the Equal Suffrage idea, although, perhaps, not one of them would have joined with us in a distinctly Suffrage Movement. The Congress proved a success in every way except financially.

The Annual Meeting of the Pioneer Association assembled in June and was our next opportunity, where the expression of sentiment in favor of Equal Suffrage was, by common consent, a marked feature of the proceedings.

The Willamette Chautauqua Assembly met in July, and gave us as usual a Woman's Day, which, as in former years, proved the most successful day of the Assembly, both popularly and financially. Herr Anton Schott, the world-famed Wagnerian tenor; Dr. Frances Woods, who is now in Manila as one of Clara Barton's most valuable aids; Alice Moore McComas and daughters, of Los Angeles, Cal.; and our own Mrs. W. H. Games, assisted our State President in the exercises of the day, over all of which Colonel R. A. Miller, President of Chautauqua, himself a Suffragist, was so jubilant, that he has given us an Amendment Jubilee Day, for our Assembly in 1899, which, if our President had consented, would have been called Abigail Scott Duniway Day.

The various moral, financial and labor reform movements throughout the State are all, with a few exceptions, in favor of Equal Suffrage. Among them may be enumerated the Woman's Christian Temperance Union, the Woman's Club Movement, the Good Templars, the State Grange, the Knights of Labor, the Printers' Union and the Brotherhood of Engineers. While none of these named are strictly Suffrage Organizations, the fact that they, like many of the churches and all of the leading men of all political parties, are ready at any time to avow their sympathy with the cause, naturally gives us strength.

But the crowning success of the year, over which we exult, is the submission of our Amendment to the vote of our late Legislative Assembly, by twenty-five to one in the Senate, and forty-eight to six in the House of Representatives. We cannot too strongly commend our President's method in conducting the campaign for 1900, since we feel that her quiet, unostentatious manner, dispelling prejudice and opposition, left the Legislators free to act, without instructions from their constituents. This Legislature invited our leader to address both Houses while in regular session, the first time in the history of Oregon such an honor was ever conferred upon a woman.

Another important event, over which Suffragists are happy, was the invitation by the Legislature to Mrs. Abigail Scott Duniway to take a prominent part in the joint proceedings of the two Houses in honor of our forty years of Statehood.

As a Suffrage Organization we do not claim, or even desire, much numerical strength. Experience has taught us that States that win Suffrage are those wherein the objective work is focused among a few leaders, through whose judicious management the cause of Equal Rights is allowed to permeate all other associations of whatever name or order.

FRANCES E. GOTSHALL,
Corresponding Secretary of the Oregon Equal Suffrage
    Association.

CHAPTER XVI.

How To Win the Ballot.

THE following address was delivered by myself before the National Convention of the National American Woman Suffrage Association, May 2nd, 1899, at Grand Rapids, Michigan, and is given here as the shortest way at my command for telling many truths that Eastern readers ought to read:

Coming as I do from the far Pacific, where the sun at night sinks into the sea, to greet a convocation of co-workers from the far Atlantic, where the sun at morn rises out of the sea; and standing here, upon the central swell of the Middle West, where the sun at high noon kisses the heaving bosom of the mighty inland sea that answers back to East and West the echoing song of liberty, I realize the importance of my desire to speak to the entire continent, such tempered words as shall help to further unite our common interests in the great work that convenes us.

The first fact to be considered, when working to win the ballot, is that there is but one way by which we may hope to obtain it, and that is by and through the affirmative votes of men. We may theorize, organize, appeal, argue, coax, cajole and threaten men till doomsday; we may secure their pettings, praises, flattery, and every appearance of acquiescence in our demands; we may believe with all our hearts in the sincerity of their promises to vote as we dictate, but all of this will avail us nothing unless they deposit their affirmative votes in the ballot box.

Every man who stops to argue the case, as an opponent, tells us that he "loves women," and, while wondering much that he should consider such a declaration

necessary, I have always admired the loyal spirit that
prompts its utterance. But, gentlemen,—and I am proud
indeed to see such a fine audience of you here tonight—
there is another side to this expression of loyalty. Not
only is our movement not instigated in a spirit of warfare between the sexes, but it is engendered, altogether,
in the spirit of harmony, and inter-dependence between
men and women, such as was the evident design of the
great Creator when he placed fathers and mothers,
brothers and sisters, in the same home and family. We
are glad to be assured that you "love women," but we
are doubly glad to be able, on proper occasions, and in
every suitable way, to return the compliment. No good
Equal Suffragist will any longer permit you to monopolize
all the pretty speeches about the other sex. Every good
woman in the world likes men a great deal better than
she likes women, and there isn't a wise woman in all this
goodly land who isn't proud to say so. We like you,
gentlemen, and you cannot help it. We couldn't help it
if we would; we wouldn't help it if we could. You like
us, also, because you cannot help it. God made the sexes
to match each other. Show me a woman who doesn't like
men, and I will show you a sour-souled, vinegar-visaged
specimen of unfortunate femininity, who owes the world
an apology for living in it at all; and the very best thing
she could do for her country, provided she had a country,
would be to steal away and die, in the company of the
man who doesn't like women. In order to gain the votes
of men, so we can win the ballot, we must show them
that we are inspired by the same patriotic motives that
induce them to prize it. A home without a man in it,
is only half a home. A government without women in it,
is only half a government. Man without a woman is
like one-half of a pair of dislocated shears. Woman without man is like the other half of the same disabled im-
plement. Male and female created He them, saith the

GROUP OF EQUAL SUFFRAGISTS

THE LATE MRS. ELIZABETH LORD
Vice President of Oregon Equal Suffrage
Association

ESTHER POHL LOVEJOY, M. D.
President of Oregon Everybody's Suffrage
League

MRS. EMMA GALLOWAY
President of Yamhill County Equal
Suffrage Association

MRS. SARAH A. EVANS
President of Oregon Federation of
Women's Clubs

MRS. C. M. CARTWRIGHT
President Woman's Auxiliary of Oregon
Pioneer Association and Charter
Member of O. E. S. A.

MISS FRANCES E. GOTSHALL
Corresponding Secretary and Equal
Suffrage Publisher
A Prohibitionist

MRS. MARY P. COOKE
Charter Member of Oregon Equal Suffrage
Association 1872

Higher Law, and to them God gave dominion "over every living thing upon the earth"—except each other.

Thirty years ago, when I began my humble efforts for securing the enfranchisement of women, away out upon the singing shores of the Pacific Sea, men everywhere imagined, at first, that the movement was intended to deprive them of a modicum of their liberties. They ought to have known this idea was absurd even then, as they have always had the power to both oppose or allow themselves to be ruled by women. But they thought legal supremacy over them was what women were after, and they met their own theory with hoarse guffaws of laughter. I had previously had much experience with the genus masculine, not only with my good husband, but with a large family of sons.

It is needless for me to tell you, after this confession, that I am not young, and you can see for yourselves that I am no longer handsome.

The fact that men, for the most part, contented themselves in those early days of the Suffrage Movement, with exhibitions of ridicule, I accepted as a good omen. If you wish to convince a man that your opinion is logical and just, you have conquered the outer citadel of his resentment when he throws back his head and opens his mouth to laugh. Show me a solemn-visaged voter, with a face as long as the Pentateuch, and I will show you a man with a soul so little that it would have ample room to dance inside of a hollow mustard seed. Having tickled your opponent with a little nonsense, that at first was necessary to arrest his attention, you must then be careful to hold the ground you have gained. Your next step must be to impress upon all men the fact that we are not intending to interfere, in any way, with their rights; and all we ask is to be allowed to decide, for ourselves, also as to what our rights should be. They will then, very naturally, ask what effect our enfranchisement will have upon their politics. Visions of riotous scenes in political conventions will arise, to fill them with apprehension, as the possibility occurs that women, if enfranchised, will only double the vote and augment the uproar. They will recall partisan banquets, at which men have tarried over cups and pipes until they rolled under the table, or were carried off to bed on shutters. Very naturally, men, everywhere, object to seeing reputable women, and especially their own wives, engaged in such excesses. But our mighty men of the Pacific Northwest are troubled very little by these vagaries. They realize, as they sleep off the results of their latest political banquet, that at every public function in which their wives participate, there is a notable absence of any sort of dissipation. They remember that in former times, before good women had joined them, in the mining camps, mountain towns, and on the bachelor farms, that such scenes as sometimes transpire today, at men's great gatherings, were once so common as to excite little comment. It was the advent of good women in the border territories that changed all this, and eliminated the bad woman from social life, just as the ballot will eventually eliminate the bad woman from political life, where she now reigns supreme among men, having everything her own way. By the very charm of good women's presence they brought these changes about on the Pacific Coast, in social life, till men began to wonder how they had endured the old conditions, before the women joined them. Now, quite naturally, they are learning to apply this rule to politics; and so our men of the Pacific Coast are not alarmed, as many men are in other states, lest women, if allowed to become equal with themselves before the law, will forget their natural duties and natural womanliness. If, however, any man grows timid, and exhibits symptoms of alarm, as they sometimes do (even in Oregon), lest the balloted woman will forsake the kitchen sink, at which she has always been "protected" (without wages), or abandon the cooking stove, the rolling pin, the wash tub and the ironing board, at which she has always been shielded (without salary), we remind him that housekeeping and homemaking are, like everything else, undergoing a complete process of evolution. We show him that there is no more reason why every loaf of bread should be baked in a different kitchen than there is why every bushel of wheat should be ground in a different mill. We show him that the laundry is destined, hereafter, to keep pace with the threshing machine; the creamery with the spinning jenny and power loom; the fruit cannery with the great flour mill; the dish washer with the steam-driven mangle, and the bakery with the ready-made clothing store.

When women have been voters long enough to have acquired recognition of their own equal property rights with men, the servant girl problem will settle itself. When that time comes there will be no more work left to do in the home than the wife and mother can perform with comfort to herself and household; and the servant girls of today will then find systematic employment in the great factories, where food and clothing are manufactured by rule. This evolution has already begun with the woman typewriter. You see her everywhere; pretty, tidy, rosy with a ribbon or flower at her throat, intent upon her work and sure to get her pay. Then can the mother, for the sake of herself, her husband, and children, preserve her health, her beauty, and her mental vigor. Then can she be an adviser in the home, the state, the church, and the school, remaining so to a ripe old age.

But women can never have the opportunity, or the power, to achieve these results, except in isolated cases, till they are voters and lawmakers; and never even then, till they have had time to secure, by legislation, the equal property rights that they have earned with men from the beginning.

All evolution proceeds slowly. Women, under normal conditions, are evolutionists, and not revolutionists, as is shown by their conduct, as voters, in Wyoming, Colorado, Utah and Idaho. Your ideal, hysterical reformer, whose aim in life is to put men in leading strings, like little children, doesn't hail from any state where women vote.

Mary A. Livermore, at the head of the Sanitary Commission during our great internecine war; Clara Barton, President of the National Red Cross Society, and Oregon's own Mrs. Creighton, President of the National White Cross Association, have each proved the capacity of the American woman for rescuing the race from the awful consequences of war; while every soldier proves, by the very fact of his existence, that some mother has borne a son at her peril, perhaps to be shot in battles that woman might help to avoid.

The very best housekeepers and homemakers in America are among the Equal Suffrage platform workers, the editor of the "Ladies' Home Journal" to the contrary notwithstanding. They may know better than to ruin their eyes over Mr. Bok's latest fad in "Battenburg" or shatter their nerves over his mental creations in crazy stitches, but they can, and do, raise men and women, like the sons and daughters of Lucretia Mott, Mary A. Livermore, Emily B. Ketchum, Elizabeth Cady Stanton, Lilly Devereaux Blake, Abigail Scott Duniway, Lucy Stone Blackwell, Elizabeth Boynton Herbert, Harriet Beecher Stowe and Julia Ward Howe.

But, your most important point, if you hope to win the ballot at all, is to convince the average voter, that, in seeking your liberties, you are equally anxious that he shall preserve his own. You may drive, or lead, a horse to water, but you cannot make him drink. Nor can you lead any man to vote for your enfranchisement till you have first convinced him that by so doing, he is not placing you in a position where you may, if you choose, trample upon any of his rights, whether they may be fancied or real, healthful or harmful. Every woman knows she cannot rule her husband. The man who would be ruled by his wife would not be worth corralling in the chimney corner after she had driven him home. What is true of men in the abstract, is equally true of men in the aggregate. I cannot too strongly impress upon you, good sisters, the fact that we will never get the ballot till the crack of doom, if we persist in demanding it as a whip, with which to scourge the real or apparent vices of the present voting classes. If we can make men willing to be reformed, they will then reform themselves.

Here is where woman has, in the last two decades, made her greatest blunder. Whenever she demands the ballot, not simply because it is her right to possess it, but because by its use, she expects to reconstruct the genus man by law, on a basis of her own choosing, she only succeeds in driving nails into the closed coffin lid of her own and other women's liberties.

Men know, intuitively, that the right to representation in the legislature is a right as inestimable to us as to them; that it is formidable to tyrants only. They do not believe themselves to be tyrants, and will resent the implication that they are such to the bitter end. They also know that women, in giving existence to the soldiers, suffer their full share of the penalties and perils of existence, equaling all the horrors of war. So, when they say, "Women must fight if they vote," it is easy, in the awful glare of the tragedies of the present year, to convince them in the words of Joaquin Miller, Oregon's greatest poet, that "The bravest battles that ever are fought, are fought by the mothers of men."

When men claim to represent us, it is not difficult, if we are always careful not to make them angry, to prove to them that men never say, if any woman is accused of crime, "May it please the Court and the jury, I represent this woman, punish me."

No man, save Jesus of Nazareth, our divinely commissioned Elder Brother, has ever yet appeared before the bar of God, or man, and offered himself as propitiation for the sins, debts, or taxes of women.

Many good men object to women doing jury duty. They often frighten timid women by saying, "How would you like to be locked up in the Jury Room with eleven men?" I can't understand why so many men imagine that if women should once be allowed their right to vote, they would never, thereafter, do anything else but vote, vote, vote, vote! Nor can I comprehend another fancy, equally absurd, that, just as soon as women are voters, they will all be compelled to sit all the time on juries; and everyone of those unfortunate jurors will always have as many little children as poor John Rogers of historical memory; and no matter what the state of her health and the needs of her neglected husband, and "nine small children," etc., she will still be on the jury; and that jury will always be composed of one woman and eleven men. Such assumptions are too absurd for refutation; but for the fact that they sometimes bring out negative votes, we would not notice them. Men and women always have been, and always will be, excused from jury duty—for cause.

Again, we can never win the ballot by demanding it in the interests of any particular "ism," union, party, sect or creed. In our Pacific Northwest, the majority of the voters stand ready to grant us the ballot whenever we demand it on the broad basis of individual and collective liberty for ourselves; and we will never get it otherwise.

Our friends east of the Rocky Mountains were amazed and electrified, in the autumn of 1883, by the announcement that the Legislature of Washington Territory had extended the ballot to women.

Less than four years later, after a few self-imported agitators had made strong attempts to use the women's ballots for the enforcement of sumptuary legislation, to which the men objected (even while pretending to approve it, till they got the women into a trap), women everywhere were dumfounded by the action of the politicians of the Territory, who retaliated by shutting down the iron gates of a State Constitution in the women's faces, leaving them as ex-voters on the outside of the temple of liberty, with their hands tied.

The men of Washington are not yet over their scare, nor will they be till women have made an effort to convince them that the eyes of the great majority are now open, and they will never be entrapped in such a way again.

I pray you do not misunderstand me, friends. I wage no war upon any organization, or upon any person's political or religious faith. Catholics have just as good right to their religious opinions as Protestants. Republicans have just as good right to their political bias as Democrats, and Socialists have just as good a right to their reformatory fancies as Prohibitionists. Yet, if any one of these great armies of opposing opinions should claim Equal Suffrage as its chief dependence for success, and the great National American Woman Suffrage Association, or the Suffrage Association of any State, should become the champion of its special "ism," we should, henceforth, be unable to rally to our standard any appreciable vote, save that of the particular sect or party with which the voters of opposing sects or parties should believe us allied. We need all the votes we can get from all parties to win.

If I, as a member of the Presbyterian Church, for instance, should have gone before the legislature of Oregon, seeking the submission of our Suffrage amendment as a measure for enforcing the Presbyterian creed, think you that the members of the Catholic Church, or of the Protestant Churches of other denominations, sitting in that assembly, would have electrified the suffragists of this nation by voting almost solidly for our amendment, as allies of the Westminster catechism?

A year ago, when our second semi-annual convention of the Oregon Congress of Women was in session, it was boldly proclaimed by a zealous advocate of sumptuary legislation, that Susan B. Anthony, the venerable and venerated President of the National Woman Suffrage Association, had declared herself a worker for the ballot as the sworn advocate of only one idea. I wrote at once to our beloved President, who never fails us at a critical period, asking for facts over her own signature, and received for answer, her unequivocal denial of the allegation that she was allied, in the Equal Suffrage work, with any sort of sumptuary legislation, or any other side issue under the sun. This declaration, which I caused to be published in the secular papers, set the minds of the voters at rest on that score, and enabled Dr. Annice F. Jeffreys and myself to go before the legislature free from all handicaps.

When the question of sumptuary legislation confronted us at the capitol, we explained that equal suffragists everywhere believed with Gail Hamilton that the only way to reform a man is to begin with his grandmother. This frank announcement removed the last vestige of legislative hostility, and gave us the submission of our Equal Suffrage amendment, practically without opposition. Potential grandmothers do not trouble our politicians overmuch. The present possible rewards of office drive remote probabilities to the wall.

The year 1900 is the period fixed by law for the final vote upon our pending Suffrage amendment, and we need have no fear for the result, if we can keep the fact before our voters that our demand for the ballot is not engendered by emotional insanity.

The men of our Pacific Northwest are a noble lot of freemen. The spirit of enterprise which led them across the untracked continent to form a new empire, beside our sundown sea, was a bold and free spirit; and the patient heroism of the few women who originally shared their lot had in it the elements of grandeur.

There are lessons of liberty in the rockribbed mountains that pierce our blue horizon with their snow-crowned heads, and laugh to scorn the warring elements of the earth, the water and the air. There are lessons of freedom in our broad prairies that roll away into illimitable distances. There are lessons of equality in the gigantic, evenly-crested forest trees that rear their hydra heads to the vaulted zenith and touch the blue horizon with extended arms. There are lessons of truth and justice in the very air we breathe, and lessons of irresistible progress in the mighty waters that surge and sweep, with super-human power, between the overhanging bluffs of our own Columbia, the "River of the West."

My state is the only one represented this year, in this great Convention, in which an Equal Suffrage Amendment is pending. The opportunity has come to us, as to the women of no other state, to claim the dawn of the 20th century as our year of jubilee. To work in unison with each other, and with the women of the older states, crystallized with constitutions hoary with the encrustations of long-vanished years, and compel them to look to the free, young, elastic West, for the liberties they cannot get at home, is the proud ambition that commands my presence here tonight. Help us with your wisdom, your sympathy, your co-operation, good friends; and

when we shall have been successful at the ballot boxes
of our state, thus adding a star of the first magnitude
to the already bright constellation of our four free states.
which now illumine our Northwestern heavens, we will
entertain you with a national jubilee to celebrate our
liberties, as the most fitting accompaniment to the dawn
of the 20th century which patriotism can devise. Then
shall liberty, newly born, be christened with a new name,
selected for her by an octogenarian Oregonian, now confined with the infirmities of age in a New York hospital,
who sent our Equal Suffrage Association as a message of
congratulation, when the telegraph proclaimed the news
that our amendment had passed the Legislature, the
magical greeting, "A child is born, and her name is
Alleluia."

(We failed to win the ballot in all of our Pacific
Coast States till thirteen years after the above address
was given; but its facts appeal, today, with even greater
force, to men and women in every state where votes of
men are needed to secure the blessings of liberty and
responsibility, or the right of self-government for all
the people, "by no means excluding women.")

CHAPTER XVII.

Success in Sight.

T HIS address was delivered by myself before the National American Woman Suffrage Convention, in Washington, D. C., February 14, 1900, and appeared in "The Oregonian" the following morning :

The Paradise of the Pacific Northwest, from whose summer lands and sun-down seas I have traveled four thousand miles to greet this brilliant gathering, was, until within the past few years, so remote in time, as well as in distance, from the older settled portions of this North American continent, that nobody living outside of our great bailiwick, except Susan B. Anthony, had discovered the woman's side of our progressive history, with which she became acquainted by personal contact in 1871. But even Miss Anthony found on reaching our shores, nearly 30 years ago, that the awakened woman of the latter half of the 19th century had, prior to her advent, discovered herself.

When the historic expedition of discovery, headed by Lewis and Clark, began its famous journey of exploration in 1804, it started westward from a point east of the Mississippi river, and extended its transcontinental travels through the almost unknown country now known as the Middle West, till it came, at last, to Oregon, leaving its families at home. The results of that important journey will remain through all time, to mark the tracks it left upon this nation's topographical and commercial history. But, of the ultimate results of their researches, the men who managed it had no dream; still less did they imagine that, ere the dawn of another century, the co-existence, and necessary co-association, of wives and mothers in all the great and small affairs of life would echo back, across the Rocky Mountains, and from under the shadows of our own sea-bathed Sierras, the fact that the most important discovery of the century had been made when the woman of the great West discovered herself. If Lewis and Clark and their no less intrepid companions were with us in the flesh today, they would see vast armies of men, as valorous and adventurous as themselves, still engaged in making new discoveries in the physical geography of the United States. And they would see these modern Argonauts, reaching out, guided by a destiny they could not foresee or fathom, to raise the standard of individual and collective liberty in the gem-studded waters of the Pacific Ocean and the Asiatic seas. Then, in turning the searchlight of their expanded vision northward, they would see yet other companies of men, reaching out into the hyperborean altitudes of remote Alaska, accompanied (as Lewis and Clark's expedition ought to have been) by mothers, wives and daughters, who are proving themselves as strong in endurance and as intrepid in danger as their fathers, husbands and sons.

They would see, too, no matter whether they turned their searchlight, from their viewpoint, toward the East or West, that whether the modern adventurer had pitched his tent upon the granite heights of Sumpter, or toward the South to the tree-clad hills of Oregon's Bohemian district; no matter whether they bivouacked among the frozen crags of Chilcoot Pass, or on the humid borders of Cape Nome; no matter if they camped under the mountain edges of modern Skagway, or rested at Metlakahtla, that the virtue of the forest maiden would not be disturbed as of yore—nor would the dusky wife of the aboriginal man be tempted to populate the new world with half-caste children, to become the Ishmaelites of new generations, like the son of one Argonaut I have in mind, who, when asked, after being convicted of murder, to state why sentence of death should not be pronounced upon him, turned savagely upon his pious father and cursed him roundly for having married an Indian woman.

When I was asked to include in my remarks, tonight, a brief recital of the progress made during the century by the mothers of the race, in the far-off corner of our continent from which I come, these facts crowded themselves upon me for expression, hence this introduction.

Nowhere else, upon this planet, are the inalienable rights of women as much appreciated as on the newly settled borders of these United States. Men have had opportunities, in our remote countries, to see the worth of the civilized woman, who came with them, or among them, to new settlements, after the Indian woman's day. And they have seen her, not as the parasitic woman who inherits wealth, or the equally selfish woman who lives in idleness upon her husband's toil, but as their helpmates, companions, counsellors and fellow-homemakers, rejoicing with them in the homes they have earned together, and in the sons and daughters they have reared, in the hope that each would follow, in the other's steps, the good old plodding paths of industry and peace. In spite of theories or regrets, the world is moving, and woman is moving with it—not always, maybe, in the best chosen paths, for we are no wiser than our brothers—but always moving onward, in some direction, toward a higher goal. There came a time in Oregon, in the days when Washington, Montana and Idaho were as yet a part of Oregon's territory, when men said to the intrepid women who were helping them to subdue the wilderness, "You shall be endowed with property rights of your own, other than those dependent upon the meager possibilities of gift, devise and inheritance." And they bestowed upon women, under an act of congress, originated by themselves, great tracts of virgin acres, making freeholders of our women pioneers.

During the limited period of the early "fifties," while this act, known as the donation land law, was in force, large numbers of married women joined their husbands in Oregon, and availing themselves of their opportunity, became original owners of the soil; and it is safe to say, that, such is every sane woman's innate love of home, not to speak of her oftentimes inordinate desire to possess a home of her own, that if the law had not been repealed unto this day, there need not be a resident man in all the states of the Pacific Northwest, of which Oregon was the mother, who would not today be in joint possession, with his faithful family, of an abode having its foundation in the soil, from which no speculator could dislodge him. Woman always was and always will be, the best and truest friend of man. And I say again, as I have often said before, "God bless the men! We couldn't.do without them if we would; we wouldn't if we could."

And yet, it is well known that the very best men are not always the most prosperous.

I have here a copy of the transactions of the Ninth Annual Reunion of the Oregon Pioneer Association, in which I find the following testimonial from the pen of Hon. Jesse Applegate, to the memory of his faithful wife, who died in 1881. Mr. Applegate says: "She was a safe counsellor, for her untaught instincts were truer and safer rules of conduct than my better informed judgment. Had I oftener followed her advice her pilgrimage on earth might have been happier; at least, her strong desire to make all happy around her would not have been cramped by extreme penury." Ah, many have been the women of my bailiwick, who, like Mrs. Applegate, have "gone to their graves in deep penury," whose "untaught instincts," if they had been possessed of equal rights before the law, would have accompanied their "strong desire to make their husbands and all around them happy and prosperous,"—a desire that could have been gratified to their heart's content, if their lives had not been cramped by poverty, through the political suppression of the "untaught instincts" that come to woman as the gift of God, though often denied her by the laws of man.

In an address made by myself before the Pioneer Society at its tenth anniversary, I said, alluding to the foregoing incident, and I repeat it here: "It was a tardy recognition of a noble woman's worth that brought forth the deep wail of regret that I have quoted. But no tongue or pen can depict the hopeless anguish of the bereaved husband, who frankly confessed, in his hour of desolation, that 'her life might have been longer and happier' if 'he had oftener followed her advice.'" There never lived a kindlier, manlier man than Jesse Applegate, whose great bereavement opened his blinded understanding and made him, ever after, to the day of his death, an uncompromising equal suffragist, whose many relatives are now following his example; and if, with his great soul and manly goodness of heart, he was so unjust to the best and dearest friend God ever gives to man, what shall we say of the lives of many—alas, how many—other women, with husbands less noble than he, whose toil has brought them no recompense, very little appreciation and far less of liberty?

In former times, every woman, no matter how lowly, possessed some sort of a home in which she was always toiling. She was the world's first crude manufacturer, the world's first homemaker; and she still desires, always, above everything else, to be her own homekeeper. But the world is changing front. Her spindle and her loom are gone. Steel and steam have despoiled her of the primitive means of livelihood which kept her comfortable, busy and content. Still, she must earn, or help to earn, a livelihood. Very few men possess the Midas touch that turns the things they handle into gold.

The woman who "keeps boarders for company," is

a close second to the wife who "makes dresses for diversion," or "teaches school for recreation," or goes out washing "for amusement." These words are not spoken in disparagement of the many men who are financial failures, nor would I reflect in any way upon the far lesser number who possess the Midas touch. I am simply stating facts, germane to the question at issue, through the observance of which our border statesmen have grown both just and wise.

Our pioneer women had not long been property holders before they became taxpayers. Then, gradually, the truth dawned upon them, as they toiled to pay the taxgatherer, that "taxation without representation is tyranny," and "governments derive their just powers from the consent of the governed." By and by the son of the pioneer grew up and left the farm, with its old-fashioned, meager equipments, which satisfied the good old father, who, while he lived, had tried in vain to curb the aspirations of the boy. And the son became an inventor, an actor, a speculator, a printer, a publisher, a lawyer, a miner, a preacher, a teacher, a doctor, a prize-fighter, a soldier, a banker, a broker, an editor, a politician, a merchant—an anything but a plodding, half-way tiller of the soil his parents loved.

Then the daughter, finding the young man had left the farm, came also to the city, and began to crowd her brother in the race for livelihood. The young man co-operated with his fellows and built a clubhouse—and still the maiden was alone. But she would work cheaper than he, chiefly because she could not run life's race with him except in ruinous competition. So she lived in a 7 by 9 room with an oil stove and a folding bed; and more and more she crowded him to the wall. And it was a life of independence compared to that which she had left. Her meager wage sufficed for food and clothes and shelter. She had discovered herself, and for a time she was satisfied. She was not compelled to marry from mercenary motives, and would not wed a coronet unless love crowned the contract and cleanliness of character, equal to her own, accompanied the nuptial bond.

And so it has gone on and on, until another stage in her development has come. And, like the bird, which, tethered at the end of a short line, rejoices in its enlarged circuit when the line is lengthened, until at last nothing will satisfy it but freedom altogether, the young woman has tried her partial emancipation from old-time environments; and now, she is no longer satisfied. She sits alone at night in her little chamber and watches the career of her brother, upon whom there are fastened no political fetters, and sees him reach the United States senate, or become the president of a bank, or the head of a great department store. She watches a sister, who became the parasitic wife of him of the Midas touch, and beholds her, sheltered in a gilded mansion, between which and herself there is a great gulf fixed; or she reads of her as presiding languidly in her palace, at a meeting called to oppose the political liberties of such toiling women as herself. She cannot have a gilded or even an humble home, for herself, because there is no man left to marry her, and her wages hardly support her daily existence. So she says, "What means that favored woman's wealth to me? This box wherein I sleep is not a home! I toil at half wages, and I am ostracized from the society in which my favored sister and brother shine. I have no hope in posterity, for I cannot marry. But I must live, and I am not content!" So she is calling to her brother bachelor in the United States Senate, or her married brother in the Hall of Representatives, and to all men in the ballot-booths of Oregon, saying, "Men and brethren! The times are out of joint! Old things have passed away, but not all things have become new. There are no fetters on you! Why should we wear manacles?" When you say "keep to your home," she is compelled, alas, to answer that she has no home to keep! When you remind her that "marriage is her proper sphere," she is confronted with the fact that the modern bachelor is not a marrying man.

So she quotes Elizabeth Cady Stanton and Susan B. Anthony, and Olive Schreiner and Charlotte Perkins Gilman, in her dreams, and repairs the next morning to her schoolroom, where she teaches the Declaration of Independence to a class of 50 girls and less than half a score of boys!

Among married women and sweet girl graduates, the attempt to make the best of their present environment within the limited circle bounded by their strained lariats results in the formation of women's clubs. And while, as yet, these institutions are mere travesties upon the clubs of men, they do suffice to ease somewhat the tension of their tethers, which many of them are unconsciously, but none the less certainly, striving to snap in twain, with every prospect of success.

I now come to my reasons for heading my address with the inspiring caption, "Success in Sight!" The never-fettered men of Oregon are becoming as weary as ourselves of these times that are out of joint. So they have submitted, by the vote of their representatives in the legislature, an amendment to our state constitution, in which they say, "No person shall hereafter be prohibited from voting on account of sex." This amendment they propose to ratify at the coming June election. And, while we shall miss, in the campaign now pending, the powerful aid of the late lamented Senators Mitchell and Dolph, the financial backing and manly votes of Hon. W. S. Ladd and J. B. Montgomery, of revered memory; the influence of Hon. Henry Failing, and his lamented father, Josiah Failing, Esq., who have passed to the skies; while we no more hear the honored voice of Oregon's Chief Justice, M. P. Deady, raised in our behalf, nor the encouraging words of the long line of our governors who have gone, in the fullness of time, to their long, long home, we have scores of leading men yet left to speak for us, whose names I now withhold for prudential reasons, lest, as was done one time by women in the Territory of Washington, the enemy be forewarned and their defeat invited and secured, through the caucus and conventions of the political machine.

For the same reason, I resist the strong temptation to name, in this connection, the many associations and fraternities of men who have signified by their votes, in their different orders and fraternities, their determination to give us their affirmative votes at the ballot-box next June. But I do take pride in mentioning, with no fear of disaster, the Emergency Corps and Red Cross Society of our State, organized through the mobilization of our volunteers, during our war with Spain, and maintained in active working order as long as there was work for them to do. It would, indeed, humiliate our returned veterans, were they to see these noble women defeated at the June election. These women, who, though tethered at the end of the governmental lariat, have royally earned their liberties by toiling to feed and comfort the soldiers, to whom women had given life, exhibiting such largeness of liberty and such statesmanship in administration of the army affairs as has challenged the admiration, not only of our own returning volunteers from Asiatic seas, but of those from Idaho, Montana, Nebraska, Dakota and Washington, all of whom were cheered and feasted, and sent on their way rejoicing, amid the glad acclaim of music, guns and bells. And the homeless wife, and sweet girl graduate are hearing all this and taking courage. They do not want to rule over men. It would be useless for any woman but an anti-suffragist to attempt to control men's votes, and none other tries. Our cry is for an equal chance with man in the great arena of work. Not many of us could be office-holders, and very few, in any State where women vote, aspire to office. The men of Oregon are tired of seeing their wives and daughters rated in the political category of idiots, insane persons, criminals and Chinamen. A delightful calm has settled over our political arena, but we believe it is the calmness that precedes the success that is in sight.

I wish that I had time to tell you of the mighty possibilities of fair young Oregon. Her capacity for homes is as unlimited as is the azure of her skies on her fairest days. Her people are prosperous and progressive and their spirits are as free from fads as the air they breathe. They do not like professional agitators, but they love liberty. To you, Miss Anthony, our honored leader and guest, whom it is my privilege to salute, in this hour of your serene young age, I say in conclusion, that my chief desire and prayer to God, on this great occasion, is that the government of these United States shall proclaim you a free and independent citizen, as you of right ought to be, at least long enough to get used to your liberty, before you are called to the skies. Your life has been a noble example of what Ella Wheeler Wilcox calls "the splendid discontent of God," which I am honored by repeating, ere my allotted time is up:

> The splendid discontent of God
>   With chaos, made the world,
> Set suns in place, and filled all space
>   With stars that shone and whirled.
>
> If apes had been content with tails,
>   No thing of higher shape
> Had come to birth; the king of earth
>   Today would be an ape.
>
> 'Tis from the discontent of man
>   The world's best progress springs.
> Then feed the flame (from God it came)
>   Until you mount on wings.

CHAPTER XVIII.

Preparations for Campaign of 1910.

THE Executive Committee of the State Equal Suffrage Association decided, after our defeats at the general elections of 1900, 1906 and 1908, to adopt a new line of departure, by adding a tax-paying clause to a new Constitutional Amendment, to be submitted to the electorate at the polls in 1910. In adopting this measure, we acted on the advice of experienced politicians of much prominence. The increased negative vote on a proposition, made unpopular by the campaign that had wrecked us in 1906, had convinced us of the necessity of attempting some variation in our lines of action, to interest the general public, outside of our beaten pathway, which the majority of men were opposing, ostensibly because of the sameness of our often attempted, and as often defeated, efforts to amend the Constitution along the same old lines.

"Why don't you try a different proposition?" asked a sagacious leading editor, who requested us to withhold his name from publication. "I have given your next line of action some serious consideration," said another, "and I don't see why you shouldn't add a clause to your next appeal, providing that no person who is a taxpayer shall be denied the right to vote on account of sex." Then another, the Governor of Oregon, said, alluding to the above suggestion, "Wouldn't it be a good plan to add a tax-paying clause, that will interest the women, and men also, so they'll start a controversy outside of your suffrage organization? That question will compel the women to think about 'taxation without representation', and when they go to the office of the County Clerk to pay their taxes, they will pay them under protest."

GROUP OF EQUAL SUFFRAGISTS

MINERVA HENDERSHOTT EATON
Leading Suffragist of Eastern Oregon
& Prohibitionist

MRS. IMOGENE BATH
Auditor of Oregon Equal Suffrage
Association

MRS. LOUISE BRYANT TEULLINGER
Noted Press Correspondent of Portland,
Oregon. An Active Suffragist

MRS. SOLOMON HIRSCH
President Portland Equal Suffrage League
and Society Leader

THE LATE MRS. H. A. LOUGHARY
A Prominent Oregon Suffragist and Path-
breaker of 1879

MRS. MINNIE WASHBURNE
President of Lane County Equal Suffrage
Association. Republican

MRS. KATE BONHAM
Financial Secretary of State Equal Suffrage
Association

I laid these ideas before the next meeting of the Board; and, although the proposition was not intended to forestall further attempts to secure full suffrage as our ultimate object, we concluded to try a half-step under the following initiative petition:

"To the Honorable F. W. Benson, Secretary of State of the State of Oregon:

"We, the undersigned, citizens and legal voters of the State of Oregon, respectfully demand that the following proposed amendment to the Constitution shall be submitted to the legal voters of the State of Oregon, for-their approval or rejection, at the regular general election to be held on the 8th day of November, A. D. 1910, and each for himself says: I have personally signed this petition. I am a legal voter of the State of Oregon; my residence and postoffice address are correctly given after my name.

TAXPAYERS' SUFFRAGE AMENDMENT.

Section 2 of Article II of the Constitution of the State of Oregon shall be and hereby is amended to read as follows:

"Section 2. In all elections not otherwise provided for by this Constitution, every citizen of the United States, of the age of 21 years and upwards, who shall have resided in the State during the six months immediately preceding such election, and every person of foreign birth of the age of 21 years and upward, who shall have resided in this State during the six months immediately preceding such election, and shall have declared his intention of becoming a citizen of the United States, one year preceding such election, conformable to the laws of the United States on the subject of naturalization, shall be entitled to vote at all elections authorized by law. It is expressly provided hereby, that no citizen who is a taxpayer shall be denied the right to vote on account of sex."

It was also decided to make only such noise about

the next campaign as would be necessary to make each step of our proceedings legal.

Petitions, validating our next amendment campaign, were gathered with little difficulty. The taxpaying clause appealed satisfactorily to business men, who had begun to fear what they called "freak legislation," which appeared to be making progress among irresponsible and nomadic citizens, under the Initiative and Referendum. Our 38th Annual Meeting was held November 28, 1908, in the Convention Hall of the Portland Commercial Club, and was largely attended by a well-pleased audience. We did not meet in the evening as a delegated body, the annual election having been effected by correspondence, under the able management of Miss Myrtle Pease, Corresponding Secretary; Mrs. A. Bonham, Financial Secretary, and Miss Elma Buckman, Recording Secretary, who counted and ratified the votes.

The speakers of the evening were Reverend J. Whitcomb Brougher, Reverend W. R. Bishop, Miss Myrtle E. Pease, Reverend Harrison Barrett, Clara B. Colby, and Abigail Scott Duniway.

* * *

The following Open Letter was officially ordered by the Executive Committee to be sent to as many leading business men of the State as we could reach by post, calling attention to the following facts, compiled from historic records of all countries, by Alice Stone Blackwell, editor of "The Woman's Journal," and Recording Secretary of the National Woman Suffrage Association:

Portland, Oregon, ———, 1909.

Dear and Honored Sir:

Anticipating our Equal Suffrage Campaign Election, it has been officially planned to memorialize yourself, and as many other leading business men of the State as we can reach with the following statistical information:

"Seventy years ago, women could not vote anywhere, except to a very limited extent in Sweden, and a few other places in the Old World. In 1838, Kentucky gave School Suffrage to widows with children of school age. In 1850, Ontario gave it to women, both married and single. In 1861, Kansas gave it to all women. In 1867, New South Wales gave women Municipal Suffrage. In 1869, England gave Municipal Suffrage to single women and widows. In that year, Victoria gave it to women, both married and single, and Wyoming gave full Suffrage to all women. In 1871, West Australia gave Municipal Suffrage to women. School Suffrage was granted in 1875 by Michigan and Minnesota; in 1873 by Colorado; in 1877, by New England; in 1878, by New Hampshire and Oregon; in 1879, by Massachusetts; in 1880, by New York and Vermont.

"Municipal ballot was granted South Australia in 1880. In 1881, Municipal Suffrage was granted to single women and widows of Scotland. Nebraska gave women School Suffrage in 1883. Municipal Suffrage was given by Ontario and Tasmania in 1884, and by New Zealand and New Brunswick in 1886. In 1887, Municipal Suffrage was granted in Kansas, Nova Scotia and Manitoba, and School Suffrage in South Dakota, Montana, Arizona and New Jersey. In the same year, Montana gave taxpaying women the right to vote upon all questions submitted to taxpaying citizens.

"In 1888, England gave women County Suffrage, and British Columbia and the Northwest Territory gave them Municipal Suffrage. In 1889, County Suffrage was given to the women of Scotland, and Municipal Suffrage to single women and widows in the Province of Quebec. In 1891, School Suffrage was granted in Illinois. In 1893, School Suffrage was granted in Connecticut, and full Suffrage in Colorado and New Zealand. In 1894, School Suffrage was granted in Ohio, Bond Suffrage in Iowa, and Parish and District Suffrage in England, to women, both married and single. In 1885, full Suffrage was granted in South Australia to women. In 1896 full Suffrage was granted in Utah and Idaho.

"In 1898, the women of Ireland were given the right to vote for all offices, except members of Parliament; Minnesota gave women the right to vote for library trustees; Delaware gave School Suffrage to taxpaying women; France gave women engaged in commerce the right to vote for Judges of the Tribunal of Commerce, and Louisiana gave taxpaying women the right to vote on all questions submitted to taxpayers. In 1900 Wisconsin gave women School Suffrage, and West Australia granted full Suffrage to women, both married and single.

"In 1901, New York gave taxpaying women, in all towns and villages of the state, the right to vote on all questions of local taxation; Norway gave them Municipal Suffrage, and the Kansas Legislature voted down almost unanimously 'amid a ripple of amusement,' a proposal to repeal Municipal Suffrage. In 1902, full Municipal Suffrage was granted to all women in Federated Australia, and State Suffrage to the women of New South Wales; in 1903, Bond Suffrage was granted to the women of Kansas, and Tasmania gave women full Suffrage. In 1905, Queensland gave women full Suffrage. In 1906, Finland gave full Suffrage to women, and made them eligible to all offices, from members of Parliament down.

"In 1907, Norway gave full Parliamentary Suffrage to the 300,000 women who already had Municipal Suffrage, Sweden made women eligible to Municipal Office, Denmark gave women the right to vote for members of Boards of Public Charities, and to serve on such Boards, and England, with only 15 dissenting votes, out of the 675 members of the House of Commons, made women eligible as Mayors, Aldermen, County and Town Council-

lors. In 1898 Denmark gave women the right to vote
for all offices except members of Parliament, and Michigan had just adopted a new constitution, containing a
clause granting Suffrage to taxpaying women."

With these facts before us, added to the recent remarkable progress of the movement of the Municipality
of Chicago, the adoption of full Suffrage in the whole of
Federated Australia, and the activity of the leaders of the
movement in Washington, California and Oregon, with
the enfranchised States of Colorado, Wyoming, Utah and
Idaho, laughing in their sleeves at the men of Oregon,
whom they accused of being afraid of the women of their
household, and giving that accusation as a reason for
men having voted us down last June, we believe the time
has come to so far respect the conservatism of the voters
of our state as to offer them a compromise. We are, therefore, asking them for a constitutional amendment, providing that no citizen who is a taxpayer shall be denied the
elective franchise on account of sex.

We are not proposing to govern men. All we ask
is the power to march, side by side, with our husbands,
fathers, brothers and sons, enjoying, equally with them,
the rights made necessary to us by the changed conditions
of modern times, which have driven so many women out
of homes into the business and wage-earning world, in
defense of homes and property rights, which they are
paying taxes to maintain.

We have thousands of women who pay taxes, mostly
upon little homes or lines of business they are conducting
for support of themselves and families, who are looking
eagerly for the enactment of a law or amendment to the
Constitution, in accord with the foregoing facts. We
would respectfully request your aid in securing the passage of such an amendment, thus relieving us and you
of the necessity of continuing the expenditure of further
effort by our weary workers for liberty along this line.

The slogan of our campaign is, "No Taxation Without Representation." The eyes of the enfranchised women of the four states to the east of us, and those of the enfranchised women of the world, are turned with patriotic interest upon Oregon. She alone holds the key to the present situation in the United States of America. It rests with her voters to decide whether she will take the lead in this important progressive movement or leave the honor of victory to Washington, Montana or California, which are now marching in our rear, hoping to overtake and distance us in the race toward liberty, which we believe public-spirited Oregonians will not permit.

Respectfully submitted by the Oregon State Equal Suffrage Association.

ABIGAIL SCOTT DUNIWAY, *President.*

MYRTLE E. PEASE, *Corresponding Secretary.*

SARAH A. EVANS, *Member of National Committee by favor of the State President.*

CHAPTER XIX.

Is Prohibition Wise?—A Reactionary Struggle.

EVERYTHING in human experience emphasizes the fact, that when any particular craze takes possession of the minds of any considerable portion of the people, the men and women who are its chief promoters become incapable of coherent reasoning, and many of their followers, unconsciously to themselves, become the victims of hallucinations that overstep rational bounds. Previous to the delivery of an address, as recorded in a foregoing chapter, I had fully expected the National Woman Suffrage platform to remain as I had found it in former years, an open court, where the leading advocates of votes for women could assemble annually to discuss every phase of the movement, with an eye single only to the best means for its promotion, including the fearless discussion of every difficulty to be met and overcome. But I was destined to be cured of my delusion as to the righteousness of the motives of the prohibition movement, when Dr. Anna Shaw, now President of the National American Woman Suffrage Association, came into our Equal Suffrage field as a National Officer of the Woman's Christian Temperance Union. It was not till much experience in my vocation as publisher and editor of "The New Northwest," and much activity as a public lecturer, that my mental eyes were opened to the broader vision that enabled me to rise above the narrow light that led me to behold at last the vast area of human needs to which the average reformer is too often blinded by the one-idead craze of a narrow environment.

The women of Washington Territory were enfranchised in November, 1883, by legislative enactment.

At that time there was no general alarm among business men, and their great army of coadjutors—the moderate drinkers, who, though opposed to prohibition, are recognized as men of temperate habits. There was then no apparent probability of an uprising, engendered by clergymen, fostered by politicians and inflamed by women, which would cause such an upheaval among voters as would end, as it did, in the disfranchisement of the women of Washington Territory, on the threshold of Statehood, and create a nation-wide uprising against Equal Suffrage among men engaged in the liquor traffic and their immense array of manufacturers, consumers and supporters, beginning in the soil and ranging through all the ramifications of commerce and trade.

A FACT OF HISTORY.

The following public address exhausted the Sunday and weekly editions of "The Oregonian" at the time of its republication under the unusual excitement of prohibition in 1906. It has been so often called for since out of print, and especially since the defeats of the Equal Suffrage Amendment in Oregon in 1906-08-09-10, caused as nobody disputes by the combined efforts of professional prohibition leaders and the voting adherents of the liquor interests (the former championed by a preacher of some prominence, and the latter by a notoriety-seeking woman, whose motives were too transparent to deceive any intelligent person) that its reproduction in this history has become imperative.

It was first given before the annual convention of the National Woman Suffrage Association in Washington, D. C., in February, 1889, and was afterwards circulated, through thousands of leaflets, in the Equal Suffrage campaign of Oregon of 1900.

My theme was "Ballots and Bullets," and I said:

Madam President: In presenting my theme before this convention, I realize the magnitude of my task as I rise to perform the most irksome and yet the most necessary duty that has ever devolved upon me since the beginning of my public career.

It is an easy matter to address an assembly like this along the lines which custom has made comparatively popular; but necessity now demands a deviation from established usage; and it has become the duty of an humble leader, coming from the confines of the far Pacific, to discover and divulge the fact that the present lines of action (as approved by a majority of our beloved and respected co-workers on the Eastern border) is not the policy for the great National Woman Suffrage Association to pursue to win. For this reason, this humble leader must sound an alarm. She sees that our ships are being scuttled, and she would be recreant to every duty to which her sacred obligation calls her, did she hesitate to speak the truth, the whole truth and nothing but the truth; and that is what, with the help of God, I shall try to do tonight.

I confess that I enjoy a controversy with an enemy. I like to puncture his pet prejudices and play havoc with his hoary sophistries. But when I am called, by the sacredness of my trust, to differ from friends whom I love, and show them that their zeal is out-running their discretion; that their efforts are acting as boomerangs to batter down our own breast-works and lay them in ruins at our feet, I realize the peril of my position, and would gladly delegate my duty to another, if one could be found who would undertake to perform it.

Oregon is the mother state of the Pacific Coast, and originally embraced the present states of Washington, Idaho and much of Montana. School suffrage was granted to the women of Oregon, Washington and Idaho, almost without the asking, prior to 1883, when full suffrage was given to the women of Washington Territory by legislative enactment, amid almost universal rejoicing.

It is a matter of history that for fifteen years prior to that enactment, your humble speaker had traveled, alone, over Oregon, Washington and Idaho, enduring toil, hardship, privation, ridicule, sneers and vituperation, and steadily overcoming all sorts of obstacles. It was through these experiences that I learned the necessity of using the same tact in dealing with men, in all our work for ballots, that nations had long before learned to exhaust, when dealing with each other, before resorting to force, or the argument of bullets.

Every woman knows she cannot rule her own husband. The man who would consent to be ruled by his wife (if against his will) would be so poor an excuse for manhood that she wouldn't consider him worth corralling in the chimney corner after somebody had driven him home. What is true of men in the abstract is equally true of men in the aggregate. Learning this fact, I proceeded, very early in my public career, to make the most of it; so I said everywhere, "Gentlemen, in our demand for the ballot we are not seeking to rule over you. We only ask for our enfranchisement because we desire freedom for ourselves. We recognize your right to liberty and the pursuit of happiness, with yourselves as the only proper judges of your own methods in that pursuit. And we most earnestly and respectfully demand a like recognition, on your part, of our right to the pursuit of liberty and happiness for ourselves, by methods of our own choosing, so long as they do not conflict with your prerogatives."

The Declaration of Independence and Preamble to the Constitution of the United States formed the basis of my many sermons through all those weary years. If any other line of argument had been pursued we could have made no headway with our voters; for you must yet learn to bear in mind, my sisters, one fact of which most of you seem strangely to have lost sight: we can only secure our right to vote by and through the consent of voters; and we have only gone ahead in the prosecution of our case when we have succeeded in gaining men's consent. Whenever our demand for our right to vote is based upon an alleged purpose to take away from men any degree of what they deem their liberties, or own right of choice, we simply throw boomerangs that recoil upon our own heads.

Every woman who stands behind the prison bars of her present political environment, reaching her manacled hands to men, who hold the key to the locked gates of constitutional law, through which she alone can gain her liberty, and says to them, "Give us the ballot, and we'll put down your whiskey!" only arouses a thousand men to say by their votes, "Very well, we won't give you the ballot and that will settle it. You sha'n't have it at all if you are going to use it as a whip over us."

And right here, in the face and eyes of the temporarily fashionable fad of prohibition, I declare that as a temperance woman, I am opposed to prohibition on principle. I have raised to manhood a large family of sober sons, who have wended their way to school and office, past the drug store and the groggery, all their lives. I never preached prohibition to them and never talked temperance in their hearing, except occasionally to say (alluding to some drunken man), "Boys, you know that if you should go astray, the world would say it was your mother's fault. She has dared to deviate from established custom by publicly advocating woman's right to equality with man before the law. Men say boys are what their mothers make them and I accept the verdict. If you go wrong, your mother will bear the full blame for her own failure to make you what you ought to have been."

Madam President, that was always argument enough.

My boys needed no prohibitory law to keep them sober, nor will the son of any woman whose guiding star is liberty and self-dependence. I have always left money, sweetmeats and other things that other people's children might be tempted to steal, within my children's reach. I would say by word and deed, "I trust you," and they were proud to prove worthy of the trust. It is liberty that the mothers of children need; then responsibility and self-dependence naturally follow. But I recognize the right of others to hold different views, even if wrong; and their right to exercise their opinions is as sacred to me as my own, so long as they do not, by a mistaken policy, overthrow a greater work through their excess of zeal.

At the time the women of Washington Territory received enfranchisement—on the 23rd day of November, 1883, when Governor Newell signed the suffrage bill amid the mingled hallelujahs of Olympia's guns and bells—the Woman's Christian Temperance Union was of recent origin on the Coast, and was looked upon by the mass of voters in the Pacific Northwest as being quite as harmless in its way as the average woman's prayer meeting. Its rank and file were not suffragists. They had never lifted voice or finger to secure their right to vote, but had often sat in the sanctuary singing, "Where Is My Wandering Boy Tonight," when the little hoodlum was kicking up a rumpus at my suffrage meetings.

A constitutional amendment for extending the right of suffrage to women was pending in Oregon at the time the women of Washington Territory were enfranchised, and great caution was needed, lest by excess of newly awakened prohibition zeal, we should scare the voters into ambush, where, behind the coverts of the law, they would be on the alert to strike us down. I had already scented the lurking danger that menaced us from the coverts of the liquor power—not liquor sellers only, for their numbers are limited, but liquor buyers and drinkers, who comprise everywhere the very large majority of the voters. So I came over here to our National Convention in 1884, and by the co-operation of our suffrage forces organized a "still hunt" campaign of our own, through which I verily believe we would have been successful at the June election of that year if it had not been for the Woman's Christian Temperance Union, which, though feeble in Oregon, was reinforced by hired lecturers from the East, who held suffrage meetings of their own in the interest of prohibition agitators, which nullified our "still hunt" method, and quite naturally aroused the ballot-handed liquor league, and its constituents, the voters, against us almost as a unit, everywhere.

I had previously made arrangements with the Republican and Democratic central and county committees of Oregon by which, if the W. S. A. would furnish the ballots ready printed, they would handle "yes" tickets in such a way that fair play could be secured for us at the ballot boxes, and these committees, in turn, authorized the local committees of both parties to furnish bands and halls for the immense meetings of the campaign that awaited me at the county seats all over the state. I remember such a meeting at Pendleton, one of our principal eastern Oregon towns. A crowd had gathered at the opera house, the band was in attendance, vocal music by local talent was provided, and when the lecture hour came I made my way with great difficulty through the throng to the platform. There I was met by the excellent wife of the Congregational minister, president of the newly organized local W. C. T. U., who had never attempted to attend a suffrage meeting before in her life. This lady informed me that Mrs. Mary Clement Leavitt was present; that she had been speaking for several evenings in the church to a small W. C. T. U. audience, and she wanted her to be heard, before leaving the town, by the general public. Though I knew that I would not at that time have been allowed to speak on the W. C. T. U. platform at all for fear I should say "ballot," I could not afford to violate a principle of liberty by checking freedom of speech on a suffrage platform. So I asked Mrs. Leavitt to the seat beside me. Then, after an hour's talk by myself on the fundamental principles of a republican form of government, during which men frequently tossed their hats to the ceiling in token of their appreciation of our cause, I introduced Mrs. Leavitt as "a distinguished 'round-the-world ambassador of the Woman's Christian Temperance Union, who hailed from Boston." The dear little one-idead woman came to the front and said: "The Woman's Christian Temperance Union, which I have the honor to represent, is not a Woman Suffrage Association. The vast majority of our women are vehemently opposed to woman suffrage. They claim that our work is devotional and religious, while the woman suffrage work is, as you know, political. But our leaders have learned, to our sorrow, that we can do very little toward securing prohibitory legislation, before Congress or legislatures, because women do not have votes. So we are gradually learning to accept woman suffrage as 'a short-cut to prohibition.' "

When the speaker took her seat the band began playing (to drown my effort to reply) and the crowd filed out, leaving that great audience of voters, two-thirds of whom were probably full of whiskey to their necks, to organize against us secretly, which they did to such purpose, all over the state, that when election day came, a few weeks later, every man who could be bought, cajoled or prejudiced against our amendment was voted, by their orders, against our unballoted hosts, while we sat with "our hands on our mouths and our mouths in the dust," in powerless despair, our work of years overthrown in a day, while the Woman's Christian Temperance Union remained as benignantly and self-righteously oblivious to the ruin it had aroused the enemy to bring down upon our devoted heads as Mrs. Leary's cow.*

But we still had hopes for Washington Territory, where the women had secured full suffrage before its W. C. T. U. was out of its swaddling clothes. Women were voters in that Territory for three and a half years, notwithstanding the fact that repeated unsuccessful attempts to defeat them were made by men—attempts which nobody could parry but those who were acquainted with all the leading politicians, and knew every inch of the ground. It is needless to say to this convention that the attempts of leading men and women to secure a constitutional convention of woman suffragists was frustrated at this critical period by the untimely invasion of Mrs. Clara B. Colby and other self-imported Eastern Suffragists, who created a "hurrah" campaign that completed the ruin the W. C. T. U. had begun.

In January, 1886, when Washington was on the eve of Statehood, a Legislature met which had been chosen at the election of 1885, largely by women's ballots. Both political parties had endorsed woman suffrage during the campaign, and the security of the measure seemed permanent. But in the meantime the prohibition wave that had arisen in the East, had swept over the women and preachers of the churches, and designing politicians, the kicked-outers of other political parties, massed themselves among them as its leaders. Clergymen who, by the very nature of their calling, are as full of impracticable business methods as inexperienced women, combined their forces all over the territory as promoters of local option and they said to the Woman's Christian Temperance Union, which they patted, petted, paid and praised, till it was no wonder it thought itself holier than the

---

*It was this cow that kicked over a lamp and created the great Chicago fire.

woman suffragists: "Women are Voters! Now is the time to show the world what you can do with the ballot" —forgetting that no ballot is in force in any State at this date of human development, unless there is a latent bullet behind it.

The Legislature convened at Olympia in the very midst of this excitement, and the Woman's Christian Temperance Union, led by an enthusiastic little lecturer from a little Pennsylvania village, backed secretly by the National Liquor League, which worked hand in glove with it (though it did not know it), had no difficulty in securing just such prohibitory legislation as it asked for under Territorial government, while men who were secretly opposed to prohibition chuckled over their success as strategists, as they prepared to vote it down at the polls.

At that time my own home was over-shadowed by the trailing wing of Azrael. My beloved only daughter was in the last stages of a fatal illness, and my duty kept me at my darling's bedside. Women, wives of the members of the Legislature in some instances, wrote to me, saying: "The cause of woman suffrage is being drawn into a trap! Come over and help us to protest against this prohibition movement, which (under the guise of local option) will surely destroy our suffrages, if it is not checkmated." I answered, "Now is your time to lead. Checkmate this movement while there is yet time! I cannot leave my post at home!" But the husbands of these women would not permit them to act, unless I would lead them, and receive in my own breast all the barbed arrows of the combined whiskey and prohibition elements. And, as no other woman could be found who was willing to meet the crisis, women's freedom went by default, and the frenzied friends of prohibition were made the cat's-paw of the liquor league at its will.

Need I tell you the result? In every precinct, no

matter how the vote on local option went, the women got the blame. If a precinct went wet, prohibition shriekers cried: "There, don't you see that women will not vote our way?" If a town went dry, the men who opposed prohibition would say: "There, we told you so! The women and the preachers are all fanatics together!"

In the spring of 1886, seeing the danger that threatened women's ballots at the next territorial election, I went to Walla Walla to sound the alarm. But I found a boycott against me in all the churches. So I was compelled to go to the residence of the widow of a brewer, from whose husband I had in former years often rented an opera house for suffrage meetings, before church pulpits had been opened to women at all.

The brewer's widow, at first indignantly denied my request. She said, and mark you, Madam President, there is a lesson here: "When we came to Walla Walla, the town was little, and it was dead already, but my husband brought with him ten thousand dollars. I earned more than half of that money myself, a-washin' for miners at Canyon City. But the money was not mine! Women had no rights! So my husband, he start a brewery. He buy the people's barley; he subscribe to churches and bridges and schoolhouses; and by and by he build this brewery. I scolded, for I don't like the business! But what could I do? Women had no rights. By and by he die, and leave me a mortgage of forty thousand dollars. You know he helped you for woman's rights when the churches wouldn't! When the suffrage law was made, I, too, was glad; but now comes prohibition! Women's votes will shut up my business. Interest will come due, I cannot pay. Taxes will come due, I cannot pay. By and by comes a sheriff and turns me and my children in the street. You call it Christianity! I call it robbery! No; you can't have my hall."

I assured her that she greatly misunderstood the

spirit of Christian women (as I then thought I understood it), if she believed that they intended to raid or loot her means of livelihood, and provide her nothing in return! I told her we would gladly help her to pursue a different business, if she would let us; and I added, "Come out tomorrow night and hear me speak in your hall, and I will present your side of the question to the women." She answered like a flash: "You would not dare! Women would ostracize you! You don't know the spirit!"

I assured her that I had dared greater things, and after a little parley I hired her hall for two nights. On the first evening the hall was packed, in spite of opposition meetings held by prohibitionists in all the churches. My theme was "Woman's Opportunity." I told the new voters that the present conflict was forced upon them by the combined efforts of their friends, who were blinded by zeal, and their enemies, who, alert from self-interest, were determined to lead their ballots into a trap. In telling the story of the brewer's widow, I added: "Last night, after I had left her house, I paused on the sidewalk, under the blooming locust trees, and looked up at the moonlight, shimmering through the leaves, and lying in lambent sheen on that brewery, a great pile of mortar and masonry, held down by that widow's mortgage; and I thought 'here is woman's opportunity.' If, instead of joining men in this conflict for prohibition, which, even if successful at the ballot box, cannot be enforced, except by bullets, you will utilize your newly acquired power by forming a corporation to buy or lease that great building —if you will convert it into a cannery, or creamery, or both, and give employment to that woman and her children, and to the wives and children of all the men in your midst, whose means of livelihood are now in jeopardy, the fame of your philanthropy and common sense will go out to other portions of our goodly country and the success of your business methods will inspire the voters of all other states and territories to emulate the example of the men who gave you the ballot. Then, in due time, under the happy environment of a free motherhood, a race of men will spring up who will not be slaves to appetite, and prohibition and drunkenness will die a natural death."

This proposition took immensely with the women that night, but the next morning's papers, after being interviewed by prohibition agitators, contained awful criticisms, under flaring scareheads, accusing me of pandering to the liquor interests; and all the women of the churches, except the leading suffragists, whose protests were lost in the clamor, accepted the story of a whiskey-soaked, loud-mouth prohibition agitator from the brothels and saloons of Portland, who said, "Mrs. Duniway has sold out to whiskey!" and the prohibitionists, repeating the slander, cried, almost with one accord, "Away with such a woman from the earth!"

Dear friends, why prolong the story? That ex-brewer's widow still runs her dead husband's business. The men voters of Oregon and Washington still drink intoxicating liquors whenever so inclined, as they always will, whether women vote or not; and the women ex-voters of the State of Washington find themselves with the iron gates of a state constitution shutting them out from the exercise of their liberties, while they are left to chant mournfully: "Whiskey recovered from the fight; 'twas woman's vote that died!"

As I conclude, I must crave your indulgence while I repeat an illustration often used by myself in that memorable struggle, because I feel that its potency is yet to be required in other places, perhaps for years to come, ere women learn the ins and outs of one-sex politics, against which they seek blindly to do battle, with their own hands in manacles.

The story goes that a man was walking on the beach

and came to a little bayou, leading from the ocean, up which a salmon was struggling, favored by the tide. The man had a scythe on his shoulder. The bayou was so narrow that he could step across it; and with all his mind on the alert, possessed by the one idea that he must have that salmon then and there, he brought down the handle of his scythe to knock the fish upon the head, but it eluded his blow, and the blade of the scythe came down upon his own neck with such force that it severed his head from his shoulders.

Dear friends, let us seek first the kingdom of liberty and its power; then all other blessings can be gradually attained as fast as they can be understood and assimilated by a free people, led by men and women who respect everybody's rights.

If in anything I have said tonight, I have given any one of my sincere co-workers a moment's pain, I can only say I am sorry, but I must not withhold the facts. In spite of our blunders we are marching on! The fiat has gone forth and men and women together will alike be free!

CHAPTER XX.

Affiliation With Prohibition a Blunder.

M Y BELOVED Eastern co-workers, including such eminent women as Lucretia Mott, Lucy Stone, Julia Ward Howe, Susan B. Anthony, Mary A. Livermore, Elizabeth Cady Stanton, Matilda Joselyn Gage, Dr. Clementine Lozier, Frances Dana Gage and Lillie Devereaux Blake, had welcomed me from the Pacific Coast as an important acquisition from a new field of labor. On several occasions, the program committee of the Annual National Conventions had assigned me the position of near, if not actual, valedictorian. I went, therefore, to the platform in 1889, fully imbued with the belief that my coadjutors would receive my message in the same spirit of love for the truth, and for themselves and the cause, in which I had laid other propositions before them.

My address of the evening was received with unbounded approbation from the audience, if one could judge by the applause of the multitude. I was delayed at the close of the meeting by introductions, congratulations, and invitations for lectures in various places till after the other speakers had left the hall, leaving me to return alone to our headquarters at the Riggs House. I was very tired when I reached the hotel, and on entering the dining room for a cup of tea, took a vacant seat at table between Anna Shaw and Susan B. Anthony. Miss Shaw had made her debut on the platform the same evening, speaking before I did, and proving herself a ready, catchy, witty, eloquent and voluble orator. I did not realize at the moment that she was a head officer in the Woman's Christian Temperance Union; therefore, I was quite taken a-back when Miss Anthony, who had evi-

GROUP OF EQUAL SUFFRAGISTS

LATE MRS BESSIE ISAACS SAVAGE
Leading Suffragist of Washington in State
and Territorial Days

MRS INA B. GARRIOTT
Who Initiated Eight-Hour Bill for Oregon's
Working Women, in Oregon
Legislature

MRS ROSS CARTER
Recording Secretary National Council of
Women Voters of Idaho

THE LATE A. H. H. STUART
Olympia, Wash. Mother of Women's Clubs
in Northwest and Co-Worker with Mrs.
Duniway in Founding Equal Suffrage

MRS A. E. CLARK
Active Suffragist of Portland Oregon

ALICE R. NUGENT
President of Oregon's Good
Government Club

THE LATE LILLIE DEVEREAUX BLAKE
A Leading Suffragist of New York

dently begun negotiations with her for coming as a worker into the Woman Suffrage field, said to me, in re-pellant tones, "Mrs. Duniway, you shocked a great many good people by your speech tonight!" "Glad to hear it," I said hastily. "Time was when you shocked good people, and that was the way you got your start." The conversation was changed to other topics; but I could see that I was *de trop*, so I drank my tea and hurried away, realizing that our peerless leader was about to be dominated by a new force, led by a comparatively young, inexperienced but ambitious woman, whose ready-made eloquence and ebullient wit had captivated her physical senses.

I met Miss Anthony in a hotel corridor the next morning and tried in vain to convince her that her proposed new alliance would hinder the enfranchisement of women, which we could never obtain except by a majority of the votes of men. I told her frankly that this alliance would create a conflict between the two opposite extremes of force and freedom, that would defeat them both. But she was obdurate. "If I can reach the women of the churches through the national offices of the W. C. T. U. I shall not hesitate to do it," she said, with emphasis. "But when we get up a conflict between a voteless class and a great political body, armed with ballots, can't you see that the voteless class will get the worst of it?" I asked, my heart thumping hard. She shook her head, and my protest being of no avail, I returned to the Pacific Northwest, and began a diligent search for lines of least resistance.

I had observed that the waters of the great rivers that seek the Pacific Ocean begin as lakes or as rivulets, away up in the fastnesses of the Oregon mountains, receiving the added flow of thousands of affluents in their winding journey toward the sea. I had noticed in my long stage rides, when journeying to distant settlements to carry the gospel of Equal Rights to every accessible

point in my arduous itinerary, that stage coaches, like
rivers, do not waste their energy in futile attacks upon
the steepest and rockiest obstructions, but seek easier
ways to reach their destined goal. Therefore, seeing that
it would be impossible to divert the public mind, or mind
of the average voter, from a belief that women, if enfranchised, would hurl themselves as a unit against obstacles, which, if not overcome, would divert the channels
of trade from natural sources and compel men to seek
a market for the products of the soil into the commercial,
manufacturing and transportation interests, which voteless women are alike powerless to meet, I began to study
and analyze the proposed prohibition of the liquor traffic,
just as I had previously studied and was continuing to
study and analyze the prohibition of woman's right to
vote.

* * *

From an accumulated array of old letters, sufficient
in quantity to fill a half-bushel measure, I have selected
at random some eminent opinions, showing the difficulties
that have lain in the way of the success of the Equal
Suffrage movement, by apparent co-operation between
the opposing principles of force and freedom, which I
shall include herewith as an introduction to arguments
that follow. These will show the need of dispelling almost
universal belief of men engaged in the liquor traffic, and
their numerous, almost universal patrons, the liquor buyers and consumers (whom the agitators of prohibition
perversely ignore) by proving to my readers that women
are as generally divided in their opinions of dealing with
the liquor problems as are men.

The late Henry B. Blackwell, of Boston, leader in
the Equal Suffrage Movement from 1870, writing to me
under date of April 2nd, 1889, speaking both as a Suffragist and Prohibitionist, said, "I fully agree with you
that the Woman's Christian Temperance Union is over-

estimating its political power. It makes a serious mistake in trying to unite its forces with the Woman Suffrage Movement. I know its charge, that you in opposing such an affiliation 'are bribed by the liquor elements,' is a serious one and hard to bear in silence. But such a charge, being false, will die out as time passes, and your work for liberty will be all the stronger when the present fanaticism dies out. Just ignore all such accusations, and simply take pains to show the voters of the Pacific Coast that prohibition does not exist in states where women vote, and that the states where prohibition exists are not under Woman Suffrage."

Lucy Stone Blackwell, wife of Henry B. Blackwell, writing, May 7th following, said: "I regret the attitude of the W. C. T. U. toward you, personally. It is too bad that you have been slurred by it through a paragraph that crept unobserved into an issue of 'The Woman's Journal.' But never mind. You are too well known as a temperance woman, often speaking for it in public, and as the mother of a large family of sober sons who are working with you for Woman Suffrage, to let such accusations annoy you. Prohibition is not the only cure of the drink evil. It is only a method."

The late Susan B. Anthony, writing from San Francisco, in 1896, said: "My personal belief as to prohibition, pro or con, is nobody's business but my own, but I have done all I could to keep the two questions (Woman Suffrage and Prohibition) separate in the California Woman Suffrage Campaign. The two movements cannot successfully unite to win for either cause. But I am glad to see women awakened from their apathy through any movement that is backed by the churches, since so many of them cannot be aroused in any other way. Don't mind it if they do assail you. It will amount to nothing more at last than the fly on the ox's horn."

The late Amasa Scott, writing from Craftsbury, Ver-

mont, April 7th, 1889, said, referring to the foregoing
lecture: "I see the danger that imperils the suffrage
cause through the efforts of women to combine the two
elements of force and freedom. The prohibition movement, which you call 'a craze,' recalls a similar movement in my childhood's days, in Vermont, when a few
pious men became so violently fanatical that they cut
down their apple trees because hard cider was made of
apples, and destroyed their peach trees because the fruit
was used for making brandy. But the agitators came to
their senses after the craze had run its course, and the
present agitation will cease when its chief promoters can
no longer make money by it. Alcohol isn't the only thing
that intoxicates the people. But fanaticism always 'sobers
off' when the stimulant that inspires it has expended its
force. So many women have been impoverished so long
in their homes by drunkenness that it isn't any wonder
they get excited by the preaching of prohibition in pulpits. By putting the collection in their own pockets (as
lecturers) they get a stimulant stronger than whiskey."

The late Laura DeForce Gordon, a pioneer Woman
Suffrage leader, writing from Lodi, Cal., in 1874, said:
"I am, as is well known, an advocate of temperance in all
things; but I am not in favor of the Church's style of
preaching prohibition as we see it done in the nineteenth
century. If I think I need a glass of wine, I do not intend
that any one but myself shall be allowed to say I shall or
shall not take it."

The late Mrs. Sarah Knox Goodrich, writing from
San Jose, Cal., in 1887, said: "I claim the right of every
normal man and woman to judge personally, as to
whether we shall take a drink or not, ourselves only
being the judges. I believe, with you, that drunkenness
is a disease, preventable in its earlier stages, and that its
cure lies in equal rights for women, which are placed at
present in peril by the conflict between Prohibition and

whiskey, in which whiskey holds the mastery through the money power and the power of the ballot."

The late Colonel and Mrs. John A. Collins, of San Francisco, said in a joint letter, written April 2nd, 1874: "The present attitude of the Church toward the prohibition of the liquor traffic, together with its well-known hostility to Woman Suffrage, has created an unfortunate combination in which the party with votes has the chief advantage. The suffrage cause was making splendid headway in California when the Women's Crusade aroused the voting elements of the state against it. This power must be placated in some way before we can get votes enough to win."

The foregoing excerpts, chosen at random from the great pile of letters at my left, are sufficient to show the trend of public sentiment among the leading thinkers of their time who did not hesitate to support my contention that the Woman's Christian Temperance Union in trying to connect the two opposite elements of force and freedom, were indefinitely postponing the day of woman's full enfranchisement.

I am also in possession of many scores of letters from prominent men and women in different cities of Oregon, Washington and Idaho, all in harmony with the quotations above selected; but as most of these writers have not yet passed to the Unseen, and I do not wish to cause any one of them, or their surviving friends, to become such victims as I have been to the fanaticism and falsehoods of the prohibition craze, from which I have long been immune, their names are lovingly withheld in this recital.

I am not attempting, as stated elsewhere in these pages, to compile the facts embodied in this history in exact chronological order. I prefer to place them in the order of their re-unfoldment before me, as I come across them among a necessarily heterogeneous array of

old letters and manuscripts, many of them yellow with age
and some of them so badly faded as to be partly un-
decipherable. My only aim is to state the truth, in which
future historians will bear me out, long after I shall have
passed to the silent majority. The fair-minded men and
women who are prohibitionists at this writing (in this
year of Grace 1914) will after awhile become convinced
of the untenability of the present line of spasmodic efforts
to control the individual will of the people by the vote of
a temporarily excited electorate. They will then have
learned that noisy irresponsible hired agitators will often
secretly disobey the laws they make to govern others;
and having grown weary of the sham, imposition and
failure that result from the brain-storms of fanaticism,
they will turn their attention to human needs, human
desires and human responsibilities, now placed in jeopardy by the substitution of sporadic law.

CHAPTER XXI.

Origin of Woman's Clubs in The Pacific Northwest.

THE following letter is condensed from a reply to a letter received by me from Mrs. Carrie Chapman Catt, a valued friend, who has since become famous and is now the able and popular President of the International Woman Suffrage Association of the World.

As will be seen by quotations following, we had had some differences of opinion over "plans of work in campaign states"; but these differences were happily dissipated as her experience increased; and now, for many succeeding years, our friendship has not suffered a break. The facts of my letter, herewith submitted, are given in this chapter to show that my objections to the imported invasion of outside managers in local campaigns did not begin with Dr. Shaw, although she was as well aware of them before she took charge of our Oregon Equal Suffrage Campaign in 1906, as she was after her methods had caused the defeat of two consecutive campaigns that followed.

My letter to Mrs. Catt was dated August 2nd, 1898, and only that part of it is here given which is necessary to show that I have not changed my original opinion in regard to the management of campaign states up to the time of present writing.

Among other things, I said: "When Miss Anthony was in Portland in 1896, attending the Congress of Women, she told me, as you also have done in writing, that the Idaho people resented the work of the National Association. She said Idaho people had been so 'cranky' about it, that when they did finally make a plan for herself and Anna Shaw to come to Boise for a meeting, 'we just let them alone.'

"I said to Miss Anthony, 'What would you think of the irony of Fate, if Idaho wins and California loses?' She answered, 'Impossible! California is managed by our trained workers from the East.' " I asserted in my letter to Mrs. Catt that the system of invasion by the National W. S. A., into states where amendments had been submitted by the home workers, and sidetracking such workers, was not the true purpose of a national organization. I said: "When a state is pregnant with a pending Equal Suffrage Amendment, our local workers must be supported in their efforts to deliver the goods. To drain the state dry through the efforts of imported workers at such a time is not statesmanlike. * * * Your plans must be reconstructed or they never can become National. * * * When we have great meetings, and invite your workers to come to us, under our supervision, to help us animate public sentiment, it is your duty, as National officers, to respond, and use national funds to meet your expenses.

"It is also your duty to invite our state co-workers to your National Conventions, as Miss Anthony formerly did, and reciprocate the honors we extend to you. * * * The plan for precinct organization after an amendment is submitted, I have always urged; but it should also be managed by home workers, who understand the home situation, and know the home sentiment."

* * *

Early in January, 1897, I was favored with a copy of the Rochester (New York) "Herald," to which I sent the following letter, in reply to a report from our beloved National President, Susan B. Anthony, concerning the way in which the Equal Suffrage Constitutional Amendment was carried in Idaho. The "Herald" said: "She (Miss Anthony) spoke briefly of the work that had been accomplished by the Campaign Committee of the National Association in the interest of Woman Suffrage. She declared that through the Committee's earnest work was due the fact that Idaho had declared in favor of granting the franchise to women." To this I replied, through the "Herald," saying: "While the workers of the East and West are a unit as to the desire of women to secure the ballot, there are radical differences of opinion as to the reasons why the West advances more rapidly in the work than does the East.

"You will see by the enclosed open letter * * * that many years of pioneer work had been done for the Suffrage Cause in Idaho, chiefly among the voters, to bring public sentiment up to a point that would justify them in submitting an amendment to a referendum vote, before any national organization was attempted at all." Continuing, I said: "I would by no means under-rate the work of our co-laborers in the East; but we have other Pacific Coast States to carry, and it is just as necessary for us to keep before the people the fact that we look to voters within the borders of those states for victory, as it was necessary to pursue the same course that has carried Idaho. We all concede the devotion to the cause of our beloved and honored Miss Anthony. We gladly accord to her and her cabinet of co-workers due credit for their earnestness, brilliancy and eloquence. We love them every one, and hope to have them visit us often, as invited guests; but we are thoroughly convinced by our many Western defeats, under their management, that every locality is its own best interpreter of its own plans of work."

In justice to Mrs. Catt, I am proud to record the fact that she appeared before the nominating convention of the two political parties during our Suffrage Campaign in Idaho, and secured the adoption of a resolution in each, asking the support of the voters at the polls. Having accomplished this excellent work, she did not remain to overdo it, but gracefully retired from the state, leaving the cause in control of the people who had created it.

* * *

The Woman's Christian Temperance Union's upheaval was at its height in the Territory of Washington, in the years of 1885 and 1886, and, while men were gathering their forces to defeat the Equal Suffrage law under the constitution of an incubating state, my wide-awake and ever loyal coadjutor, the late Mrs. Abby H. H. Stuart, of Olympia, called upon me one day at the home of Mrs. Clara E. Sylvester, another faithful ally, and stated that it would not be possible to carry the Suffrage Movement to victory by any direct action under present conditions, and she had started the Woman's Club Movement in Olympia as a necessary step in the progress of the cause. I saw at once the force of her logic, but explained that it would be a difficult step for me to take, as I was publishing the Equal Suffrage paper, "The New Northwest," in open advocacy of votes for women, and had burned my bridges behind me. "So much the better!" she explained, with her characteristic animation. "Nobody expects you to change your tactics. You can go right ahead, throwing hot shot wherever you can find a target! The Woman's Club Movement will give women who oppose the Suffrage Movement (or think they do) an opportunity to divest themselves of their prejudices."

I do not remember that Mrs. Sylvester, a prominent Suffragist, approved the plan at the time, or that she ever united with the Woman's Club Movement; but Mrs. Stuart's idea, which struck me as both logical and necessary (because of such facts as are fully recorded elsewhere), came opportunely to rescue the Suffrage Movement from a deadlock, from which there seemed to be no way of escape till Mrs. Stuart found a way. Her original Club consisted of fifty women of the little capital city

of Olympia, and was organized along lines that were national and have always been practical.

* * *

The Equal Suffrage Cause had become almost quiescent in Oregon for the same reason that had led voters to
forsake the cause in the Territory of Washington. So I
corresponded frequently with Mrs. Stuart about starting
up the Club Movement in my own state. But it was not
until the spring of 1894, that we thought the time had
come to begin our initial club work in Oregon.

When Mrs. Stuart came to Portland for this purpose,
we did not deem it wise to call a meeting at my home,
known everywhere as Equal Suffrage Headquarters, nor
did we think it best for me to appear at the preliminary
meeting. But, after the first meeting, held at the home of
the late Mrs. W. W. Spaulding, and after Mrs. Stuart had
returned to her home, I thought I could risk attending
the next one, which convened in the parlors of the Hotel
Portland, where, at my solicitation, approved, as I distinctly remember, by motion of Mrs. L. W. Sitton, I had
the honor to name the second and fourth Fridays of the
month as our regular Club days, and to announce our
purpose to inaugurate the movement on planks so broad
that every woman, no matter what her belief on other
questions, could unite with all of us by excluding "politics, temperance and religion." I also had the honor of
being the first woman in Oregon to suggest the formation
of the State Federation of Woman's Clubs, which I did
at that meeting.

But my example as a club woman didn't always agree
with my precepts, and I was frequently called to order by
some good suffragist, and was sometimes deeply humili-
ated as a result of throwing hot shot, myself, among
women, who for a long time went out of their way to
emphasize their thought that they were opposed to Equal

Rights for their sex, which, nevertheless, they were unconsciously promoting. A prominent leader in this opposing faction was the late lamented Mrs. J. C. Card, the first President of the Portland Woman's Club, a capable and useful leader, and my personal friend, over whose prejudice against votes for women, I would sometimes rap her with good-natured raillery. She passed away in the midst of her social usefulness, during my term as President of the Club, and no one mourned or missed her more sincerely than myself. She always said she would vote if she had the chance, but was opposed to getting the chance, or permitting any other woman to get it.

The early demise of Mrs. A. H. H. Stuart cut short her hope of seeing the enfranchisement of women in Washington and Oregon; though she was gladdened before her transition with the success of the Movement in Idaho, for which she always gave grateful credit to my analysis of prohibition before the Constitutional Convention at Boise in 1889. The women of the Pacific Coast owe to her memory a debt of lasting gratitude.

* * *

It was my good fortune to attend the Annual Meeting of the Oregon Federation of Woman's Clubs in 1913, at Hood River, where an opportunity was given me, as its first Honorary President, to pay tribute to the memory of the deceased members of the Federation, who had shared with Mrs. Stuart and myself the secret of our original intention in starting the Club Movement. I had the melancholy pleasure of eulogizing at that meeting the late Mrs. E. L. Smith of Hood River, whose acquaintance I had formed in Olympia in 1871, at the time of my first visit to the Legislature of Washington in the company of Susan B. Anthony. Mrs. Smith became identified with the Suffrage Movement during that visit and continued my consistent co-worker and friend to the day of her death in Oregon. Like Mrs. Stuart and myself, she believed the Suffrage Cause could be best promoted by following the lines of least resistance, and for that reason became an active club woman, whose good husband and surviving daughters always sustained her loyally.

Our next important loss to Equal Suffrage and the Club Movement during the year 1913, came in the passing of Mrs. Myrtle Pease-Hatfield, who became a leading club woman of Forest Grove at the time of her marriage, and so continued up to the time of her tragic and untimely death. She became Corresponding Secretary of the State Equal Suffrage Association at the time of our open rupture with the Woman's Christian Temperance Union, in the fall of 1906. (See Chapter XXIII.)

The State Equal Suffrage Association never had much money. Its annual membership of one dollar, not meeting the greater part of its expenditures, compelled us to rely upon the independent contributions of progressive people of all associations, or beliefs, of "whatever name or nature"; and our Executive Committee gladly permitted Miss Pease to accept a salaried position of the Boys & Girls Aid Society, under whose auspices she traveled over the state for six consecutive years, bringing us frequent tidings of the quiet progress of the Equal Suffrage Movement among the voters in almost every county. To the quiet and logical presentation of the Suffrage cause among men, wherever her other duties called her, the women of Oregon owe more gratitude for their enfranchisement than to any other agency, except that accorded by the state to my unaspiring self.

Deep gratitude is also due to the memory of Mrs. W. W. Spaulding, under whose auspices our movement was inaugurated. Mrs. Spaulding had long been a widow, and was childless,—the death of her only son having preceded that of her husband by many years. As a Club Woman, she was active and aggressive till failing health compelled her retirement, though she often chuckled quietly over the progress the Equal Suffrage Cause was making under another name.

The next shining light to pass from our Woman's Club in Portland, was Mrs. Julia H. Bauer, with whom I had become a co-worker in the Suffrage cause in Walla Walla in 1872. Mrs. Bauer joined the State Equal Suffrage Association after coming to Portland to reside, a few years later. She became an active member of the Woman's Club, and was widely known as a Shakespearean interpreter and Esperanto teacher. Her eldest daughter, Emilie Frances Bauer, who now resides in New York, has acquired international fame as a musical critic and literary analyst.

Our next shining light to be called from the Woman's Club Movement into the higher life, was Mrs. Elizabeth Lord, of The Dalles, Vice-President of the State Equal Suffrage Association. Mrs. Lord was a woman of majestic presence and splendid literary attainments, a pioneer of the early '40s. As a leader in every good work in her home city, she allied herself with the Club Movement, as so many others had done for the primal purpose of promoting the Suffrage cause. Her beautiful home was always the center of hospitality, kindly cheer and literary advancement.

It now becomes my melancholy pleasure to name in this connection the untimely passing of Mrs. Martha A. Dalton, a charter member of the Portland Woman's Club, and distinguished as one of the three founders of the Oregon State Equal Suffrage Association. She was for seven years the Chairman of the Club's Federation Headquarters at the Annual Meeting of the Willamette Valley Chautauqua Association, where she became widely acquainted with men and women of national reputation. Of dear, devoted Mrs. Dalton, to whose memory my tears are falling as I write, I can say, as I change the subject, that no matter who else might forsake her original standard bearer, she was always true. She remained a member of the Executive Committee of the State Equal Suffrage Association up to the time of her death; and, though a prohibitionist, always agreed with my efforts to hold the Suffrage Movement aloof from affiliation with the Woman's Christian Temperance Union, after it got into politics.

* * *

It was my destiny to be elected as seventh president of the Portland Woman's Club at the regular election in June, 1902. I could not have been more astonished at this election than if I had been suddenly appointed as Minister Plenipotentiary to the Court of King James. I was not in good health. My long vigil during my husband's illness had left me a widow in 1896, heartbroken, and an easy prey to ailments similar to those that befall an overworked stage horse, which limps along in the harness for years without the possibility of being turned out to grass. But I had kept up my correspondence with leading voters in Oregon, Idaho and Washington to such an extent that I was hardly thinking any more about the need of a Woman's Club Movement, when I received a telephone message one day from Mrs. A. H. Breyman, a gifted member of its Board, urging me to attend the election. I hurriedly obeyed the summons, but did not reach the meeting till the ballots were counted, naming me as President, and Mrs. Sarah A. Evans (afterwards President of the State Federation) as Vice-President of an influential body of women of which I was made Honorary President, being so elected for life. I am pleased to add that the Federation is the most popular and influential body of women in Oregon. It is still nonpartisan, but its members wield a vast influence for good, as voters.

CHAPTER XXII.

The National Convention Meets in Oregon.

MUCH to the relief of our patient State Executive Committee, the Initiative and Referendum Amendment to the State Constitution was adopted by the voting element at the general election in 1902, enabling our coadjutors to emerge from ambush under a new departure for which we had been quietly working since our near-victory of 1900, which had brought us to within less than two per cent of a majority vote. This amendment having been declared constitutional by the State Supreme Court, permitted us to escape into the open with comparative safety, since all controversy over the necessity of securing a two-thirds majority of all the votes cast by men at the previous election upon any other question than Equal Suffrage, though silent on this one proposition, should be counted among the "noes."

We, therefore, decided to resubmit our amendment thereafter, whenever necessary, by petition, hoping that we might get it on the ballot for a general election, the next one to be that of 1904. But again, our real opponents, of the prohibition party, proved their determination to prohibit Equal Suffrage by elbowing our workers aside, until after it was too late to secure final acceptance of our petition by the Secretary of State within the legal time limit. We, therefore, decided to postpone further open agitation till the time should approach for preparation for the June election of 1906. It was vainly hoped that, before the next election, the prohibition question, which had come up in local option form, would be settled and out of our way.

* * *

In the meantime, the 37th Annual Convention of the National American Woman Suffrage Association met in Portland, from June 28th to July 5th, inclusive, in 1905, in a convention which disarranged our plans. This convention was held in the beautiful First Congregational Church, Park and Madison Streets, and was largely attended at every session. Susan B. Anthony, our beloved National Honorary President, favored every session with her gracious presence and made many brief, witty and reminiscent remarks, delighting all who heard her.

Mrs. Carrie Chapman Catt, a noted National leader, spoke frequently, her charming presence and irrefutable logic being met with unstinted praise. Dr. Anna Shaw, the brilliant National President, eloquent attache and afterwards legatee of Miss Anthony, was in her glory.

Alice Stone Blackwell, the able and indefatigable Recording Secretary of the National Association, daughter of Henry B. and Lucy Stone Blackwell, and editor of the "Woman's Journal" of Boston, was a conspicuous figure, whose unique way of calling attention to her newspaper was amusing, attractive and original.

Cora Smith Eaton (King), a young, vivacious and pretty physician, and Laura Clay, relative of Henry Clay, a stately, earnest and logical advocate, were introduced as National Auditors and made happy responses.

The convention was called to order at the opening session by President Shaw. Prayer was offered by Reverend Elwin House, pastor of the church. Greetings were offered by Dr. Viola M. Coe on behalf of the Oregon Equal Suffrage Association. Responses followed by Mrs. Mary Woods Swift of the National Council of Women; Mrs. Lucia Faxon Additon, for the National Woman's Christian Temperance Union; Mrs. Clara H. Waldo, for the National Grange; Mrs. F. Foos, for the National Federation of Labor; Mrs. Nella H. Lamson,

Group of Equal Suffragists

MISS FLORENCE ROBERTS
Idaho President of National Council of
Women Voters

MRS. EMMA SMITH DEVOE
Who Led the Equal Suffrage Campaign for
Washington in 1910. President Na-
tional Council of Women Voters

BERTHA KNOTVOLD MELLETT
Member of Executive Committee of
National Council of Women Voters,
Tacoma, Wash.

SENATOR JAMES H. BRADY
Ex-Governor and Present U. S. Senator of
Idaho. Chairman and Founder of the
National Council of Women Voters

MRS. C. H. McMAHON
Auditor National Council of Women
Voters, Salt Lake City, Utah

VIOLA MAY COE, M. D.
Acting President who led Equal Suffrage
to Victory in 1912. Oregon's President
of National Council of Women Voters

DR. CORA SMITH KING
Treasurer National Council of Women
Voters, Washington, D. C.

for Ladies of the Maccabees; Mrs. A. H. Breyman, for
the Forestry Association, and Dr. Mary A. Thompson
for the Henry George League. Abigail Scott Duniway's
Centennial Ode, inspired by the Lewis and Clark Exposition, was read in a masterly manner by Mrs. Sylvia
McGuire.

The evening session was opened by prayer, offered
by Rabbi Stephen S. Wise of the Synagogue Beth Israel,
now of New York. Addresses of welcome were offered
by Governor George E. Chamberlain (afterwards United
States Senator); Mr. T. C. Devlin, representing Hon.
George H. Williams (Mayor of Portland, who was ill);
Hon. Jefferson Myers of the Lewis and Clark Exposition,
and Abigail Scott Duniway for the Pioneers of the Pacific Northwest. The response by Carrie Chapman Catt
was an appropriate and eloquent expression of welcome
from the National Vice-President at Large. Music, by
Masters Wayne and Earl Coe, was a marked feature of
the evening, and the annual address of President Shaw
was a comprehensive review of the National and International progress of the Equal Suffrage Movement.

The business session of Friday morning was opened
with prayer, offered by Reverend H. M. Barden. Henry
B. Blackwell, of Boston senior editor of the "Woman's
Journal," gave a report on Presidential Suffrage for
Women, and Ida Porter Boyer, of Pennsylvania, reported
for National Libraries. The reports of State Presidents
of Suffrage Associations were submitted in person or by
proxy by Frances Griffin of Alabama, Lydia Robinson
of Arizona, Mary Simpson Sperry of California, Minerva
C. Welch of Colorado, Isabella Beecher Hooker of Connecticut, Martha Cranston of Delaware, Mary C. Talbot
of District of Columbia, Rose Y. Colvin of Georgia,
Marion K. Bowles of Illinois, Mary J. Coggeshall of Iowa.

The evening session, Carrie Chapman Catt presiding,
was opened by Father Black of Portland, who offered

prayer. Eloquent and logical addresses were given by Ida Husted Harper of Indiana, Colonel C. E. S. Wood of Oregon, and Mary C. C. Bradford of Colorado. Mrs. Evan Spettinger, of Portland, gave a delightful reading, followed by congregational singing of "America" and benediction by Reverend Eliza Tupper Wilkse of California.

The Friday afternoon session convened at the Exposition Grounds, at which the State Federation of Women's Clubs was represented by Mrs. Sarah A. Evans, the Woman's Christian Temperance Union by Mrs. Lucia Faxon Additon, the Young Women's Christian Association by Mrs. Cleveland Rockwell, the Woman's Medical Association by Dr. Esther Pohl, Daughters of American Revolution by Mrs. Warren E. Thomas. Greetings were tendered delegates from the four free states, Wyoming, Colorado, Utah and Idaho, and responses were given by delegates from Massachusetts, California and New York, followed by an address from Dr. Frances Woods of South Dakota. An inimitable and charactertistic recitation of an original poem was given by Charlotte Perkins Gilman of New York.

The last survivor of the Organization of the Provisional Government of Oregon, Hon. F. X. Matthieu, sent Mrs. Duniway a complimentary bouquet of yellow flowers, which she accepted with a complimentary speech. A reception to delegates and friends was held in the Oregon State Building, which concluded the exercises of the day.

The Saturday morning session was opened July 1st by prayer offered by Reverend E. S. Muckley. Reports of progress were submitted from Kansas, Kentucky, Louisiana, Maine, Maryland, Massachusetts, Michigan, Wisconsin, Minnesota, Missouri, Nebraska, New Hampshire and New Jersey. Reports of the Literature Committee were submitted by Carrie Chapman Catt of New

York and Elizabeth Hauser of Ohio on distribution of same. The afternoon session was opened by prayer offered by Reverend Burgette Short, Mary Holland Kincaid presiding. A Press Conference following proved a most impressive and instructive symposium, conducted by Ida Husted Harper, Ellis Meredith, and Reverend Eliza Tupper Wilkse. The local daily press was especially interested in this conference, and favored the public with excellent reports. An address by W. S. U'Ren, author of the Initiative and Referendum, closed the proceedings of the afternoon.

The evening meeting was opened by prayer, offered by Reverend J. Whitcomb Brougher. Dr. Anna Shaw occupied the chair. A charming solo was given by Mrs. Susie Gambell Whitehurst of Portland, and was succeeded by instructive addresses by Ella S. Stewart of Chicago, Stephen A. Lowell of Oregon, Antoinette Brown Blackwell of Massachusetts, Mary J. Coggeshall of Iowa, and Gail Laughlin of Maine.

Susan B. Anthony occupied the pulpit of Reverend Dr. Brougher in the White Temple on the following Sunday, Charlotte Perkins Gilman preached at the First Congregational Church, Laura Clay and Mrs. Abigail Scott Duniway occupied the pulpit of the Taylor Street Methodist Church, and Reverend Eliza Tupper Wilkse presented the Equal Suffrage gospel from the Unitarian pulpit. Not a word of expostulation, or a single quotation, or command, from St. Paul, exhorting women to "keep silence in the churches," was heard at any of these meetings, nor was any woman commanded to obtain the spiritual information she required by "asking her husband at home." All of this goes to show the elasticity of modern interpretations of Holy Writ, that, like the Constitution of the United States, or of any state in the Union, can be waived to suit the progress of civilization and enlightenment, for which Jesus came, "To break every yoke and let the oppressed go free."

* * *

The officers and organizers of the National Woman Suffrage Association remained in Oregon after the National Convention to take charge of the campaign for the election of 1906, against my earnest protest. I had watched the results of imported national domination of other state campaigns; and I knew as well before as after our forthcoming campaign in Oregon, that we could not win unless permitted to complete our near-victory at the next Referendum Election in 1906.

I had seen the national method defeat apparent success in Kansas in 1894, and in California in 1896. I had seen Colorado win in 1903, when the National Association had no faith whatever in the prospects of victory and so did not attempt to control the campaign; and I knew, by the part I had taken in Idaho, by preventing a long struggle of National domination in 1895-96, that the election in our favor, in that state, had resulted by keeping its management under local control.

But I made a serious mistake by authorizing our delegates to the National Woman Suffrage Association in Washington in 1904 to invite the National Convention to meet in Oregon in 1905. I thought it would be a good opportunity for our home people to meet our National co-workers, whom I desired to "show off" in my home bailiwick. I got up, for the convention, the first great program of leading local voters they had ever met anywhere. The Lewis and Clark Centennial Exposition was attracting thousands of outside visitors, who attended the convention, which was a brilliant success from start to finish. But, when our National Officers saw the Oregon situation, they decided to remain and conduct the forthcoming campaign themselves, along their own original lines. Foreseeing this, after inviting the National Convention, and when it was too late to countermand its coming, I had resigned my office as State President, in order that I might be in a position to resume my work after the defeat, that I instinctively felt was forthcoming and inevitable, and lovingly told them so.

As has always been the case, in any state where any Equal Suffrage Campaign has been brought before the voters by local managers, we had a few ambitious but practically unknown women in Oregon, who attached themselves to the National Officers, and had no difficulty in convincing them "that Mrs. Duniway was injuring the cause." In this scheme for side-tracking the State Manager of the Movement, they were ably assisted by Clara B. Colby, a self-imported Suffragist, whose eccentric orbit carries her, unheralded, into every locality on two continents, where other people have brought victory into tentative prominence, though she never remains long enough at a time, in any one place, to accomplish any purpose to which she aspires.

I had insisted, when resigning my position as State President, upon my right to name my successor, and had chosen Mrs. Viola M. Coe, an able and tactful woman, to whose management, and that of our reorganized State Executive Committee, the women of Oregon are indebted for leading us to victory through the votes of men at the State Election of 1912.

CHAPTER XXIII.

Rebuffs and Resumptions After Defeat.

OUR DEFEAT of 1900, came so near a final victory as to attract the irrepressible ambition of our gifted National President, and her official co-workers, who had never been able to secure the submission of an Equal Suffrage Amendment by the Legislative Assembly of any State in the Union. The adoption of the Initiative and Referendum Amendment to our State Constitution aroused their determination to take possession of our next campaign on their own responsibility. Not anticipating their design, but being desirous of maintaining harmony and extending every possible honor to our National Officers, I, as State President, empowered Dr. Annice Jeffreys-Myers and her husband (Hon. Jefferson Myers, chairman of the Oregon branch of the pending Lewis and Clark Exposition) to act as delegates to the Annual Convention of the National American Equal Suffrage Convention which was to meet in Washington, D. C., in February, 1904. It was the desire of our State Executive Committee to "show off" the National Association before an Oregon audience, after which it was expected that they would return to their homes, glad to continue co-operating with us, under our direction. But their convention, unfortunately for Oregon, produced the opposite effect from that which the Oregon workers had anticipated.

We had wished our voters to see for themselves that our National leaders were capable, brilliant, eloquent and logical. We had hoped that they would leave the State after the convention was over, carrying pointers, suggesting our plan of work to other states, and that by assisting us financially to a moderate degree, they could

assist both themselves and us. But the sequel proved
that we had "reckoned without our host." Having never
before been able to encounter the popular co-operation of
all of the leading men in any State of the Union, and
remembering that Oregon had come within one and one-
ninth per cent of a victory in 1900, the National officers decided to remain and manage our next Equal
Suffrage Campaign themselves to accomplish this purpose. So they held a supposedly secret conclave with a
few of my ambitious eleventh-hour opponents and decided to "take the Duniway bull by the horns." But
their secret "leaked," and the "bull," hoping that by
some unforeseen hocus-pocus we might "loop the loop"
and win anyhow, retreated to the rear of their procession
and carried their banner on the tips of her little horns.

* * *

I had long known, because of almost universal personal acquaintance, acquired by many years of itinerancy
in the cause, that the best and most intelligent and influential men of my great bailiwick were quietly leading
us to victory. I also knew that the women of Wyoming,
Colorado, Idaho and Utah had been enfranchised, almost
without the asking, by the votes of men, who had not
been aroused into stubbornness by a rataplan and tam-
bourine campaign, carried on as in defeated states under
National domination.

Before resigning my post as President, during the
National Campaign, I had demanded the right to name
my successor; and my choice fell upon Mrs. Viola M.
Coe, who proved the right woman in the right place, of
whose splendid work more will be added in another
chapter.

Susan B. Anthony, of whose memorable work in
my chosen bailiwick I have made mention elsewhere, who
had been compelled to resign from the National Presi-

dency on account of advancing years and failing health, had chosen as her successor Mrs. Carrie Chapman Catt, who retained the chair for two years, until her own failing health compelled her to decline re-election. Dr. Anna Shaw was elected as her successor in 1904. This remarkable woman, an oratorical genius of the highest order, first came into the Suffrage Movement at the National Convention in Washington, D. C., in 1889. Very few of our National delegates knew at the time she had come into our camp that she was an ally of the Woman's Christian Temperance Union, a comparatively new organization, of which she was a National officer, an aggressive leader and a popular lecturer.

* * *

The Woman's Christian Temperance Union, composed of well-meaning, conscientious women, backed as it is by most of the orthodox churches, is well organized everywhere; and it became a convenient receptacle for the meetings of Dr. Shaw and her hired auxiliaries in Oregon during the National Campaign of 1905-6, which swamped and wrecked us, and held us down for six successive years. It is true that our National President attempted, ostensibly, to keep the two opposing principles of Prohibition (which binds), and Equal Suffrage (which liberates), as separate questions before the people; but her example and precept didn't coalesce, and example proved the stronger element in the estimation of voters at the polls.

In closing up the business of an ephemeral State Executive Committee, after our National Campaigners had left us to our fate in 1906, we found that we owed the National Association forty-two dollars and fifty cents, or ten per cent of the membership dues they had gathered during their stay of eighteen months among us, thus showing that about four hundred and twenty women had contributed a dollar each, during its long-drawn dream of imported "campaign education."

Our National President and her Corresponding Secretary departed for a junketing journey to Europe after our first defeat, and their imported organizers went away on less expensive outings for their summer vacations, leaving the writer with her discouraged allies, to take up the burden of reconstruction under greatly augmented difficulties. By this time the Woman's Christian Temperance Union, encouraged by the uplift that Dr. Shaw's campaign had given, concluded that the time had come to take over our stranded Suffrage Cause and carry us with it as "a tail to the prohibition kite." The time for our State Annual Meeting came on in November, 1906, and the few insurgents, led by Clara B. Colby, known everywhere as a walking delegate, or free lance, in all important Suffrage gatherings, got up a typewritten ticket, intended ostensibly to put the incoming President of the State Woman's Christian Temperance Union in the chair, as putative President, with her peripatetic self as President *de facto,* under the name of Vice-President. It is only necessary to add in this connection that the scheme didn't work. I was elected back to the Presidency by an overwhelming vote. The annual meeting included many of the old guard who had been spectators at a distance during the National Campaign; and I was ably assisted ever after by loyal committees of men and women till our final victory was won at the November election of 1912.

The following officers were elected in 1906, and re-elected annually until victory was won:

President, Mrs. Abigail Scott Duniway, 292 Clay St., Portland, Ore.; vice president at large, Mrs. Elizabeth Lord, The Dalles, Ore.; corresponding secretary, Mrs. Elizabeth Craig, 173 16th St., Portland, Ore.; recording secretary, Miss Elma Buckman, 42 E. 18th St.

N., Portland, Ore.; financial secretary, Mrs. A. Bonhain, 14th and Everett Sts., Portland, Ore.; treasurer, Mrs. W. E. Potter, Hunter's Station, Portland, Ore.; auditors, Mrs. F. Eggert, The Hobart Curtis; Mrs. M. A. Dalton, Portland, Ore.; Mrs. Imogene Bath, Hillsboro, Ore.; 1st vice president, Mrs. C. M. Cartwright, 215 7th St., Portland, Multnomah Co.; 2nd vice president, Mrs. Clara Waldo, Macleay, Marion Co.; 3rd vice president, Mrs. Emma Galloway, McMinnville, Yamhill Co.; 4th vice president, Dr. Anna B. Reed, Lebanon, Linn Co.; 5th vice president, Mrs. Eva Emery Dye, Oregon City, Clackamas Co.; 6th vice president, Mrs. Minerva B. Eaton, Union, Union Co.; 7th vice president, Mrs. Rose M. Skenck, Toledo, Lincoln Co.; honorary president, Mrs. Henry Waldo Coe, 387 12th St., Portland, Ore.; member of national committee, Mrs. Sarah A. Evans, 225 7th St., Portland, Ore.; 8th vice president, Prof. Helen Crawford, Corvallis, Benton Co.; 9th vice president, Mrs. Minnie Washburn, Eugene, Lane Co.; 10th vice president, Mrs. Henry Sengstacken, Marshfield, Coos Co.; 11th vice president, Mrs. H. A. Stewart, Port Orford, Curry Co.; 12th vice president, Mrs. Elizabeth L. Lord, The Dalles, Wasco Co.; 13th vice president, Mrs. Imogene Bath, Hillsboro, Washington Co.; 14th vice president, Mrs. J. H. Trullinger, Astoria, Clatsop Co.

The outcry of the disgruntled minority, which had entered the meeting fully expecting to capture the association in the interests of prohibition, was both loud and deep. The newspapers published column after column of correspondence attacking me over my devoted head, accusing me by innuendo and otherwise, as far as the press would let it go, of "conciliating the liquor interests."

If any sentimentalist imagines that women, as a class, are better or wiser than men, he has but to attend one such an aftermath as that which followed the defeat of the attempted "merger" to dissipate his delusion. The open fight against the "Duniway bull" was discontinued after awhile, but the secret plottings of a small minority were not discontinued, as was proven in our last successful campaign, when our national treasury fund, that belonged by every principle of practice and honor to the State Association, was diverted to a committee of the local Woman's Club.

* * *

A wise general will use every means in his power to discover the strongholds of his enemy. Finding the conflict between the eleventh-hour suffragists and the liquor traffic irrepressible, I began in 1906, immediately after my re-election to the chair, to penetrate the strongholds of the latter by subscribing to its journals. Knowing its publishers were being misled by the widespread supposition that Equal Suffrage was "a tail to the prohibition kite," I sent newspaper clippings from every available source, gathered through the Press Clipping Bureau, to such journals, to show that prohibition and liberty could not possibly pull together, and it was not the object of any intelligent believer in the equality of rights for all the people to attempt such a coalition. For a long time the liquor journals ignored such clippings; but they were finally led to see, through the open rupture between the Oregon Equal Suffrage Association and the Woman's Christian Temperance Union, that prohibition wasn't our fight, but liberty was our goal. I had learned from bitter experience of former years to avoid exposing myself to the barbed arrows of professional "temperance" orators, so I didn't even tell my Executive Committee that I was studying the liquor journals at home, or sending them any clipped items of fact. It was not that I feared the opposition of our Board, but I knew some of its members were listening to the gossip of defeated agitators, and I was sincerely afraid that the cause would be injured, if it became known that I was studying the question from every discoverable angle.

For the well-intentioned solicitude of many of my closest friends, who knowing me thoroughly, sought to shield me from the unjust assault of fanaticism, I am truly grateful; but I have learned from long experience that calumny and misrepresentation will always fail of their object in their last analysis, so I had nothing to fear.

I have long known that nothing but Equal Rights for the mothers of men will ever enable the wives of drunkards to free themselves from the evils of intemperance; and these rights for wives and mothers having begun of achievement through votes for women in enfranchised states, will ultimately accomplish their inevitable purpose. The subjugation of womanhood is the beginning of all evil. Eliminate the cause and freedom and enlightenment will gradually overcome the evils of the tyranny, intemperance and ignorance we now deplore.

ARGUMENT IN VOTERS' PAMPHLET.

The Oregon State Equal Suffrage Association presented the following joint resolution to the Legislative Assembly in 1907, which passed the Senate, only to be killed by the House,—an act which drove us back to our petition work and secured for us another vote at the general election of 1908:

"Portland, Oregon, February 6, 1907.
To the Honorable Body, The Legislative Assembly of the State of Oregon.
Gentlemen:

The undersigned, on behalf of your friends, the taxpaying, law-abiding women of Oregon, most respectfully appeal to you to submit to the electors of the state (in common with other proposed amendments) the following:

HOUSE JOINT RESOLUTION:

Be it resolved by the House of Representatives, the Senate concurring, that the following amendment to the constitution of the State of Oregon be and the same hereby is proposed:

That section 2 of Article II of the Constitution of the State of Oregon be amended to read as follows:

'Section 2. Qualifications of electors. The elective franchise in this state shall not hereafter be prohibited to any citizen on account of sex; and at all elections not otherwise provided for by this Constitution, every citizen of the United States of the age of twenty-one years and upwards, who shall have resided in this state during the six months immediately preceding such election, and every white person of foreign birth of the age of twenty-one years and upwards who shall have resided in this state during the six months immediately preceding such election, and shall have declared his or her intention to become a citizen of the United States one year preceding such election, conformable to the laws of the United States on the subject of naturalization, shall be entitled to vote at all elections authorized by law.'

We are asking this favor of you as an act of courtesy to us, and because we believe you will be proud to relieve us of the further labor and expense that will otherwise be necessary to complete and verify our initiative petitions, for which, at great inconvenience and cost to ourselves, we have already procured about half of the signatures required by law.

I have the honor to be, now and always,

Yours for Liberty,

ABIGAIL SCOTT DUNIWAY,

President Oregon State Equal Suffrage Association.

MYRTLE E. PEASE,

Corresponding Secretary."

Having failed in our efforts before the Legislature, we took advantage of the new Constitutional Amendment known as "The Initiative and Referendum," and secured a place by petition on the ballot for. the next general election. The National body having declined to assist us in the petition work, unless under its own plan of invasion, we were surprised and delighted to receive a contribution of three hundred dollars from Laura Clay of Kentucky, an individual member of the National Board, which enabled us to complete the petitions without exposing our financial straits as a society, to the assaults of the State Branch of the "National Association Opposed to the Further Extension of the Elective Franchise to Women."

The following open letter was ordered sent:

To Every Liberty-Loving Voter of Oregon:

The undersigned, representing, as we believe, the large majority of the women of Oregon, are happy to embrace this opportunity, accorded to us through your initiative petitions, to lay before you a few of our many reasons for believing you will be as proud to extend to us, at the coming June election, your courteous invitation to join you in full and free possession of the elective franchise, as were the gallant men of Wyoming, Colorado, Idaho and Utah, who bestowed full rights of citizenship, almost without solicitation, upon every law-abiding woman within her borders.

This movement, which began in Oregon in 1871, grew so rapidly, under the guidance of pioneer men and women and public-spirited law-makers, that the Legislative Assembly enacted, in autumn of 1872, a married woman's sole trader bill, enabling a wife to hold her own earnings, if necessary, as her own property, by registering her intention with the county court. Stimulated by this small beginning, the growth of public sentiment in favor of equal property rights for women has placed Oregon women far in advance, as self-earning property-holders, of women of any other State in the Union, except the four States wherein they already vote.

But, although we are taxpayers, we are not yet full-fledged voters. This handicap brings the wage earnings of women into ruinous competition with wage-earning voters, and is a disability from which we believe you will be glad to relieve us by your votes next June, in the interest of both halves of the people.

This movement grew from the small official beginning in 1872, above noted, until the year 1884, when your representatives submitted for us, by legislative enactment, a constitutional amendment at the State election of that year, which brought us 11,223 votes. Our proposed amendment was again submitted to a vote of one-half of the people in the year 1900, and the "yes" vote had by that time grown to 26,265. The amendment was again submitted (always by men) in 1906, and the "yes" vote rose to 36,902.

For causes that are wholly eliminated from the present campaign (and we hope from all future State campaigns for equal rights, and, therefore, need not be explained in this letter) the "no" vote of 1906 was for the first time proportionately increased; but the readiness with which men have responded with their signatures to the large initiative petitions, through which you have reopened our case, is an assurance to us of your success in our behalf at the June election of 1908, for which we are patriotically expectant and profoundly grateful in advance.

If any of you say you are weary of this agitation, we answer in all seriousness, so are we. So weary are we that we believe you will, in mercy, not compel us to repeat this struggle in the year 1910, as we surely must if you fail us this time.

If there shall yet remain a few women who should attempt to repeat their former protest against this appeal for equal rights for other women, of which they are unable or unwilling, from their viewpoint, to see the need, we trust your practical good sense will prove to them, through your affirmative votes in our behalf, that our enfranchisement, while enlarging *our* opportunities, will in no way encroach upon their rights or liberties.

If any man objects to extending to his wife and mother the power of the ballot from the fear that if they become his equals, they will neglect or forsake the home, we shall depend upon you to divert his mind from such a fallacy, by recalling the fact that the home instinct is inherent in woman, and cannot be created or destroyed by laws of men's or women's making. If he does not know, of his own accord, that there are many hundreds of men and women in Oregon, who could not have the semblance of a home to keep, under present industrial conditions, if women did not go outside to earn or help to earn the means to rent or support a home in ruinous competition with balloted men, just let him alone; his delusion is chronic, and he is past recovery.

This movement for the enfranchisement of your closest friends, the mother-half of the people of Oregon, is wholly non-partisan, non-sectarian and non-political. We are not seeking to make laws to govern men. We believe as implicitly in men's fundamental right to self-government as in our own, and we are awaiting your invitation, through the ballot box, to the possession of our inalienable right to equality with you before the law, which we prize for the same reasons that you prize it, and we believe it will be a pleasure to you to bestow it upon us exactly as it would be our pleasure to extend it to you under reversed conditions.

ABIGAIL SCOTT DUNIWAY,
President Oregon State Equal Suffrage Association.

Mrs. Henry Waldo Coe, Honorary President.
Mrs. Elizabeth Lord, Vice-President.
Mrs. C. M. Cartwright, Second Vice-President.
Sarah A. Evans, Member of National Exec. Com.
Miss Elma Buckman, Recording Secretary.
Mrs. W. E. Potter, Treasurer.
Mrs. A. Bonham, Financial Secretary.
Myrtle E. Pease, Corresponding Secretary.
Mrs. Elizabeth Eggert, First Auditor.
Martha Dalton, Second Auditor.
Mrs. Imogene Bath, Third Auditor.

List of Vice-Presidents by Counties:

Baker, Mrs. Harvey K. Brown; Benton, Prof. Helen Crawford; Clackamas, Mrs. Eva Emery Dye; Clatsop, Mrs. J. H. Trullinger; Columbia, Mrs. E. H. Flagg; Coos, Mrs. Henry Sengstaken; Crook, Mrs. Ada Millican; Curry, Mrs. H. A. Stewart; Douglas, Mrs. Ida Marsters; Gilliam, Mrs. Clay Clark; Grant, Mrs. Ida Niven; Harney, Mrs. Frank Davey; Jackson, Mrs. Hattie S. Day; Josephine, Mrs. L. L. Mangum; Klamath, Mrs. O. C. Applegate; Lake, Mrs. C. U. Snider; Lane, Mrs. Minnie Washburne; Lincoln, Mrs. R. A. Bensell; Linn, Dr. Anna B. Reed; Malheur, Mrs. Tina Chambers; Marion, Mrs. Clara H. Waldo; Morrow, Mrs. Florence Whitehead; Multnomah, Mrs. C. M. Cartwright; Polk, Mrs. Walter L. Tooze; Sherman, Mrs. Ella Slayback; Tillamook, Mrs. Emma Morrison; Umatilla, Mrs. S. A. Lowell; Union, Mrs. Minerva B. Eaton; Wallowa, Mrs. Elizabeth Oakes; Wasco, Mrs. Elizabeth Lord; Washington, Mrs. Imogene Bath; Yamhill, Mrs. Emma Galloway; Wheeler, Mrs. J. S. Stewart.

The subjoined eminent opinions in behalf of the Equal Suffrage Amendment were included in the voters' pamphlet and sent to all voters:

No reason can be given for man suffrage that cannot be urged with equal force in favor of woman suffrage.—The late U. S. Senator J. N. Dolph.

I have nothing but words of commendation and praise for equal suffrage, and will gladly welcome the day when women are permitted to vote in all of the different States and territories, and at all elections.—Governor Frank R. Gooding of Idaho.

I hope that this State will give women the ballot, and I hope that every State will do it.—Geo. E. Chamberlain, Governor of Oregon; afterwards United States Senator.

Bad women do not exert an appreciable influence in politics. The fact that women vote in Wyoming does not interfere in any way with home duties, nor with the pleasant relationships of family life.—Bryant E. Brooks, Governor of Wyoming.

The salvation of this Republic depends upon the enfranchisement of its mothers.—The late W. S. Ladd.

This demand for the enfranchisement of women is right. It is just. No man has any right to vote against it.—Jefferson Myers.

I believe the enfranchisement of women will elevate the standard of citizenship.—Colonel R. A. Miller.

I am naturally conservative, but I advocate woman suffrage because it is right.—The late Solomon Hirsch.

One of the great advantages which has come to us from woman suffrage is the fear on the part of the machine politicians to nominate for public office men of immoral character, or to defeat those who have maintained a reputation for honesty and decency.—Judge B. F. Lindsay of Colorado.

I go for all sharing the privileges of the government

who assist in bearing its burdens, by no means excluding women.—Abraham Lincoln.

Over and above all, suffrage is the woman's right, and no fair, just man will deny her that right. While we may defend equal suffrage upon the ground of expediency, it is not a question of expedience, but of justice. —Ex-Governor Alva Adams of Colorado.

I do not in the least believe in the patient Griselda type of woman. * * * I believe in the woman's keeping her self-respect, just as I believe in the man's doing so. I believe in her rights just as much as I believe in the man's, and indeed, a little more. * * * No family can become all it should be if the mother does not keep in touch sufficiently with outside interests and what is going on in the world to become an intellectual stimulus to her children.—Theodore Roosevelt.

I look for and earnestly desire the enfranchisement of the women of Oregon at the June election of 1908.— U. S. Senator Jonathan Bourne.

The fact is, and can readily be verified, that the advent of women into the political arena has had the effect of raising the moral standard to a much higher degree than it was before.—Governor Jesse T. McDonald of Colorado.

The moral delinquencies from which many men suffer may be traced to the disfranchisement and consequent moral irresponsibility of mothers.—The late U. S. Senator John H. Mitchell.

Utah has been an equal suffrage State ever since statehood was granted, and my observation has led me to believe that the results of giving the franchise to the women have been beneficial.—Governor John C. Cutler.

I have always assisted the women of Oregon in their efforts to secure the ballot. Of course women should vote.—U. S. Senator C. W. Fulton.

The right of suffrage should be denied to no citizen.

save as punishment for crime. * * * I favor equal suffrage, not only as a matter of justice, but as a moral and educational force in the nation.—Willis S. Duniway.

I congratulate the women of Oregon, and anticipate success for them in the present equal suffrage campaign. John Barrett, President of the Bureau of Pan-American Republics.

Every man ought to be ashamed to oppose equal rights with himself for his wife and mother at the ballot box or anywhere else.—Dr. Henry Waldo Coe.

(Endorsed)

Filed February 3, 1908.

F. W. BENSON, Secretary of State.

CHAPTER XXIV.

Washington Campaign of 1910—National Council of Women Voters.

THE LEGISLATIVE ASSEMBLY of the State of Washington met in January, in 1909, and submitted an equal suffrage amendment to the electorate of the state, for a referendum vote in November, 1910. The proposed submission of the amendment passed the House of Representatives without difficulty, the majority of its proponents expecting the Senate to bear the responsibility of effecting its defeat by a negative vote. A committee of representative women of the State Equal Suffrage Association held a headquarters during the entire session and kept anxious watch over the deliberation. The leading Senator, to whom belongs the credit of the final vote in the Upper House, was Mr. George U. Piper, who adroitly led the fight to a finish. Mr. Piper is a loyal son of my beloved old-time friends of Albany, Oregon, the late Judge and Mrs. Piper, whose older son, a brother of the Washington State Senator, is managing editor of the Portland "Oregonian."

The victory in the Washington Legislature was received by the suffragists of the nation with universal rejoicing. Then began an earnest controversy between myself and a few newly established leaders of the Washington suffragists, who disagreed with me as to the advisability of turning the coming campaign over to the management and domination of the National Association. The annual convention of the National leaders was held in Seattle in the month of June, succeeding the submission of the proposed amendment, which resulted in a fortunate rupture between the leaders of the Atlantic and Pa-

GROUP OF EQUAL SUFFRAGISTS

ELIZABETH CADY STANTON
In 1912 Deceased

DR. CLEMENCE LOZIER
In 1873 A Prominent Suffragist
Deceased

ANNA HOWARD SHAW
President National Woman Suffrage
Association

MRS. CARRIE CHAPMAN CATT
President International Woman's Suffrage
Association

LUCY STONE
Early Suffrage Leader Founder of The
Woman's Journal Deceased

MARY G. HAY
President State Federation of New York
Federation of Woman's Clubs

MRS. SARAH KNOX GOODRICH
Early Suffragist of California
Deceased

cific coast, and culminated later in the organization of
the National Council of Women Voters.

The National officers having retired from the field
after a stormy succession of several days' sessions, the
local, or State managers of the campaign, succeeded in
successfully conducting the movement with commendable
cleverness. They had no wreck of a national defeat to
clear away, as we were compelled to do for six succeeding
years, in Oregon, before reaching a victory. Mrs. May
Arkwright Hutton, of Spokane, had control of a large
following in eastern Washington, and managed her part
of the program with ability and tact. Mrs. Emma Smith
DeVoe, president of the State association, was aided by
a loyal State Executive Committee, with whose co-
operation she traveled extensively, proving her sagacity
by enlisting the aid of the press in all localities. Her plan
of work, issued in collaboration with my own, which was
successfully used in Oregon in 1912, was issued to workers, as follows:

"We will canvass every precinct in the State, according to the latest poll list. At first this may seem to be a
herculean task, but not so; for we have many willing
workers in every county and precinct in the state. In
every county we will have a central committeeman, who
from her county map, will note and bound each precinct
in her county. She will then appoint an active, intelligent
worker in each precinct, whose duty it will be to secure a
list of voters from the poll books. This precinct committeeman, with her helpers, will ascertain how each voter
stands on the woman suffrage question and record the
same on blanks furnished her. When her work is completed, she will turn her records over to the chairman of
the central committee, who will forward them to the State
headquarters. By this method we will know where to
do our work and not consume time on people who are
already converted."

While it is not claimed that this work was done as completely as was desired in either state, enough of it was done to enlist the co-operation of leading men and women in every county.

But the crowning act which secured the adoption of the amendment in 1910 was the wording placed upon the final ballot, which was made to read as follows:

"For the proposed amendment to Article 6 of the Constitution relating to the qualifications of voters within this State.

"Against the proposed amendment of Article 6 of the constitution relating to the qualifications of voters within this State."

For this consummate piece of strategy the credit belongs, of right, to State Senator Piper, who, having had much experience in engineering the political machine, knew how to catch the affirmative votes of thousands of men in whom the one word "woman" would have aroused intense opposition. The vote at the polls was more than two to one in favor of the amendment, many thousands of men complaining, after it was too late to enlighten them, that they hadn't known the meaning of the proposed amendment or they would have voted it down. In chronicling this incident I am led to exclaim, in words I am not wise enough to coin myself,

> Great God! on what a slender thread
> Hang everlasting things!

* * *

The following account of the formation of The National Council of Women Voters, from the facile pen of Dr. Cora Smith Eaton, is condensed from the National Review. The chronicler hereof was a witness and participant at the great ratification jubilee, which followed at the opera house in Tacoma, Washington, in the following January and can vouch for its accuracy:

" 'What are you going to do, now that you have the vote?' wired the 'New York Times' to Mrs. Emma Smith

DeVoe, of Tacoma, Wash., the woman who had planned and led the victorious campaign. They published her answer in their issue of November 19, 1910. It was the keynote to what followed. It began: 'We have won. We are going to rest now. We must think.' Beware of the woman who thinks. She is apt to 'start something.' In this case, the woman laid the problem of 'What next?' before the man who had been her chief adviser throughout the Washington campaign,—no lesser man than the Governor of Idaho, Mr. James H. Brady.

"Mrs. DeVoe went to Boise, Idaho, for one more conference in the governor's mansion. There again before the blazing logs in his wide fireplace, around the great table in his stately dining room, and on the wide sunny piazza, where Governor Brady was most content, they held council. When it was over, Governor Brady issued a call to the governors of the other four suffrage states. This document stands unique in history and here it is:

'Whereas, on November 8th, 1910, the electors of the State of Washington voted a constitutional amendment giving the women of that State the right of suffrage, making five states west of the Missouri River that have placed this Godgiven right in their hands.

'I, James H. Brady, Governor of the State of Idaho, and Chairman of the advisory board of Washington Campaign Committee, of said state, believe that the time has arrived when the enfranchised women of the West should extend a helping hand to their sisters in the Eastern and other states in securing the ballot; and I hereby call a convention, to be held in the city of Tacoma, Washington, on January the 14th, 1911, for the purpose of organizing an association of national scope of the Women Voters of America; and I hereby appoint Margaret S. Roberts, of Boise, Idaho, as delegate to said convention, with full power to act on all matters coming before the same, and I respectfully request the Governors of all the states where women have the right of suffrage to appoint one delegate to said convention, with authority to organize a national association.'

"There was prompt concurrence by all the governors of enfranchised states, each of whom named and duly authorized a woman Commissioner for this important meeting. Governor Brooks, of Wyoming, named Mrs. Zell Hart Deming, of Cheyenne; Governor Shafroth, of Colorado, named Mrs. Mary C. C. Bradford, of Denver; Governor Spry, of Utah, named Mrs. Susa Young Gates, of Salt Lake City, and Governor Hay, of Washington, named Mrs. Virginia Wilson Mason, of Tacoma.

"These Commissioners met on the morning of January 14, 1911, Governor Brady, himself, calling them to order and stating the object of the meeting. The scene was laid in the large colonial home of Mr. and Mrs. John Q. Mason, in Tacoma, in the long living room, the fir logs crackling in the fireplace, the bright sunshine outside reflected from the dazzling snow that had fallen the day before. The snowstorm was memorable, because unusual in the Puget Sound country, where all winter gentle rains keep the lawns green and the English daisies blooming in the grass. It was as though Tacoma had prepared a snowy winter scene to make the women from the Rocky Mountain States feel quite at home.

"The Commissioners adopted a brief constitution, which is given in full below:

CONSTITUTION.

'Article 1. Name—The name of this organization shall be the National Council of Women Voters.

'Article 2. Object—This council shall be nonpartisan. Its object shall be to obtain equal suffrage in other states; to change conditions in our own states for the betterment of men and women, of children and the home, and to claim justice for women in the political, social and economic world.

'Article 3. Officers—The officers of this organization shall be: President, one vice-president at large, one vice-president from each enfranchised state; (the president of each state council shall be, by nature of office, the vice-president of her state). The appointees of the governors of the enfranchised states shall serve in this capacity until the next meeting of the council; recording secretary, corresponding secretary, treasurer and auditor.

'These officers shall constitute the board of managers, five of whom shall be a quorum. This board is empowered to transact all business of the council in the intervals between conventions.

'The officers shall be nominated and elected by ballot and shall serve until successors are elected.

'Article 4. Committees—The board of managers shall appoint all standing committees. Special committees may be appointed by the president.

'Article 5. Meetings—Meetings shall be subject to the call of a majority of the board of managers and shall be annual or bi-ennial.

'Article 6. Amendments—The constitution may be amended by a majority vote at any meeting of the council regularly called by a majority of the board of managers.

'Article 7. Roberts' Rules of Order shall govern the deliberations of this council.'

"The Officers elected were: President, Mrs. Emma Smith DeVoe, Tacoma, Washington; vice-president-at-large, Mrs. Harriet G. R. Wright, Denver, Colo.; corresponding secretary, Mrs. Berthe Knatvold Kittilsen, Tacoma, Washington; recording secretary, Mrs. Leona Cartee, Boise, Idaho; treasurer, Dr. Cora Smith King, Seattle, Washington; auditor, Mrs. C. H. McMahon, Salt Lake City, Utah.

"The afternoon of the same day, a brilliant reception was held at the home of Mrs. Mason, the Washington Commissioner, followed by a dinner and reception tendered by the Tacoma Commercial Club. A great mass meeting was held in the evening, packing Tacoma's largest theater to the topmost gallery. The Governor of the State of Washington, the retiring Governor of the State of Idaho, the special Commissioners and the officers-elect exchanged felicitations on the platform, celebrated the emancipation of 175,000 Washington women and hailed the organization of the National Council of Women

Voters. Mrs. Emma Smith DeVoe presided. The orator
of the evening was James H. Brady, the originator of the
movement. The greatest enthusiasm greeted his message
to the women voters of the United States.

"Mr. Brady is a man of imposing presence, with a
ruddy, wholesome, almost boyish face, the eyes twinkling
with humor, and lighting up his otherwise serious expression. His voice and manner are those of the born
orator, his message that of the philosopher, whose vision
is equality and justice applied to men and women alike.
By one stroke of executive genius he had assembled the
machinery that bids fair to prove the greatest power for
the extension of suffrage in our country. The most applauded portions of his speech were these:

'Over 400,000 enfranchised women of America are today speaking through this convention to the world; and
when your labors are finished there will have been formed
an organization that represents, not only this army of intelligent workers, but also an association that will go forth
into other states and secure for your sisters that right which
belongs to every American citizen—the right to express by
their ballot their will on all questions affecting every aspect
of our civic life.

'Too often, men and women who have achieved their
own rights lapse into indifference as to whether these rights
are assured to others. Your meeting and organization is to
overcome this tendency in human nature and to record the
fact that the strength and experience of five equal suffrage
states is at the disposal of the other states of this Union.
You have made successful campaigns—your methods of
success you place at the disposal of others. You have had
experience with equal suffrage. The results of actual trial,
you offer to others as an argument founded on fact.'"

Ex-Governor James H. Brady is Junior United States
Senator from Idaho at this writing, and, like our Oregon
Senators, George E. Chamberlain and Harry Lane, is
proud to come from a state where women vote. The last
annual election of the National Council of Women Voters, a non-partisan organization, with headquarters at

Tacoma, Washington, chose the following National officers:

Honorary President, Mrs. Abigail Scott Duniway, 170 Ford Street, Portland, Oregon.

President, Mrs. Emma Smith DeVoe, 605-606 Perkins Bldg., Tacoma, Wash.

Corresponding Secretary, Mrs. Bertha Knatvold Kittilsen, 605-606 Perkins Bldg., Tacoma, Wash.

Recording Secretary, Mrs. Leona Cartee, 1011 No. 8th St., Boise, Idaho.

Treasurer, Dr. Cora Smith King, 63 The Olympia, Washington, D. C.

Auditor, Mrs. C. H. McMahon, 38 Caithness Apts., Salt Lake City, Utah.

VICE-PRESIDENTS.   Gained full suffrage in

Wyoming—Mrs. Ida Harris Mondell, Newcastle.....1869
Colorado—Mrs. Mary C. C. Bradford, State House, Denver 1893
Utah—Mrs. Rose Less Sutherland, Salt Lake City....1896
Idaho—Miss Margaret S. Roberts, Boise............1896
Washington—Mrs. Virginia Wilson Mason, 2501 No. Washington St., Tacoma 1910
California—Mrs. Mary McHenry Keith, 2207 Atherton St., Berkeley 1911
Oregon—Dr. Viola M. Coe, 841 Lovejoy St., Portland.1912
Arizona—Mrs. Frances W. Munds, Prescott.........1912
Kansas—Mrs. Bertha Felt Thompson, Garden City....1912
Alaska Territory—Mrs. Cornelia Templeton Hatcher, Kuik, Alaska 1913

CONGRESSIONAL COMMITTEE.

Dr. Cora Smith King, Chairman, 63 The Olympia ....Washington, D. C.
Mrs. Ida Harris Mondell....................Wyoming
Mrs. Annie Hamilton Pitzer...................Colorado
Mrs. Rose Lee Sutherland........................Utah
Mrs. Fred T. Dubois............................Idaho
Mrs. Sabina Page Morton.................Washington
Mrs. John W. Raker........................California
Dr. Viola M. Coe...............................Oregon
Mrs. Henry F. Ashurst........... ....Arizona
Mrs. William H. Thompson....................Kansas
Mrs. James Wickersham......................Alaska

Mrs. May Arkwright Hutton, of Spokane, leading suffragist of eastern Washington, said to me, in discussing the National situation: "We are having no quarrel with our brilliant sister co-workers of the Eastern States. They make no greater mistake, when they take possession of a Western campaign, than we should surely make if we should try to manage their local affairs for them. They do not understand the freedom-loving, patriotic spirit of our Western men."

CHAPTER XXV.

Appreciated Assistance.

THE following report is condensed, by permission, from the graduating thesis of Mr. A. T. Kronenberg, an alumnus of the University of Oregon of 1913, and is compiled from the National History of Woman Suffrage, Vols. III and IV, and from files of the "Morning Oregonian," selected from February 14, 1894, to November 17, 1912:

"While the equal suffrage amendment of 1894 was pending, awaiting the electorate of the following June, our capable and conscientious United States Senator, the late Joseph N. Dolph, favored the Oregon State Equal Suffrage Association with an able and comprehensive letter for general publication, and in a speech before the U. S. Senate, commended the adoption of the amendment as a measure of justice and right. Leading clergymen, especially of Portland, preached in favor of woman suffrage, prominent among whom were Rev. T. L. Eliot, pastor of the First Unitarian Church; Chaplain R. S. Stubbs, of the Church of Sea and Land, and Rev. Frederick R. Marvin, of the First Congregational Society. Not one influential man made audible objection anywhere.

"The state had been carefully districted and organized, neither labor nor money being spared in supplying 'Yes' tickets for all parties and all candidates and putting them everywhere in the hands of friends, for use at the polls. But no sooner had the polls been opened than it appeared that the campaign was one of great odds. Masked batteries appeared in the open in every precinct, and multitudes of men who are rarely seen at the polls except at a general election, crowded forth to strike down the manacled and voteless women. Railroad gangs were driven to the polls like sheep, and voted against the amendment in battalions. But, in spite of all this opposition, nearly one-third of the vote was thrown in its favor, requiring a change of only about one-fourth of the opposing vote to have given victory to the cause; thus proving, to the amazement of its enemies, that they had a formidable opponent to confront in future elections.

"Seeing that the election had demonstrated the impossibility of receiving a fair, impartial vote at the hands of the lawless multitude, whose ballot outweighed all reason and overpowered all sense, Mrs. Duniway went to the Legislature in 1885 and secured the aid of friends in introducing the following bill:

" 'Be it Enacted by the Legislative Assembly of Oregon, that the elective franchise shall not hereafter be denied to any person on account of sex. This act to be enforced from and after its approval by the Governor.'

"After much parliamentary filibustering, the vote of both houses, in joint session, stood 34 to 54. This vote, coming so soon after the defeat at the polls, was regarded as the greatest victory yet won, notwithstanding its lack of a two-thirds majority, as required by law.

"Following this defeat the advocates of the movement, facing an unequal fight, made no open organized effort for ten years, although much was done by letters to the press, written almost wholly by Mrs. Duniway, who was lecturing in Idaho and sending characteristic communications to the Oregon newspapers.

"Returning to Portland in 1894, and finding that nothing had been done by others to carry the movement during her long absence from the state, Mrs. Duniway issued a call for an open meeting to be held at her residence on the coming Fourth of July.

"The attendance was large, and the proceedings were spirited, resulting in a temporary reorganization of the scattered forces. A committee was formed to convene weekly, meeting thereafter for six consecutive years, bringing reports of progress throughout the state, gathered mainly from newspaper articles in different papers, and especially from "The Oregonian."

"Woman's day was celebrated in the Horticultural Convention in October following, by invitation of its president, Judge William Galloway.

"On October 27th, a mass meeting was held at the Marquam Grand Theater, in Portland, at which a permanent state reorganization was effected and a constitution ratified, which had previously been prepared by the executive committee.

"In February, 1895, the association received from the legislature, a resolution for the submission of a woman suffrage amendment, which it would be necessary for a subsequent legislature to ratify. The annual meeting of the state association was held in Portland, November following of that year, conducted in as quiet a manner as possible, in order not to arouse the two extremes of society, consisting of the slum classes on the one hand, and the ultra conservatives on the other.

"The convention of 1896 met in Portland November 16th. Mrs. Duniway was changed from honorary president to acting president. Mrs. H. A. Laughary was elected honorary president. Dr. Annice F. Jeffreys was chosen as vice-president at large; Ada Cornish Hertsche, vice-president; Frances E. Gotshall, corresponding secretary; Mary Schaffer Ward, recording secretary; Mrs. A. E. Hackett, assistant secretary; Mrs. J. C. Pritchard, treasurer. These state officers remained the same until 1898, when Mrs. W. H. Games was chosen recording secretary, and Dr. Viola M. Coe treasurer.

"The year 1896 was spent in continuous effort, on the part of the state officers, to disseminate equal suffrage sentiment, in more or less direct ways, so that other organizations of whatever name or nature, might look upon the proposed amendment with favor. The executive committee decided, early in the year, to hold a Woman's Congress and secure the affiliation of all branches of women's philanthropic and literary effort under the management of the State Suffrage Association. Just at that time an amendment campaign was going on in California, in which Susan B. Anthony was very active; and the Oregon Association resolved to obtain her attendance at the Congress to be held in June, with Miss Anthony as its chief attraction. * * * No matter what was the subject of each speaker's address, little suggestions and sentiments in regard to the equal suffrage question and the proposed constitutional amendment were thrown into the talk, to show the individual feelings of the speakers, whether they lived in Oregon or other states adjoining its borders. The late Mrs. Sarah B. Cooper, the noted philanthropist of San Francisco, was a special attraction, and added many converts to the growing cause.

"The next public meeting of that year was held in July at the commodious grounds of the Willamette Valley Chautauqua Association, under the supervision of the state recording secretary, Mrs. Mary Schaffer Ward. One day of the session was set aside (under management of Mrs. Duniway) as 'Rev. Anna Shaw day,' and on that occasion Dr. Shaw spoke as one inspired.

"Thirty-six regular meetings and four mass meetings were held by the Suffrage Association during the year.

"The Woman's Club had become prominent by this time, in the Pacific Northwest, under the skillful management of Mrs. A. H. H. Stuart, a noted equal rights advocate of Olympia, Washington (a co-worker with Mrs. Duniway), so that, by the suffragists joining in the organization, the current of public opinion on behalf of the proposed amendment was considerably strengthened.

"Among other societies, and clubs, which at this time voiced the adoption of the amendment, were the

Oregon Emergency Corps, the Red Cross Society, the Oregon Pioneer Association, the Grand Army of the Republic, the Woman's Christian Temperance Union, the Good Templars, the Knights of Labor, the Printers' Union, and many other associations of similar nature.

* * *

"The second Women's Congress took place in Portland in 1898, under the auspices of the State Equal Suffrage Association, forty different societies of women participating.

"Woman's day at the Willamette Valley Chautauqua, held in July, was again a great success. This time over forty different societies of men and women were represented, and such leaders as Alice Moore McComas, of California, and Dr. Frances Woods, of Iowa, were among the speakers. An invitation by the president, Col. R. A. Miller, himself an ardent suffragist, was extended to all persons to attend the meeting the following year. * * *

"In 1889, Mrs. Duniway was invited by the Legislature to take part in the proceedings of the two Houses as valedictorian, in honor of forty years of statehood.

"This year, in preparation for the election, at which the woman suffrage amendment passed by the legislature of 1889 was to be voted on, one hundred and six parlor meetings were held, fifty thousand pieces of literature distributed, and the names and addresses of thirty thousand voters, in 13 counties, collected. Mrs. Duniway did much that year in the way of speaking before various orders and fraternities throughout the state, most of which indorsed the amendment. The usual headquarters were maintained during the state fair, under the tactful management of Dr. Annice F. Jeffreys, afterwards the bride of Hon. Jefferson Myers, a prominent attorney and equal suffragist.

"At the meeting of the legislature in 1897, the women were ready and waiting for the ratification of the amendment (proposed by the assembly of 1895), but, due to a quarrel over choice of candidates to the United States Senate, the solons refused to organize for any line of business, leaving the women without ratification of their amendment for two years, until 1899, when a long-delayed opportunity arrived. Mrs. Duniway and Dr. Jeffreys-Myers were again in charge, and were recognized by prominent members and admitted to the floor of both Houses. Senator Fulton, who had been a champion of the movement in 1880 and 1882, was once more asked to bear the women's flag; but he showed little desire to take up the question on account of the numerous side issues which non-voters had requested him to present to the Assembly. For several days thereafter Mesdames Duniway and Jeffreys-Myers furnished short and pithy letters to the papers of the Capital City, answering all arguments of objection to the movement. They sent open letters to each member of the Legislature, explaining that their idea of self-government was based on equal rights for women, and was not made in the interest of any one reform. Finally, Senators Fulton and Brownell thought the time ripe for the consideration of the amendment, and had it made a special order of business. Mrs. Duniway was asked to present the claims of the women of the state, over half of whom, through resolutions of their various societies, had asked that the amendment be submitted. The roll call showed twenty-five 'Ayes' to one 'No.' In the House, after a ten-minute speech by Mrs. Duniway from the speaker's desk, the vote stood 48 'Ayes' and 6 'Noes.' During the proceedings one member had presented a large collection of documents, sent by the anti-suffrage association of women in New York and Massachusetts. The preceding autumn these same women had sent out a salaried agent (a Miss Emily F. Bissel,

of Delaware) to canvass the state against the measure.
* * *

"The succeeding campaign was very largely in the nature of a 'still hunt,' but Mrs. Ida Crouch Hazlett, of Colorado, held meetings for two months, in counties away from the railroad, doing effective work among the voters of the border. Miss Lena Morrow, of Illinois, gave special attention to men's fraternities throughout Portland, in all of which she was accorded a very gracious hearing. * * * 'The Oregonian' was the only newspaper, out of 229 in the State, that opposed the amendment. But, notwithstanding its deadly strokes, over 48 per cent of all the votes on the amendment were in the affirmative. Twenty-four out of 33 counties gave handsome majorities; one was lost by one vote, one by 23, and one by 31. The vote on the amendment in 1884 was 11,223 'Ayes,' 28,176 'Noes.' Although the population had more than doubled in the cities, where the slum vote is always against woman suffrage, the total increase of the 'Noes' of the state was only 229, while at the same time the 'Ayes' had been augmented by 15,052. * * *

"At the 36th annual convention of the National Woman Suffrage Association, held at Washington in 1904, Dr. Annice Jeffreys-Myers, Vice-President at Large of the Oregon Equal Suffrage Association, made a report of the origin and progress of the movement in Oregon up to that time. In this paper she said: 'It is not generally known that the Oregon country was the first geographical division of the world to recognize the legal individual existence of any married women. This innovation came about in 1850 by an act of congress, called "The Donation Land Law." * * * Enough financial power was gained, largely by the influence of this Act, to begin the first legally recognized movement for the enfranchisement of women, which was enacted in the Territory of Wyoming in 1869.' * * *

"During the years 1900 and 1905 there was nothing done by the Oregon Association in the way of big gatherings or conventions, at which Eastern women were asked to speak; but, whatever was done up to 1905, was accomplished in getting letters ready, and circulating petitions through the work of the executive committees of the various societies interested, particularly the State Equal Suffrage Association. In the spring of 1906 the first big meeting, since 1900, was held in the White Temple in Portland, at which about 200 members, outside of Multnomah County, were expected to attend. The conference lasted two days and two evenings, having such women as Dr. Anna Shaw, Mrs. A. S. Duniway, and Dr. Viola M. Coe to preside at the different meetings. * * * Among the many plans formed at this meeting, was one for the polling and working of the City of Portland before election day, and another for holding parlor meetings by Miss Kate M. Gordon, a southern representative, and the personal lectures of Dr. Shaw throughout the state.

"Just previous to the election there were held in Portland a series of four Sunday-afternoon meetings, to which everybody was invited. * * * Dr. Anna Shaw and Mrs. Mary C. C. Bradford, of Denver, ridiculed, and held up to scorn the men who had signed a protest against the enfranchisement measure, coming up in June, saying it was only a manifestation of the corporation and slum interests, fighting against progressive government. * * *

"After the election returns had made it clear that suffrage had lost, a meeting was held, in which plans for immediate resubmission on the question to the voters were discussed. There were apparently hopes left, for we hear Mrs. Duniway saying, 'We are determined to have the right to vote, and the men may as well let us have it now.' * * *

"The official returns for the 1906 election, show a popular vote of 'Yes' 36,902, and of 'No' 47,075, indicating a loss of 10,173. * * *

"The fatal mistake of the leaders in Oregon was that they imported the Eastern speakers, who took charge of the campaign. * * *

"A short time after the defeat of 1906, an incident occurred to cause a change in plans for the next suffrage campaigns. This was the open breach between the W. C. T. U. and the suffrage leaders. Previous to now, the W. C. T. U. had been more or less openly behind the suffrage cause; but the meeting, held following the election that year, when discussion arose as to causes for defeat, Mrs. Duniway openly said: 'It was defeated because of the activity of the Woman's Christian Temperance Union.' She said it was due to the prohibition women going into the suffrage field, wearing the thin white ribbon, that had created opposing votes. This statement was the final blow in a disagreement that had been growing for years; and in a stinging reply to Mrs. Duniway's accusation, the Union workers attempted to show that the suffragists themselves had caused the defeat by their suicidal policy. They also claimed that the suffragists in their wild struggle to gain votes, had thrown down the temperance cause and conciliated the liquor interests. After a stormy convention, in November, 1906, Mrs. Duniway was again elected president, and the Prohibitionists seceded openly.

"In June, 1907, the initial rally for the next campaign was held at Mrs. Duniway's residence, where the executive board and the working members convened. At first it was thought likely that the campaign would be worked through the Legislature of 1907, but the plan was changed to one for an initiative petition for the election of 1908. Mrs. Duniway, president of the association, emphasized the fact that this campaign would be run by the women of Oregon. A letter from Dr. Shaw was read, but no financial aid was received from the National Association. * * *

"The work went on, until election time in June, 1908, except that it was much more like the campaign of 1900, in that only the Oregon women took part. No very large meetings were held during this campaign, nearly all the efforts being centered on restoring the work to its condition in 1900. There were a few less votes for the amendment this time than in 1906, and over 10,000 more against it. The returns for this election showing 'Yes' 36,858, and 'No' 58,670. * * *

"At a meeting held at the home of Mrs. Duniway, in the fall of 1908, it was decided to file petitions for another initiative amendment for the 1910 election. * * * There was quite a change in the amendment proposed for the election in that it read: 'No citizen who is a taxpayer shall be denied the right to vote on account of sex.' * * * The success with which this amendment was started is shown by the fact that in six weeks of voluntary work in circulating petitions, more than 14,000 names of registered voters were obtained. * * *

"This amendment went down to defeat for the third time, the result being 'Yes' 35,270, 'No' 58,065. No open campaign was made this year, its proponents not having expected victory, but had offered it as a campaign touching the pockets of thousands of tax-paying women, who had begun to see that 'taxation without representation is tyranny' as they had not seen it before. This election ended the active work of the organization until May, 1911, when Mrs. Duniway began to arouse her old helpers for the final struggle, of Nov. 5, 1912. * * *

"An interesting addition to the band of workers who had been toiling for years, was in the person of W. M. Davis, Esquire, of Portland, a man hitherto very much opposed to the cause, but who now became an adherent to its principles, and was asked by Mrs. Duniway to father the movement among the legal voters in the coming campaign. * * *

"Although urged from many sides, and by some of the ablest women of the state, to begin the campaign for 1912 during the summer of 1911, Mrs. Duniway withstood all such requests until January 1st, 1912, when she felt that the time was ripe for a well-thought-out plan of attack. She then declared the 'lid was off,' and the campaign, the greatest and most enthusiastic ever seen for suffrage in Oregon, was given its final boost by the organization of a Men's Equal Suffrage Club of Multnomah County, which extended over the State.

"The first concerted effort toward establishing the principles for woman suffrage for the year 1912, was opened in Salem by a meeting held February 16, in the Hall of Representatives, by permission of Ben Olcott, Secretary of State, when Gov. West and a large gathering of suffrage leaders were assembled. The speakers for this occasion were Gov. West, Mrs. Olive England Enright, Mrs. Helen Hoy Greeley of New York, and Miss Anita Whitney of California, representing the National College League.

"At the University of Oregon, in Eugene, a College Equal Suffrage League was organized by Mrs. Greeley

and Miss Whitney. Miss Birdie Wise, of Astoria, was
made president, and the Chapter became a part of the
National College Association. Dr. Viola M.
Coe was elected president of the Portland Chapter, and Mrs. Duniway Honorary Head. * * *

"The automobile campaign which, next to newspaper
publicity, made an important part of the plans of the
State Central Committee of the Oregon Equal Suffrage
campaign, was appointed by Mrs. Duniway. Mrs. Sarah
Ehrgott, chief organizer of the Portland branch of the
College League, arranged to have autos, containing speakers, sent about the city of Portland in the evenings, making frequent short addresses from their seats in the ma-
chines wherever small groups of hearers could be found.
* * * Occasionally some of the autos were used to
advantage in the country, in distributing literature, nail-
ing up posters and giving out buttons to all who would
accept the slogan, 'Votes for Women.' * * *

"The Labor Vote in Portland and vicinity is quite
an important factor in any election, and particularly was
this vote for the enfranchisement of women one to be
gladly received by the suffragists. Although the Central
Labor Council had for some time been in favor of the
movement, and the State Federation of Labor at The
Dalles had voted for it, there was much personal work
needed in Portland among the various unions, the Building Trades Council and Socialists, to insure a favorable
answer in the coming election. Mrs. Sarah Ehrgott and
Mrs. Frank Cotterill deserve especial credit for making
most of these addresses, and for conducting the campaign
among the farmers and ranch owners of Eastern and
Southern Oregon. * * *

"On June 7, the first State rally was held at the
Hotel Portland. Addresses were made by Dr. C. H.

Chapman and Miss Anita Whitney. Reports were given by delegates from every county in the state, telling of their progress so far, and suggesting the particular needs of that vicinity. Dr. Viola M. Coe presided at this meeting, which was called as a tribute to Mrs. Duniway, who, a short time before the active campaign began, had been forced to leave her personal service on account of illness, but who had entrusted the presidency to one whom she considered able and willing to carry on the work as well as though she herself were at the helm. * * *

"The Rose Festival parade, acting under a local committee of the Woman's Club, offered for sale sandwiches from the Speedwell truck upon which their banners and pennants were displayed. The leader in this group of women, dispensing the dainty eatables prepared by the Club, which were eagerly sought for by crowds on the street, was Alice Fleming, who was then leading lady with the Baker Stock Company of Portland, and who was so interested in the sale of the delicacies that she even invaded cafes and grill rooms, always coming forth with an empty basket.

"To the Equal Suffrage Association was awarded, as the first prize, a silver loving-cup for its artistic float in the annual Rose Festival parade of 1912. This cup was presented to Mrs. Duniway, by unanimous vote of the allied Equal Suffrage Leagues. Dr. Emmett Drake, chairman of the Rose Festival committee, made a patriotic presentation speech, to which Mrs. Duniway responded from the front porch of her residence, seated in an invalid's chair. 'Is is through incidents analagous to this that votes are made for women,' said the leader. 'We can always make best progress by following lines of least resistance.' * * *

"Mrs. L. W. Therkelsen, who previous to this had been an ardent worker, but who had received no special duty or post to fill, started a new movement, to hold suffrage meetings at the various beach resorts on the Oregon coast. * * *

"The largest suffrage meeting held, up to that time in Oregon, was the one conducted at The Oaks amusement park, August 11, when Mrs. Sarah Ehrgott and Col. C. E. S. Wood addressed more than 25,000 people on the pending suffrage amendment. At the gate the visitors were met with all sorts of yellow decorations, yellow being the official color, and everywhere on the grounds were yellow posters, cartoons and mottoes. The College League, under whose auspices this meeting was held, was well represented on the ground, and its missionaries were continually moving, distributing badges and arguing for the cause. Mrs. Ehrgott made the first speech, dealing more especially with incidents of the hardships and woes of women, in order to force her way through the skepticism of the crowd. Col. Wood followed, and with his cold but logical and brilliant argument, healed the wounds the first speaker had made.

"Neighborhood clubs were formed in every direction by the Oregon State Equal Suffrage Association. Laborers hearkened everywhere to the suffrage plea. Foundry workers, lumber-yard men, piledrivers and mill-men were given opportunity to hear the plea from women themselves, who went to these respective places of industry, and with a pile of lumber, or heap of iron, as a rostrum, presented to the men in simple concise words, the cause for which they hoped to gain votes in November. * * *

"In the early part of October the committees of the various organizations and the Central Committee, outlined their plans for the last lap in the great race. * * * Free speeches, tonneau talks, Suffrage Sunday, debates and noon-day factory meetings, composed the program for the wind-up of the campaign. * * *

"One of the leading ideas coming from the College League very shortly before election, was to have 200 new posters pasted on the city bulletins, which should represent in a pictorial way the actual condition of Oregon, a state, leader of the West in so many lines, yet the only one in the midst of California, Washington and Idaho which had not yet enfranchised women. * * * After a campaign of exceptional thoroughness, Mrs. Duniway made a last appeal to the men of the state. In her plea she said that women were not seeking the power to rule over men, but only the right to keep step with them, and it was her earnest desire, after forty-two years of service, active in all except the last year, to see the men of Oregon vote as those of Idaho, Washington and California had done. * * *

"As the returns began to come in, those who were waiting in the Blue Room of the Oregon Hotel, Portland, were quite cheerful, for it was the vote from the vice and slum elements in the large cities that always had proved fatal to suffrage. Mrs. Duniway did not stay up the first night after election to hear returns; for, with her courage, as of old, she announced, as soon as the polls closed, that if they were not successful, another campaign would be begun at once. * * *

"The official figures for the measure on Woman Suffrage, which occupied the first place on the ballot this year, were 'Yes' 61,265, 'No' 57,104; showing a winning majority of 4,161 votes."

As evidence of the universal awakening just prior to the election, I am pleased to add a report to "The Oregonian" from Dr. Henry Waldo Coe, Chairman of the Na-

tional Committee of the Progressive party in Oregon, to
the effect that suffragists held the whip hand over all the
political parties. He said: "I went down to the southern
border and visited Ashland, Medford, Grants Pass and
other points. In every one of these the activity of the
suffragists was the striking feature of the place. I tried
to secure a hall and was told that it was taken for suffrage. I turned away and found suffragist meetings on
the street, and then I entered my hotel.

"Some women came to me and asked my opinion on
suffrage. Seeing that they were unaware of my identity,
I told them that the matter was one upon which I was un-
decided, and to which I had not given much thought.
Their answer was business-like, viz: 'If you want to
stop in this hotel at all, nowadays, it is about time you
made your mind up on this question, as it is interesting
everyone.'

"I tried to secure a Roosevelt Progressive speaker in
one of the towns and found he was engaged to make a
suffrage debate.

"Then, seeing that it was about time to eat, I turned
off into a small restaurant. There, at any rate, I thought
politics and suffrage would not be considered above meals;
and yet, when I took my seat, just as I was about to look
at the waiter, I found a large placard bearing the words:
'Vote 300 X Yes.'

"On going to bed, hardly had I started off to doze,
than I was awakened by the sound of a drum and fife
band. Looking out of the window, thinking this was a
Progressive meeting, I found the band was heading a
large suffrage demonstration."

CHAPTER XXVI.

Newspaper Reports.

(Compiled by L. Victoria Hampton, M. D.)

THE following corroborative chapter, compiled for these pages, is contributed by L. Victoria Hampton, M. D., a prominent physician and chemical analyst, of Portland, to whom I had regretted my disability, by telephone (owing to rheumatic lameness), to make personal investigations, for data among newspaper files, and in public libraries, without which I was seriously handicapped. The Doctor's first researches brought to light the following accounts from the Lewis and Clark Journals of June and October, 1905, from which she selected, first:

THE CENTENNIAL ODE.

Written by Mrs. Duniway and presented, in the name of 2,600 Oregon women, to the Lewis and Clark Exposition, on opening day, June 1st, 1905.

While yet the Nineteenth Century was young,
  Great Jefferson, with deep prophetic ken,
Discerned this distant West; and straight outsprung
  Through magic power of his official pen
An expedition whose results shall last
As long as Freedom's flag shall float before the blast.

And then, to make the prophecy complete,
  An Indian mother led the devious way,
Foreshadowing woman's place, which man shall greet,
  Without a protest, in a hastening day,
When womanhood, benignant, wise and free,
Shall lead him to yet greater heights of strength and
      victory.

As, through the vista of a hundred years,
  We backward turn to the Atlantic shore,
Our hearts athrob, and eyes suffused with tears—
  Almost in hearing of Pacific's roar—
The Then and Now so closely crowd the scene
That Time and Distance both but dimly intervene.

GROUP OF EQUAL SUFFRAGISTS

JANE ADDAMS
of Chicago's Hull-House Fame and Vice-
Pres. of National Council of Women Voters

MARIE D. EQUI
Fighter for Working Girls Rights. A Fearless Champion of Freedom for Women

ALICE STONE BLACKWELL
Editor of The Boston Woman's Journal.
Daughter of Lucy Stone and Henry B.
Blackwell. A reliable Statistician

THE LATE JULIA WARD HOWE
Author of The Battle Hymn of the Republic
and Noted Suffragist of Boston

RABBI STEPHEN S. WISE
Formerly of Portland Ore. Present Leader
of Settlement of Social Workers in New
York. Always Leading Suffragist

MRS. A J. WHITE
Active Worker in the Equal Suffrage Cause
in Oregon

THE LATE MARY A. LIVERMORE
Founder of the Sanitary Commission and
Leading Suffragist

Long 'ere this Nation's birth, a Master Hand,
  With mighty purposes no man foreknew,
These mountains, rivers, hills and dales had planned,
  And spread, in matchless majesty, the view
We now behold, of forest, lake and plain,
Evolved through countless ages from the heaving main.

A hundred strenuous years ago! Ah, then,
  So distant were we from our country's heart,
That Darkest Africa appealed to men
  As being nearer each commercial mart
Than Mandan District; and this Sunset Land
Was farther from their border homes than India's
    coral strand.

No steamer then had plowed the sea or stream,
  No flying ship been trained to cleave the air;
O'er all the earth no tamed electric gleam
  Was chained to duty as man's charioteer;
No cable then was laid beneath the sea,
And telegraph and telephone alike were yet to be.

And Trade and Commerce, in their infancy,
  Awaited ingenuity of man
To bring them forth in full utility,
  To build a track for iron horse to span
The lengthened trail, on which was blazed the mark
Of valiant Captain Lewis and intrepid Captain Clark.

As here, from lands anear and far, are seen
  The works of man, within these beauteous grounds,
Which water, earth and air were taxed to glean,
  And place before us, midst these sights and sounds,
Let every soul, in sweet soliloquy,
In reverence, contemplate this Nation's destiny.

From each bejeweled, bleak, Alaskan height,
  From hot Hawaii's glittering sands,
From Porto Rico's sunshine bright,
  From far Manila's sea-girt lands,
Our Starry Flag, in every breeze unfurled,
Proclaims that Freedom yet shall reign supreme
    o'er all the world.

"Only one woman has been honored by having a day set aside exclusively in her honor. October 6th was designated by the officials of the Exposition as 'Abigail Scott Duniway day,' in honor of that grand old pioneer; and pioneer she is, not only in the sense of being one of the early settlers in the wilds of Oregon, but she has been a pioneer in the ranks of those struggling for the liberty and enfranchisement of women.

"Mrs. Duniway has been a well-known and popular lecturer for many years, and it is directly through her agency that many of the laws tending toward equality and justice for women have been passed, in various states of the Northwest, as well as her own loved home state. She is an author of more than usual ability, and her various books deserve the wide popularity they have attained. Ripe in years and bright in intellect, she is one of the most honored citizens of Portland.

"The exercises of the day set aside to do her honor were not elaborate, and there was no formal programme, but all were given an opportunity to meet and greet this pioneer mother and worker of the Northwest, it being desired by those in charge of arrangements that every one have opportunity to greet the only woman thus honored.

"Mrs. Duniway has been the most conspicuous woman in the history of the Northwest, and the graceful courtesy of the Exposition officials in recognizing the inestimable value of her services in the development and progress of this state is being heartily commended by the general public."

* * *

"Previous reports, current in the newspapers at the time of publication, state that organizations, auxiliary to the National Association, were formed in Washington Territory and in the State of Oregon during a visit from Miss Anthony in 1871, but Mrs. Duniway found it impossible to hold them together after a brief period, unless she was able to answer calls to visit them at least annually, —a fact which strengthened her conviction that it was not as wise to entrust a few women, everywhere, within the iron-clad environment of a necessarily restricted organization, as it was imperative to enlist the co-operation of voters, and thus hold the approval and support of leading men outside its pale. Her plan worked admirably until after the adoption, through Territorial enactment, of a

woman suffrage law by the Legislative Assembly of
Washington in 1883. The Territory was then on the eve
of statehood; and women would have, doubtless, remained
enfranchised but for the untimely visit of an Eastern
propaganda (of prohibition), with which a few well-
meaning but inexperienced women became unduly imbued. These women, unused to the tricks of politics, were
entrapped, as voters, by a cunningly devised enactment of
a few politicians, called a Local Option Law; and Mrs.
Duniway, being at that time opposed almost everywhere
by the clergy, failed to lead such women to see that the
liquor traffic was behind this movement, and was leading
them into a trap, set for them by the National Liquor
Dealers' Association, acting under secret orders, by telegraph, from its President in Chicago. The result came,
as the suffrage leader had predicted. A new State constitutional convention was called into being in the territory in 1887, which, by electing delegates known to be
opposed to votes for women, opened the way, by an easy
trick, to close the iron doors of a state constitution in the
women's faces, leaving them disfranchised, whipped, dis-
mayed and helpless, on the outside.

"Probing deeper into similar channels of information, I find voluminous accounts of Mrs. Duniway's persistent activity in the suffrage movement, especially following the defeat of the two successive constitutional
amendment campaigns in Oregon, in 1908 and 1910. I
find that the National Woman Suffrage Association, under its president, Dr. Anna Howard Shaw, refused to assist Mrs. Duniway's administration unless under her national banner; also, that a national fund was diverted,
during the victorious campaign in 1912, to a little local
committee of the Portland Woman's Club., But, no matter who else grew weary of the struggle, we find Mrs.
Duniway always at work, supplying funds herself when
others failed, until about the first of January, 1912, when

she declared the petitions filed, for a new campaign, opened 'For the Home Stretch.'

"The National Woman Suffrage Association, which had boycotted the State Equal Suffrage Association, after Mrs. Duniway was returned to the presidency in 1906 (she having fallen seriously ill), commissioned her able ally, Dr. Viola M. Coe, to officiate as acting president. Never did field marshal in any victorious campaign do better work. Hon. Ben Selling contributed a headquarters in a business center, to which furnishings were added by loyal friends. Suffrage leagues, long moribund, sprang into existence in all directions, and prominent men in all parts of the state assisted gladly. United States Senators Chamberlain and Lane, ex-Senator Jonathan Bourne, Hon. John Barrett, of the Bureau of Pan-American Republics, ex-U. S. Senator C. W. Fulton, and the late State Printer, W. S. Duniway, never refused substantial aid. The leading press of the state sustained the campaign in every honorable way. Mrs. Solomon Hirsch, president of the Portland Equal Suffrage League; Miss Emma Wold, president of the State College League; Mrs. A. C. Newill, president of the Circulating Co-operative League, and Dr. Esther Pohl Lovejoy, president of Everybody's League, deserve special mention.

"To W. M. Davis, Esquire, a popular attorney of Portland, belongs the honor of originating the Men's Equal Suffrage League, which made its influence felt throughout the state.

"But to Dr. Viola M. Coe belongs the honor of getting votes for women on the 'home stretch.' A largely attended political banquet, managed wholly by her, was given at a popular hotel at a psychological moment, where lawyers, judges, men of every shade of political belief, preachers of Jewish, Catholic and Protestant faith, orators, professors and editors vied with each other in advocacy of the amendment and in praise of the venerable leader, who, though unable to rise to her feet, made several happy responses as guest of honor.

"With the beginning of the year 1912 the state association had made everything in readiness for what its leader called a New Deal. The equal suffrage associations of the entire state awoke at once. All sorts of suffrage associations sprang into being in almost every county and covered many precincts.

"A most unique party was given by Dr. Coe, October 22nd, shortly before election, in the great Gipsy Smith Auditorium, the occasion being Mrs. Duniway's 78th birthday. The beneficiary was carried in a wheeled chair to an artistically decorated platform, amid the applause of assembled thousands. Speeches were made by Governor West, ex-United States Senator Fulton, Col. R. A. Miller, Mayor Cotterill of Seattle, Fred Holman (president of the State Historical Society), Mr. A. E. Clark, W. M. Davis, Mrs. Hutton of Spokane, Mrs. Cartwright of California, and many others. A suffrage hymn, written by Mrs. Duniway, set to music by Mrs. A. E. Clark, was sung by an accomplished vocalist. Gov. Oswald West capped the festivities of the occasion by openly inviting the venerable beneficiary to write the forthcoming Women's Emancipation Proclamation. This document, transcribed in Mrs. Duniway's familiar chirography, was signed by Gov. West and countersigned by her, on the 30th day of November following, in the home of Dr. Viola M. Coe, in the presence of the State Executive Committee of the Oregon Equal Suffrage Association, and will find a permanent home in the state archives.

" 'Equal suffrage is bound to come,' became the general verdict after the birthday party, 'and we must not fail to adopt it while its venerable leader is here to witness the victory.'

"In conclusion, I have clipped the following report from 'The Morning Oregonian' of November 7, 1912, two

days after the election, when enough was known to make
victory assured:

"The reporter found Mrs. Duniway seated in a rocking
chair, a pillow at her head, a copy of the 'Woman's Journal'
—Oregon Suffrage issue, if you please—on her lap, her
spectacles in one hand, her other playing idly with a bundle
of letters and telegrams.

"On the table were numbers of others letters, telegrams
and items, clippings from the papers, and so on. It would
seem as if this leader did all her work by means of clippings.
Later in the interview she admitted that without them she
would not have known how to conduct the campaign.

"She was not expecting anybody, and was resting
quietly when the visitor entered the room, though she would
deny indignantly any accusation of taking an afternoon nap,
probably, in spite of the fact that her spectacles were folded
in her hand.

"The most astonishing thing about it all was that this
leader of women was not in the least excited—simply peace-
fully contented. It was as though some strange prophetic
word had told the figures on election in advance. She would
not even discuss it. It had to be. 'I knew it would come
now, but had it by any chance been delayed, we had made
arrangements whereby the fight could be renewed at once,'
and a little chuckle of delight at her forethought broke from
her lips.

" 'Now all we have to do is to wait, and wait quietly
until the Governor issues the proclamation, and he has promised to do this first in my presence.' This promise was
quoted with just a trace of apprehension, lest Governor West
should fail to remember his invitation, or her change of address. 'You see it is but right that men should still take
the lead.

" 'Then, as soon as the state has ratified the amendment, after all has been legally adjusted, I want to form a
men's and women's Good Government Union; I nearly said
League, but so many people have asked me to keep out all
such words as club, league, or society, as it would seem to
bar someone or other. This is what we want to avoid. We
desire a Federated Union, non-partisan in every way. Our
aim will be to work for what is best in government, sanitation, roads, child labor, and, above all, for rational recreation.

" 'We have refused right along to take up any special

line, for or against, the measures that have been agitating the men, for two reasons: Suffrage is allied to no party; and its own members are divided on such questions as prohibition, single tax, abolishment of capital punishment, and the like. What is more, we won our fight because in the end men realized that we were not all fanatics on some one subject, or another. No one will cure intemperance by fighting the saloons. The best antidote for liquor is not to take it at all; and when we can educate men to believe that, you have done more than any legislation will ever effect.'

"Mrs. Duniway was particularly pleased with the vote in Portland; the change from 12,000 against to a majority of 2,000 or so for it, being especially gratifying.

"The great leader sent out her best thanks to all the papers, 'The Oregonian' in particular, for she said, 'I could not have conducted my campaign without clippings from the press, and from its columns, almost entirely.' "

(From Miss Elma Buckman, Recording Secretary.)

Subsequent to my receipt of Dr. Hampton's and Mr. Kronenberg's kindly assistance in compiling data beyond the reach of a chronic "shut in," I have been favored by the following letter from our faithful Recording Secretary, Miss Elma Buckman:

"A special meeting was called, by letter from the State President, Mrs. Abigail Scott Duniway, in the Selling Hirsch Building, Portland, Oregon, March 8, 1912. Dr. Viola M. Coe was appointed Temporary Chairman and Miss Emma Wold, Temporary Secretary. Miss Buckman stated that the objects of the meeting were to effect a permanent campaign of organization, to be automatically dissolved after the expected victory of November 5, 1912.

"Mrs. Duniway requested that Dr. Coe act as Chairman of the meeting, and afterwards appointed her as acting State President for the entire campaign. Delegates present, representing the State Executive Committee, were Miss Elma Buckman, of Portland; Mrs. Elizabeth Lord, The Dalles; Mrs. Martha A. Dalton, Portland;

Mrs. Imogene Bath, Hillsboro. Delegates representing the Men's Equal Suffrage League were Mr. W. M. Davis, Mr. Albert Ehrgott, ex-United States Senator C. W. Fulton.

"Delegates representing the Portland Equal Suffrage League were Mrs. Solomon Hirsch, Mrs. J. A. Fouilhoux, and Miss Frances Wilson.

"Delegates representing Committee from Portland Woman's Club—Mrs. Caroline Dunlap, Mrs. F. Eggert, Mrs. A. C. Newill.

"Delegates representing the College Equal Suffrage League—Dr. Marie D. Equi, Miss Emma Wold, Mrs. L. W. Therkelsen.

"Officers of State Central Committee—Chairman, Mr. Albert Ehrgott; Assistant Chairman, Mrs. Elizabeth Lord; Secretary, Mrs. H. R. Reynolds; Treasurer, Dr. Viola M. Coe. To this committee, Mrs. Duniway afterwards requested the appointment as Honorary Members, Reverend T. L. Eliot, Colonel R. A. Miller, D. Solis Cohen, Esq., Hon. Ben. Selling, Ex-United States Senator C. W. Fulton.

"The following Finance Committee was chosen with power to act: Mrs. J. A. Fouilhoux, Mrs. Elliott Corbett, Dr. Florence Manion.

"Literary Committee—Mrs. Louise Bryant Trullinger, Mrs. A. E. Clark, Miss Emma Wold, Miss Blanche Wrenn.

"Ways and Means Committee—Dr. Flora Brown Cassidy, Mrs. Caroline Hepburn, Mrs. C. B. Woodruff. The full Executive Committee was composed of the Chairman, and one member from each association represented, also one member from each of the committees, including the National Representative, Dr. Viola M. Coe.

"The meeting was adjourned until March 14, 1912, at 1:30 P. M., at the headquarters of the Association, which having outgrown the offices of the accommodating

College League, was accorded other committee rooms, by invitation of Honorable Ben Selling.

"On motion of Mrs. Hirsch, it was unanimously voted to send greetings of hearty good cheer to Mrs. Abigail Scott Duniway, who was unable to attend the meeting."

In looking over the foregoing record and closing this chapter I wish to add my personal thanks to Dr. L. Victoria Hampton, Mr. A. T. Kronenberg and Miss Elma Buckman, to each of whom I owe a debt of lasting gratitude for assistance in emergency.

CHAPTER XXVII.

Mortuary Reminiscences.

IN OFFERING the concluding chapter of this autobiography to a discriminating public, I have hesitated much. Opinions differ as to the advisability of
its publication. But, on the whole, it having been my
aim, from the beginning of every successful effort in
my public career, to rely, in the last analysis, upon my
personal judgment, since I alone must be responsible
for consequences, I have decided to permit my heart
to do its own prompting; and, as my soul goes out in
love to every reader of this o'er true tale, I shall cast
conventionalities aside while paying brief tribute to my
risen dear ones, knowing well that what I say will meet
with sympathetic responses from the inner being of
many a parent's heart whose loved ones have vanished
into the realms of the unseen.

First, however, let me say that I have learned to
have no fear of the mortal change we call death, which,
in reality, is but transition, and is part of the eternal
program of life, in which everything animate must "live
and move and have its being."

The world cares little for individual sorrows.
"Laugh," says a wise philosopher, "and the world
laughs with you; weep and you weep alone." Nevertheless, there are common sorrows, appealing to the great
composite heart of our humanity, that need, more often
than they get it, the exchange of such private experiences as "make the whole world kin."

Many are the women of high positions whom I have
met, and many clergymen, scientists and philosophers,
whose fearless researches are probing, as far as mortals
have yet been able to probe, who have assisted me to a

gratifying degree, in testing the important fact that, when our loved ones depart from our earthly vision, they have merely exchanged their temporary fleshly tabernacles for better ones, "eternal in the heavens."

The first great bereavement that came to our household was the passing of our radiant, accomplished daughter, Mrs. Clara Duniway Stearns, who was endowed by nature in an uncommon degree with psychical insight. As I bent over her vanishing but glorified countenance, I exclaimed in choking accents, "I wish I could go with you, darling!" She answered, as her breath was failing, "You must stay to finish your work, Ma." * * * To go on with my unfinished work, and remain in my mortal body, to again take up life's burdens, after her dear remains had been laid away, was the first great struggle of my strenuous life. But I heeded her parting injunction, and pressed onward as before, losing my sorrow, as best I could, in pursuit of my unfinished work. She passed away in January, 1886, but I heard from her, through private psychic sources, within a month; and I have never since been able to think of her as dead.

* * *

Ten added years had folded themselves away among the irrevocable cycles of eternity, and the faithful husband of my youth was called to desert his pain-racked body, leaving me alone. "Good night, Mother!" he said to me, at midnight, on the day of his passing. "You must have some rest. Don't worry; we'll meet again in the morning." But when morning came he had lapsed into unconsciousness, from which he did not rally; and, never since, through all the mornings of nearly eighteen vanished years, have I awakened, whether from a dreamless or a dreaming sleep, failing to quote a sentence in his memory, from a dear old-fashioned hymn:

Here in the body pent,
Absent from him I roam,
Yet nightly pitch my moving tent,
A day's march nearer home.

* * *

Seventeen added years had slipped away—from August, 1896, to August, 1913—and our gifted first-born son, Willis Scott Duniway, was called to the higher life. He had been afflicted with occasional spells of heart trouble for many busy years; but his strong mentality, and the loving ministrations of his faithful wife, had sustained him through this physical affliction; and his strenuous public activities carried him forward to a useful and honorable career, over which the trailing wing of Azrael always hovered, bringing him no terrors, but inspiring him to greater efforts, till at last, he heard the welcome plaudit, "It is enough; come higher." His private and public life were alike distinguished for intelligence, fidelity and integrity.

Few of the women of today, in the full enjoyment of the blessings of enfranchisement, are able to realize, or understand, the efforts made in their behalf in the '70s and '80s of the nineteenth century, when my dear family sustained my efforts to establish a cause, of which it is to me a great consolation to remember that Willis lived to see its final achievement. He had been State Printer of Oregon for six and a half years prior to his passing, leaving behind him one and a half elective years of an unexpired term. Many voluminous press testimonials of his useful public life, commended his marvelous gifts of oratory, integrity and fidelity, but no mention was made of his, to me, the greatest of all achievements— the work he did in "The New Northwest," for nearly sixteen years, in advocacy of Equal Rights for the Mothers and Daughters of Men.

I, therefore, sent the following facts to the press,

which were widely disseminated, and for which I gratefully give thanks: "Although many of my beloved Equal Suffrage co-workers have gone to their final reward, enough remain to bear abundant testimony to my family's fealty to the Cause, and especially to the editorial work, ably and fearlessly performed by Willis, at a time when it required moral courage of the highest order to hold a young, ambitious man to his chosen duty to a disfranchised class, in the face of the most acrid opposition. No man was better pleased than he over our final victory, toward which he and my four surviving sons had at all times contributed liberally, with money, speech and pen."

In leaving, as a parting word, to my beloved readers, who have followed me, through this narrative, toward the closing activities of my earthly pilgrimage, and recalling as I write, the precious memory of "voices that are heard no more," I turn with loving confidence, from the eternal past and fleeting present, to the eternal future, which awaits us all, in the approaching bye and bye.

Six weeks after Willis had passed from mortal sight, I was favored by the following letter, sent to me by Mrs. Willis S. Duniway, my dear son's faithful wife, who found it, written October 14, 1907, stamped and addressed to me. It had not been sealed, or mailed, but my daughter found it in one of his desks in the State House, where it had been overlooked and forgotten for nearly seven years. It was sent to me, through the mail, September 3, 1914, as a message from the Land of Souls, and I shall let it tell its own sweet story, as a parting word from my devoted son:

"Salem, Oregon, October 14, 1907.
"My Dear Mother:
"The trip to my birthspot, after the lapse of half a century, in company with the good Mother who bore me, has thrown me into a reflective, not to say reverent frame of mind. The Duniway Farm! A partial clear-

ing in the wilderness! An earnest couple in life's forenoon! I keep on trying to imagine the conditions that you
and father had to face in 1853. The beginnings of civilization, government and education were there, but the
exacting need of the hour—the demand for the physical
well-being of your babes and selves—could only be met
by constant work. How well you both toiled, to make a
home in the wilderness and care for the little ones committed to you, I can comprehend in some degree, I hope.
I know the industry, energy, devotion of you both, and
the love and care you gave us, and mother dear, your own
hard experience in the June time of 1855, when in a fearful hail storm, with Baby Clara in your arms, you finally
reached a haven at Aunt Mary's, after your own cabin
home had been unroofed and wrecked; your shelter of the
babe, and keeping it warm and dry while you faced the
hail, breasted the gale and waded the icy swales—in
short, your prompt grasp of the thing to be done, with
immediate action, as soon as you met emergency—all
these are simply traits of character that have marked
your life. And, how dear father gave his strength and
enthusiasm and farm knowledge to his wilderness tasks,
I can also comprehend in some degree. The old apple
trees, set out by his honest hands, pruned and trimmed
and tended, are eloquent to me of his purpose to make
his farm home a good one. And how he loved his
and your little bairns in the isolated home, I also know.
With your deft fingers, we little ones were clothed to be
his joy, as well as yours, when people saw us; but neither
of you forgot that the need of having us good and true
in our simple lives was of vastly greater consequence
than the mere appearance we might present. The Duniway Farm! How it calls to mind the young couple, in
the morning flush of hope, bravely meeting life's responsibilities. And your good poem, mother dear, on the
'Burning Forest Tree,' is an expression, largely, of the

sentiments of a young wife and mother, who is solving the mysteries of life. Occasionally, nowadays, people are generous enough to say your boys are 'good,' and I, as one of them, realize that if we are well behaved, it is because our father and our mother gave us not only clean blood, but were our companions and helpers and guardians, who held us more by gentleness and love than by command and force. It was good for me to be at my birthspot with you, mother, and I thank you most earnestly for making the trip. Your son,

WILLIS."

* * *

The following poem, alluded to in the foregoing letter, was written on a lonely ranch in the wilds of Clackamas County, Territory of Oregon, in 1855, and widely published in the pioneer press of Old Oregon. I offered it, anonymously, to the "Oregon City Argus," and was much surprised and frightened at the prominence it achieved. It is inserted here, by special request, from an old-time co-worker of Walla Walla, Washington, and was written when I was twenty years of age:

THE BURNING FOREST TREE.

'Tis night. Slowly the orb of day
Passed through his gold-fringed curtains, grand,
And faded from our view.

    The queenly moon, with face serene,
    Now mounts her silver chariot, and soars
    In majesty, through canopies on high.

No sound is heard, save now and then the note
Of some sweet night-bird, or the common croak
Of tree-frog's call, as happily he chants
His evening melody.

    A melancholy sight now rises to my view,
    As through the deep, dark forest I gaze out
    Upon the lurid shadows.
    'Tis of a burning tree. Perhaps two centuries have lapsed
    Since first his tiny branches burst
    All gladly into life.

I dimly scan the distant years, long, long since fled,
Since thou, majestic giant, first didst stretch
Thy tender limbs to catch the dews of heaven.

Say, who inhabited these lands,
When first the wild dove cooed
Among thy trembling leaflets?
Who, what race of men, did wander round thee,
Gazing with proud fondness on
Thy well-proportioned form?

Methinks I hear thine answer,
Spoke, not audibly, but through, and in
The silence of the spheres.
"It was a noble race," sayest thou,
"Who, when my life was young, were daring,
Generous, brave.   No paleface, then,
Had e'er invaded these primeval shades,
To loot their substance or debauch their sons."

"Mayhap," said I, "a crown of thy green twigs
Has graced the brow of many a dusky maid,
While plighting vows of love and constancy
Unto her heart's best choice."

Long, cruel tongues of lurid flame
Shot upward, and the doomed tree,
A chief among his fellows, creaked and groaned.

"Ah! bravely hast thou stemmed," said I,
"Through many a passing year,
The wear of ages, and the tempest's blow.
But when the hand of man, who will not live out half thy
      days,
Is laid in skill upon thee, thou dost fall,
Nor root, nor branch, of thy great frame,
Shall stay to mark thy grave."

Again the great tree creaked and groaned.
Fierce, forked tongues of living flame
Shot toward the lurid zenith; and the moon,
As if in mourning, hid her reddening face
Behind a cloud that, like a pall,
Hung limp with fervent heat.

Great fiery branches from the big tree's frame
Let go their hold and fell with deafening crash
Upon the scorching earth, and burned
With crackling fury.

I clasped my baby, whose wide, wondering eyes
Met mine in eager questioning.   Then I prayed,
And the blest west-wind to the rescue came,
And rising high, bore the red flames
Into a fallow field; and the sweet rain
In torrents fell, and stayed the holocaust.

I closed my cabin door and cried,
"Farewell, old tree! I thank thee now
That, in thy dying hour, thou hast been
The source of calm, deep thought, to one
Who sings thy last long dirge!"

With loving deference to the request of Mrs. H. P. Isaacs, my Walla Walla friend, who counseled the publication of the foregoing lines, I cannot close this volume with a dirge. If I were writing this ode in my eightieth year, instead of my twentieth one, I should add this closing stanza:

Thou art not dead, O tree; for nothing dies.
Thou hast but changed thy form.
The waving grain, the sun-kissed fruit,
The growing edibles, which other lives
Consume for mortal sustenance,
Are vitalized through thy transition.
Life reigns—and liberty—and all is well!

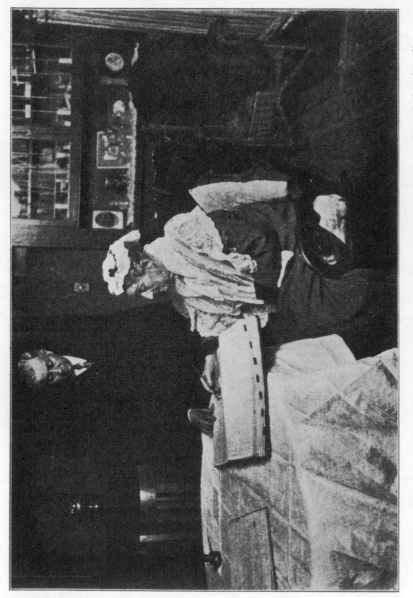

Abigail Scott Duniway, First to Register as Woman Voter in Portland, Oregon.   County Clerk Coffey, Standing.

ADDENDA

Original Path Breakers in the East.

THE following account of struggles made and conquered on the Atlantic side of the United States, while our Pacific Northwest was yet a wilderness, is from the facile pen of Alice Stone Blackwell, and is clipped from her newspaper, "The Woman's Journal," of Boston, Mass., of April 25, 1914. Eleventh-hour suffragists, as well as all original Path Breakers, will find it of absorbing interest:

Today the girl who seeks higher education finds the doors of many colleges open to her. After graduation, she has her choice among many occupations. Few young women realize how new these opportunities are. They may find both amusement and profit in a brief account of the experiences of three pioneer college girls.

First College Woman of Massachusetts.

The first woman in Massachusetts to take a college degree was Lucy Stone, the founder of "The Woman's Journal." She was a farmer's daughter, with a quick mind, eager for knowledge. But her wish for a collegiate education had a deeper root. From childhood she had been filled with indignation over the way in which she saw women treated by the laws. In those days all a married woman's property and earnings belonged to her husband; he had the sole right to the children; all the professions were closed to women, and so was every opportunity for well-paid work. Public opinion sternly condemned the very few women who spoke in public. In the eyes of many persons, it was a disgrace to a woman to write for publication, or even to belong to a philanthropic or temperance society. When Abbey Kelly Foster was appointed

upon a committee of the Anti-Slavery Society it literally
split the Association in twain.

The little Lucy early made up her mind that these
laws and customs must be changed. But one day, in
the family Bible, she came upon the text, "Thy desire
shall be to thy husband, and he shall rule over thee." At
first she wanted to die. Then she determined to go to
college and learn Greek and Hebrew, and satisfy herself
whether such texts were rightly translated.

Only One College Open to Women.

Her brothers went to college; but when Lucy expressed the wish to go, her father asked, in all seriousness, "Is the child crazy?" He would give her no help.
She picked berries and chestnuts, and sold them to buy
books. She taught school and studied, by turns. At the
low wages then paid to women teachers, it took her nine
years to earn the money to enable her to go out to Oberlin, Ohio, then the only college in the United States that
admitted women. Crossing Lake Erie from Buffalo to
Cleveland, she could not afford a stateroom, but slept
on deck on a pile of grain sacks, among horses and freight,
with a few other women who, like herself, could only pay
for a "deck passage." At Oberlin she earned her way
by teaching in the preparatory department and doing
housework in the Ladies' Boarding Hall at three cents
an hour. She was not able to go home once during the
four years, but she distinguished herself in her classes,
and thoroughly enjoyed her college course.

There Were Antis in Those Days.

She soon became known as a radical, and was re-
peatedly called before the Ladies' Board to be admonished.
The Ladies' Board was made up mostly of the wives of
the faculty, and was much more conservative than the

professors themselves. The colored people of Oberlin got up a celebration of the anniversary of West Indian emancipation, and invited Lucy to be one of the speakers, along with the college president and some of the professors. She made her address (for which nature had given her an incomparably sweet voice), and thought no more of the matter. The next day she was called before the Ladies' Board, and told that it was unwomanly and unscriptural for her to speak in public. The president's wife said, "Did you not feel yourself very much out of place up there on the platform among all those men? Were you not embarrassed and frightened?" "Why, no, Mrs. Mahan," she answered. "Those men were President Mahan and my professors, whom I meet every day in the class-room. I was not afraid of them at all!"

Bonnet Was Held Impious.

It gave her a severe sick headache to sit with her bonnet on through the long Sunday services that the students were required to attend; so she took the bonnet off. Straightway she was summoned before the Ladies' Board, and told that it was contrary to Scripture for a woman to pray with uncovered head. "But if I keep my bonnet on, I am good for nothing all the rest of the day," she said. "What account shall I give to God of my wasted Sunday afternoons?" It was finally agreed that she might sit in the rearmost pew, hidden under the gallery, and take her bonnet off.

First Woman Minister.

Meanwhile another disturber of conservatism was on her way to Oberlin. Antoinette Brown of Henrietta, N. Y., a beautiful, spiritual and very studious girl, had set her heart upon becoming a minister. Her mother urged her to go as a missionary instead. She preferred to expose her child to all the dangers of the foreign mission field rather than have her do so unheard-of a thing as try to become a minister. But Antoinette persisted, and she went to Oberlin, intending to take first the literary course and afterwards the course in theology. On the journey she was warned against a young woman of strange and dangerous notions who was studying at the college, named Lucy Stone; but the two girls soon became friends—a friendship destined to be cemented in later life by their marrying brothers (Henry B. and Samuel C. Blackwell).

Girls Might Not Debate.

The young men had to hold debates as part of their work in rhetoric. The young women of the class were not allowed to take part, but were required to attend in order to help form an audience for the boys. Lucy meant to lecture after graduation, and Antoinette to preach. Both wanted to gain practice in public speaking. They petitioned to be allowed to take part in these exercises. The professor consented. Curiosity drew a large attendance, and the debate was certainly not the least brilliant that the class had heard. The Ladies' Board and most of the faculty, however, felt that it was flying in the face of Scripture, and no repetition of the daring experiment was allowed.

First College Girls' Debating Club.

The young women organized secretly the first debating society ever formed among college girls. An old colored woman lent them the parlor of her little house for a meeting place, and they gathered there, going by ones and twos, so as not to attract notice, and when they were assembled, they "reasoned high" upon all sorts of profound subjects. Sometimes in summer they met in the woods.

Girl Must Not Read Essay.

At the end of her course, in 1847, Lucy was appointed to write an essay to be read at Commencement, but was notified that one of the professors would have to read it for her, as it would not be proper for a woman to read her own essay in public. Rather than not read it herself, she declined to write it.

Beginning in 1847, she lectured for many years through the United States and Canada, and was the first person by whom the heart of the public was widely and deeply stirred in behalf of equal rights for women. She was ridiculed in the press, was played upon with cold water through a hose when speaking, and persecuted in many ways, but she saw the cause grow and flourish. She has been called "the morning star of the woman's rights movement." Nearly forty years after her graduation, when Oberlin celebrated its semi-centennial, she was invited to be one of the speakers at that great gathering.

College Faculty Astounded.

Antoinette's troubles began when she finished the literary course at Oberlin and sought to enter the theological school. It was an unprecedented request. But the founders of the University had put into its charter a clause that all its opportunities were to be open to women. It had never occurred to them that a woman could wish to study for the ministry. Rumor said that faculty meeting after faculty meeting was held on the subject. The charter was clear, however, and there could be but one decision. At last, Prof. Morgan said to her, frankly: "Antoinette, I think you are making a mistake. I would stop you if I could. But since I cannot, I shall do my very best to teach you"; and he did.

Oberlin Men Were Generous.

She says that the men of Oberlin College in those early days were the kindest, the most generous and the most friendly that could be imagined; even those who disapproved were personally kind. The wives of the faculty, however, were much narrower. Since Antoinette could not be kept out by main force, the Ladies' Board tried to keep her out by making it impossible for her to meet her expenses.

Path Was Made Difficult.

During her literary course she had earned her way in part by teaching drawing in the lower school. The Lady Principal, Miss Adams, had promised to get her some teaching in the preparatory department to help her through the theological school also. But Miss Adams fell ill with typhoid fever. In her absence the Ladies' Board, for the express purpose of barring Antoinette out, made a rule that no graduate should be allowed to teach in the girls' department. Then Miss Atkins, the assistant principal, got up a private drawing class for her. Its members included Professor (afterwards President) Fairchild, and a number of the theological students; and it enabled her to meet all the expenses of her course.

Name Was Omitted From Graduates.

She distinguished herself in her studies, but her name was not printed in the list of theological graduates until many years later,

When she was ordained as pastor of the Orthodox Congregational Church in South Butler, N. Y., in 1853, press and pulpit thundered anathemas. When she was appointed a delegate to the World's Temperance Convention in New York, the other delegates—mostly ministers —yelled and shouted for two days running, to drown her voice. But in course of time Oberlin became very proud of her; and more than half a century after her graduation it made her a D.D. Today there are 3,405 women ministers in the United States.

First Woman Physician.

While Lucy and Antoinette were at Oberlin, another young woman, destined in later years to become their sister-in-law, was pioneering in a still more difficult path.

When Elizabeth Blackwell of Cincinnati wanted to study medicine, she took counsel with Harriet Beecher Stowe, Prof. Stowe and other friends. All said it was a good idea, but impossible of fulfillment. She was not to be discouraged. She taught, and saved the money. She studied medicine privately, first with John Dickson of Asheville, N. C., and later with Dr. Samuel H. Dickson of Charleston, S. C. Then she sought a medical school that would admit her. All those of New York and Philadelphia refused. Dr. Warrington made friendly inquiries among "some of the most intelligent and liberal-minded ladies" of Philadelphia. All replied, "No female could become acceptable to us as a practitioner of medicine."

Suggested Male Attire.

Dr. Pankhurst, who was professor of surgery at the largest college in Philadelphia, heartily approved of her trying to get a medical education, and proposed that she should enter his classes disguised as a man. To do so otherwise, he said, would be impossible. But she would not resort to disguise. After she had applied without success to ten medical colleges, that of Geneva, N. Y., opened its doors. The faculty, it afterwards turned out, had not meant to admit her; but they referred the question to the class, saying that, if a single student objected.

the request would be refused. It struck the young men as a great joke. A class meeting was held, at which the most extravagant speeches were made, and a unanimous vote was passed to admit the lady.

Desperadoes Changed to Gentlemen.

Dr. Stephen Smith, who was a member of the class, says the medical students were rude and boisterous to such a degree that it was often almost impossible for the professors to be heard, and the neighbors had several times threatened to have the college indicted as a nuisance. But as soon as the young lady appeared on the scene—"diffident and retiring, but with a firm and determined expression of face"—perfect order prevailed, and continued throughout the course.

"Either Mad or Bad."

The people of Geneva thought that she was either wicked or insane. At her boarding-house, women refused to speak to her; passing her on the street, they held their skirts aside. When the college doors closed behind her, she often felt that she had reached a refuge. There she had won the full respect and good will of both professors and students.

Experiences at Blockley Almshouse.

During the vacation, she studied in the hospital wards of the Great Blockley Almshouse of Philadelphia. The head physician, Dr. Benedict, was kind and helpful, but the young resident physicians were very unfriendly. When she walked into a ward, they walked out; and they ceased to write the diagnosis and treatment of patients on the card at the head of each bed, in order to deprive her of all assistance in her studies.

Graduates at Head of Class.

In 1849 she graduated from Geneva at the head of her class, and with the highest praise from the faculty. All the surrounding country turned out on the occasion. Elizabeth had been urged to march in procession to the church with her classmates, but refused. After she had received her diploma, however (she writes in her diary), "I was much touched by the graduates making room for me, and insisting that I should sit with them for the remainder of the exercises. Most gladly I obeyed the friendly invitation, feeling more thoroughly at home in the midst of these true-hearted young men than anywhere else in the town."

A few months ago that historic diploma was presented to Queen Margaret's College in Glasgow by Dr. Elizabeth's adopted daughter, in memory of the fact that she was not only the first woman to take a medical degree, but also the first to have her name entered on the British Medical Register (in 1859)—a privilege that she obtained as a physician with an American degree, while British degrees were still refused to women.

In the early days of her practice in New York City, she had to buy a house, because no respectable boarding or lodging house would take in a woman doctor. But this is not the place to tell of her struggles and successes. Today there are 7,387 women physicians in the United States.

Some Lessons From History.

Several points stand out clearly from these historic facts. Timorous conservatism has tried to shut every new door to women, as hard as it is trying now to debar them from the ballot-box. And the struggle has never been a fight of woman against man, but always of broad-minded men and women on the one side against narrow-

minded men and women on the other. In the words of
Mrs. Carrie Chapman Catt, "The enemy is not man, but
conservatism."

College Women Should Pay Debt.

"Bleeding feet smoothed the paths by which you
have come here!" said Abbey Kelley Foster in her old
age, to a great gathering of women. With Sarah and
Angelina Grinké of South Carolina, she had borne the
brunt of the opposition to women's speaking in public,
and had practically won that right for women, before
the time of the three college girls whose trials have been
sketched here, and against fiercer persecution than they
ever encountered. The young college women of today,
free to study, to speak, to write, to choose their occupation, should remember that every inch of this freedom was
bought for them at a great price. It is for them to show
their gratitude by helping onward the reforms of their
own time, by spreading the light of freedom and of truth
still wider. The debt that each generation owes to the
past it must pay to the future.